Democratic Legitimation of Central Bank Independence in the European Union

Cornelia Manger-Nestler • Markus Gentzsch

Democratic Legitimation of Central Bank Independence in the European Union

Springer

Cornelia Manger-Nestler
Faculty of Business
Administration and Industrial Engineering
Leipzig University of Applied
Sciences (HTWK Leipzig)
Leipzig, Germany

Markus Gentzsch
Customs Anti-Money Laundering Measures
(Division III A 6)
Federal Ministry of Finance
Berlin, Germany

ISBN 978-3-030-75114-2 ISBN 978-3-030-75115-9 (eBook)
https://doi.org/10.1007/978-3-030-75115-9

This Springer imprint is published by the registered company Springer Nature Switzerland AG.
The registered company address is: Gewerbestrasse 11, 6330 Cham, Switzerland

Preface

The independence of the European Central Bank and the national central banks in the European System of Central Banks/Eurosystem has been an important issue surrounding these monetary institutions since their establishment being the subject of numerous papers in economics, political science and law. Although, at a first glance, the normative design of the scope and limits of independence appears clear-cut, the environment in which central banks operate has changed significantly as a result of the crises of recent years and the challenges that are currently becoming more virulent. An important anchor in this "open sea" is the principle of democracy, which receives attention in central banking literature above all in the shape of democratic accountability.

This requirement is emphasised even more clearly in the case law of the German Federal Constitutional Court, which in recent years had to deal increasingly with the conformity of central bank action with the European Union law and the German constitution (Grundgesetz). The internationally controversial *PSPP decision* of May 2020 represented only a stopover on the journey of European integration, which is guided not only by the European treaties but also by national constitutional systems.

This book aims not only at better understanding the concept of central bank independence in relation to the various tasks to be performed and in comparison to other autonomy requirements under EU law but also at opening up the various approaches of democratic control of central bank action to mutual impulses.

We would like to thank *Peter Bartolomy* for helping us to differentiate between the manifold interpretations in terms of language and *Sebastian Prosche* for proofreading the manuscript. All remaining errors are ours. Moreover, we emphasise that all the views and opinions expressed in this book are ours and do not necessarily reflect the official policy or position of any institution that we belong to.

Important impulses in the drafting of the manuscript were given to us by three unknown referees, whom we would like to thank at this point. Finally, we gratefully acknowledge the donation we received from the Deutsche Bundesbank to support this project.

Leipzig, Germany
Berlin, Germany
May 2021

Cornelia Manger-Nestler
Markus Gentzsch

Contents

Abbreviations

ABoR	Administrative Board of Review
APP	Asset Purchase Programme
BaFin	Bundesanstalt für Finanzdienstleistungsaufsicht
BBankG	Gesetz über die Deutsche Bundesbank
BCBS	Basel Committee on Banking Supervision
BIS	Bank for International Settlements
BoG	Board of Governors (of the ESM)
BUWG	Banking Union Working Group
CBDC	Central bank digital currency
CFR	Charter of Fundamental Rights of the European Union
CJEU	Court of Justice of the European Union
CRD IV	Capital Requirements Directive
CRR	Capital Requirements Regulation
Data Protection Directive	Directive 95/46/EC of the European Parliament and of the Council of 24 December 1995 on the protection of individuals with regard to the processing of personal data and on the free movement of such data, OJ 23.11.1995, L 281, p. 31
DLT	Distributed ledger technology
EAPP	Expanded Asset Purchase Programme
EBA	European Banking Authority
EBAR	Regulation (EU) No 1093/2010 of the European Parliament and of the Council of 24 November 2010 establishing a European Supervisory Authority (European Banking Authority), amending Decision No 716/2009/EC and repealing Commission Decision 2009/78/EC, OJ 15.12.2010, L 331, p. 12
EC	European Community
ECA	European Court of Auditors

ECB	European Central Bank
ECB-ESRBR	Council Regulation (EU) No 1096/2010 of 17 November 2010 conferring specific tasks upon the European Central Bank concerning the functioning of the European Systemic Risk Board, OJ 15.12.2010, L 331, p. 162
ECHR	European Convention on Human Rights
ECOFIN	Economic and Financial Affairs Council
ECON committee	Economic and Monetary Affairs committee
ECtHR	European Court of Human Rights
ECU	European Currency Unit
EDIS	European Deposit Insurance Scheme
EEA	European Environment Agency
EFSF	European Financial Stability Facility
EGC	General Court
EIB	European Investment Bank
EIOPA	European Insurance and Occupational Pensions Authority
EIOPAR	Regulation (EU) No 1094/2010 of the European Parliament and of the Council of 24 November 2010 establishing a European Supervisory Authority (European Insurance and Occupational Pensions Authority), amending Decision No 716/2009/EC and repealing Commission Decision 2009/79/EC, OJ 15.12.2010, L 331, p. 48
ELA	Emergency Liquidity Assistance
EMF	European Monetary Fund
EMF Statute Draft	Statute of the European Monetary Fund, Annex to EMFR Draft
EMFR Draft	Proposal for a Council Regulation on the establishment of the European Monetary Fund of 6 December 2017, COM(2017) 827 final
EMI	European Monetary Institute
EMU	Economic and Monetary Union
EPPO	European Public Prosecutor's Office
EPPOR	Council Regulation (EU) 2017/1939 of 12 October 2017 implementing enhanced cooperation on the establishment of the European Public Prosecutor's Office ("the EPPO"), OJ 31.10.2017, L 283, p. 1
ESA	European Supervisory Authority
ESCB	European System of Central Banks
ESCB/ECB Statute	Statute of the European System of Central Banks and of the European Central Bank
ESFS	European System of Financial Supervision

ESM	European Stability Mechanism
ESMA	European Securities and Markets Authority
ESMAR	Regulation (EU) No 1095/2010 of the European Parliament and of the Council of 24 November 2010 establishing a European Supervisory Authority (European Securities and Markets Authority), amending Decision No 716/2009/EC and repealing Commission Decision 2009/77/EC, OJ 15.12.2010, L 331, p. 84
ESRB	European Systemic Risk Board
ESRBR	Regulation (EU) No 1092/2010 of the European Parliament and of the Council of 24 November 2010 on European Union macro-prudential oversight of the financial system and establishing a European Systemic Risk Board, OJ 15.12.2010, L 331, p. 1
ESS	European Statistical System
EU	European Union
FCC	Federal Constitutional Court
FinDAG	Finanzdienstleistungsaufsichtsgesetz
GG	Grundgesetz
GVG	Gerichtsverfassungsgesetz
HICP	Harmonised Index of Consumer Prices
IMF	International Monetary Fund
LoLR	Lender of last resort
LSI	Less significant institution
LTRO	Long-term refinancing operations
MFA	Macro-Financial Assistance
MiCAR	Proposal for a Regulation of the European Parliament and of the Council on Markets in Crypto-assets, and amending Directive (EU) 2019/1937 of 24 September 2020, COM(2020) 593 final
MoU	Memorandum of understanding
MRO	Main refinancing operations
NCA	National competent authority
NCB	National central bank
NGFS	Network of Central Banks and Supervisors for Greening the Financial System
NRA	National resolution authority
NSI	National statistical institutes
OLAF	European Anti-Fraud Office
OMT	Outright Monetary Transactions
PEPP	Pandemic Emergency Purchase Programme
PSPP	Public Sector Purchase Programme
Q&A	Questions and answers

QE	Quantitative easing
SI	Significant institution
SRB	Single Resolution Board
SRF	Single Resolution Fund
SRM	Single Resolution Mechanism
SRMR	Regulation (EU) No 806/2014 of the European Parliament and of the Council of 15 July 2014 establishing uniform rules and a uniform procedure for the resolution of credit institutions and certain investment firms in the framework of a Single Resolution Mechanism and a Single Resolution Fund and amending Regulation (EU) No 1093/2010, OJ 30.7.2014, L 225, p. 1
SSM	Single Supervisory Mechanism
SSMR	Council Regulation (EU) No 1024/2013 of 15 October 2013 conferring specific tasks on the European Central Bank concerning policies relating to the prudential supervision of credit institutions, OJ 29.10.2013, L 287, p. 63
TARGET2	Trans-European Automated Real-Time Gross Settlement Express Transfer System
TEC	Treaty establishing the European Community
TECSC	Treaty establishing the European Coal and Steel Community
TESM	Treaty Establishing the European Stability Mechanism
TEU	Treaty on European Union
TFEU	Treaty on the Functioning of the European Union
TLTRO	Targeted longer term refinancing operations

Chapter 1
Introduction

The first decade following the foundation of the European System of Central Banks (ESCB) in 1998 was accompanied by a stable economic environment in Europe and in the world, thus paving the way for the introduction of the single currency in 19 Member States of the European Union (EU) until now (2021). The legal framework of the Economic and Monetary Union (EMU) and the role of central banks as monetary institutions remained stable as well.

However, in the second decade the financial and sovereign debt crisis, starting in 2008, had a substantial impact on the historically evolved symbiosis between state, market and democracy causing political, social and, not least, legal upheavals.[1] The EU and its Member States implemented crisis management strategies, for instance the European Financial Stability Facility (EFSF) or the European Stability Mechanism (ESM) providing, where needed, financial assistance to euro area Member States under strict conditionality and involving the European Central Bank (ECB).[2] In respect of financial regulation, new supervisory authorities have been established and the networking of existing national and European structures has been strengthened. The role of the ECB as the core of the ESCB/Eurosystem[3] has been altered, in particular, by entrusting the management of the European Systemic Risk Board (ESRB)[4] to the ECB and thus, integrating the latter in macro prudential supervision

[1]Cf. Amtenbrink (2019), p. 311.

[2]Recital 2 EFSF Framework Agreement; Recitals 1 and 2 Treaty Establishing the ESM signed on 2 February 2012 (hereinafter: TESM). On the ESM reform, see infra Sects. 3.3.3. and 5.3.3.

[3]For details concerning the relationship between the ESCB and the Eurosystem see Manger-Nestler (2020), paras. 8.9–8.10.

[4]Established by Regulation (EU) No 1092/2010 of the European Parliament and of the Council of 24 November 2010 on European Union macro-prudential oversight of the financial system and establishing a European Systemic Risk Board, OJ 15.12.2010, L 331, p. 1 (hereinafter: ESRBR).

C. Manger-Nestler, M. Gentzsch, *Democratic Legitimation of Central Bank Independence in the European Union*, https://doi.org/10.1007/978-3-030-75115-9_1

and matters of financial stability.[5] The most significant change regarding institutional structure and functional competences has been induced by establishing the Single Supervisory Mechanism (SSM) in 2014, thereby conferring specific tasks on the ECB concerning policies relating to the prudential supervision of credit institutions.[6] As a consequence, the ECB has become an integral part of European administration and especially of the European System of Financial Supervision (ESFS) which includes at Union level, besides the ESRB, the three European Supervisory Authorities (ESAs), namely the European Banking Authority (EBA),[7] the European Insurance and Occupational Pensions Authority (EIOPA)[8] and the European Securities and Markets Authority (ESMA).[9] The ECB, as an authority responsible for micro-prudential supervision (supervisory authority[10]), exercises tasks and powers towards market participants up to withdrawing authorisations of credit institutions and imposing administrative penalties. These measures interfere with market participants' fundamental rights and are basically different from typically abstract and general monetary policy measures. The SSM as the first of the scheduled three pillars of the Banking Union[11] is complemented by the Single Resolution Mechanism (SRM) as the second pillar in which a Single Resolution Board (SRB) as a central decision-making body is primarily competent for the resolution of entities directly supervised by the ECB.[12] Although not having any

[5]Recitals 7 and 8 Council Regulation (EU) No 1096/2010 of 17 November 2010 conferring specific tasks upon the European Central Bank concerning the functioning of the European Systemic Risk Board, OJ 15.12.2010, L 331, p. 162 (hereinafter: ECB-ESRBR).

[6]Council Regulation (EU) No 1024/2013 of 15 October 2013 conferring specific tasks on the European Central Bank concerning policies relating to the prudential supervision of credit institutions, OJ 29.10.2013, L 287, p. 63 (hereinafter: SSMR).

[7]Established by Regulation (EU) No 1093/2010 of the European Parliament and of the Council of 24 November 2010 establishing a European Supervisory Authority (European Banking Authority), amending Decision No 716/2009/EC and repealing Commission Decision 2009/78/EC, OJ 15.12.2010, L 331, p. 12 (hereinafter: EBAR).

[8]Established by Regulation (EU) No 1094/2010 of the European Parliament and of the Council of 24 November 2010 establishing a European Supervisory Authority (European Insurance and Occupational Pensions Authority), amending Decision No 716/2009/EC and repealing Commission Decision 2009/79/EC, OJ 15.12.2010, L 331, p. 48 (hereinafter: EIOPAR).

[9]Established by Regulation (EU) No 1095/2010 of the European Parliament and of the Council of 24 November 2010 establishing a European Supervisory Authority (European Securities and Markets Authority), amending Decision No 716/2009/EC and repealing Commission Decision 2009/77/EC, OJ 15.12.2010, L 331, p. 84 (hereinafter: ESMAR).

[10]See Art. 2(2)(f) EBAR, as amended by Art. 1(2) Regulation (EU) No 1022/2013 of the European Parliament and of the Council of 22 October 2013 amending Regulation (EU) No 1093/2010 establishing a European Supervisory Authority (European Banking Authority) as regards the conferral of specific tasks on the European Central Bank pursuant to Council Regulation (EU) No 1024/2013, OJ 29.10.2013, L 287, p. 5.

[11]So far, there is no political consensus on a European Deposit Insurance Scheme (EDIS); see current European Parliament (2021).

[12]Recital 11 Regulation (EU) No 806/2014 of the European Parliament and of the Council of 15 July 2014 establishing uniform rules and a uniform procedure for the resolution of credit

resolution powers, the ECB's assessment whether an entity is failing or is likely to fail constitutes a necessary condition for adopting resolution scheme.[13]

Not only financial supervision and (bank) insolvency law, but also monetary policy, the ESCB's main domain due to maintaining price stability as its primary objective (Arts. 127(1) s. 1 and 282(2) s. 2 TFEU/Art. 2 s. 1 ESCB/ECB Statute), has been subject to profound changes. In order to limit negative effects of liquidity squeezes in various segments of the capital markets within the euro area, the ESCB took measures which aim at enhancing the transmission of monetary policy and thereby started to increasingly provide economic impetus. Since 2010, the ECB has chosen a mixture of different monetary policy measures comprising conventional (standard) and unconventional, i.e. exceptional and crisis-induced (non-standard) measures. Common instruments of interest rate policy have been combined with liquidity-providing operations complementing each other due to their different purposes. These measures are framed by an active communication policy which aims on directing market expectations (forward guidance).

These developments, which appear to be a transformation of the ECB from a technocratic monetary institution to a central hub of European economic policy,[14] went on despite an essentially unchanged legal framework of European primary law apart from smaller innovations in the Lisbon Treaty entered into force on 1 December 2009, by specifying the status of the ECB to become an EU institution (Art. 13(1) 6th indent TEU).[15] Especially the primacy of price stability within the ESCB's objectives and rules regarding central bank independence as *modus operandi*, now contained in Arts. 130, 282(3) s. 3 TFEU and Art. 7 ESCB/ECB Statute, remained substantially unaffected. Thus, at first glance, European central bank law seems to be based on strong constitutional provisions which can handle the functional evolution of the ECB.

However, this view does not stress enough the relationship between price stability and central bank independence and tends to neglect the legal dependence, in particular the democratic responsibility to the people and the requirement of judicial review. The evolution of an institution primarily committed to maintain price stability to an actor integrated into maintaining financial stability, exercising banking supervision and supporting economic policies leads to the question whether the high level of independence granted to the ECB can also be applied when carrying out these tasks and duties as well as exercising related powers.[16] This holds true especially for those tasks and powers which interfere with fundamental rights or cause significant economic impact, thus having paramount importance to the general

institutions and certain investment firms in the framework of a Single Resolution Mechanism and a Single Resolution Fund and amending Regulation (EU) No 1093/2010, OJ 30.7.2014, L 225, p. 1 (hereinafter: SRMR).

[13]Recital 26 SRMR.

[14]Peroni (2017), pp. 254–255 with further references.

[15]Cf. Häde (2012), pp. 421 et seq.; Amtenbrink (2019), p. 310.

[16]See also the concerns expressed by Mersch (2017).

public. Therefore, it is necessary to clarify, whether and to what extent European Union law contains democratic standards bounding and embedding central bank independence in accordance with its respective functions. In this context, other modes of autonomy encountered in EU primary and secondary law move to the fore which may help to gain conceptional comprehension of the relationship between independence and democratic legitimation within the European Union.

Research into these interrelationships is urgently needed at a time when the ECB faces a multitude of challenges. The euro area and the world economy have been undergoing profound structural changes for some time, in particular a decrease in interest rates, which reflects slowing productivity, an ageing population and the aftermath of the financial crisis.[17] The environment in which the ECB operates has been further transformed by the threat to environmental sustainability, rapid digitalisation, globalisation and evolving financial structures.[18] The ECB has therefore launched a review of its monetary policy strategy, which not only covers the objectives and means of central bank action, but also addresses communication practices.[19] The latter resulted in the project "ECB Listens" inviting euro area citizens to submit ideas and comments online.[20] In its controversial decision of 5 May 2020 concerning the Public Sector Purchase Programme (PSPP; *PSPP decision*), the German Federal Constitutional Court (FCC) also addressed, to a certain extent, matters of transparency alleging that "the Governing Council of the European Central Bank neither assessed nor substantiated that the measures provided for in these decisions satisfy the principle of proportionality".[21]

Finally, one of the greatest challenges facing the EU and the ECB is the COVID-19 pandemic associated not only with a collective public health emergency, but also exceptional economic and financial circumstances prompting the ECB to take crisis management operations to an unprecedented extent.[22] As a result, it is more urgent than ever to clarify the ECB's mandate in the triad of monetary policy, banking supervision and financial stability and to search for a stronger legal underpinning for its independence from, as well as its dependence on EU and national political authorities.

The analysis starts with illuminating the concept of central bank independence and outlining the tensions with the principle of democracy (2). Then, the multivarious tasks of the ECB on the basis of EU law will be characterised including the respective independent-related provisions (3). Afterwards, other modes of autonomy to be found within EU law will be focused on making reference to central bank independence (4). This is followed by an exploration of democratic legitimation and

---

[17]ECB, Press Release of 23 January 2020.

[18]Ibid.

[19]Ibid.

[20]ECB, Press Release of 24 February 2020.

[21]FCC, PSPP, 5.5.2020, 2 BvR 859/15 et al., para. 116.

[22]See Recitals 3 and 4 Decision (EU) 2020/440 of the European Central Bank of 24 March 2020 on a temporary pandemic emergency purchase programme (ECB/2020/17), OJ 25.3.2020, L 91, p. 1.

control of central bank action. Herein, the analysis carves out elements of an EU law-based principle of democracy and identifies democracy-safeguarding elements (5). Finally, the results of the inquiry are summarised (6).

References

Amtenbrink F (2019a) Independence and accountability in the new age of European central banking – revisiting Gormely and de Haan's 'The democratic deficit of the European Central Bank'. In: Amtenbrink F, Davies G, Kochenov D, Lindeboom J (eds) The internal market and the future of European integration – essays in honour of Laurence W. Gormley. Cambridge University Press, Cambridge, pp 305–321

European Central Bank (2020a) Press Release of 23 January. https://www.ecb.europa.eu/press/pr/date/2020/html/ecb.pr200123~3b8d9fc08d.en.html (26 February 2021)

European Central Bank (2020b) Press Release of 24 February. https://www.ecb.europa.eu/press/pr/date/2020/html/ecb.pr200224~752f11038e.en.html (26 February 2021)

European Parliament (2021) Legislative train 01.2021 – European Deposit Insurance Scheme (EDIS). https://www.europarl.europa.eu/legislative-train/api/stages/report/current/theme/economic-and-monetary-affairs-econ/file/jd-european-deposit-insurance-scheme-(edis) (26 February 2021)

Häde U (2012) The Treaty of Lisbon and the economic and Monetary Union. In: Blanke H-J, Mangiameli S (eds) The European Union after Lisbon – constitutional basis, economic order and external action. Springer, Heidelberg, pp 421–441

Manger-Nestler C (2020a) Chapter 8: The architecture of EMU. In: Amtenbrink F, Herrmann C (eds) The EU law of Economic and Monetary Union. Oxford University Press, Oxford, pp 191–213

Mersch Y (2017a) Central bank independence revisited, Keynote at the "Symposium on Building the Financial System of the 21st Century: An Agenda for Europe and the United States", Frankfurt a.M., 30 March 2017. https://www.ecb.europa.eu/press/key/date/2017/html/sp170330.en.html (26 February 2021)

Peroni G (2017) The European Central Bank (ECB) and European democracy – a technocratic institution to rule all European States. In: Daniele L, Simone P, Cisotta R (eds) Democracy in the EMU in the aftermath of the crisis. Springer, Heidelberg, pp 249–264

Chapter 2
Central Bank Independence and Democracy

2.1 The ESCB, the Eurosystem and the ECB: Institutional Aspects

The performance of the ECB's tasks can only be measured and evaluated within its institutional framework. For this reason, it is necessary to briefly present the ECB's position within the ESCB and the Eurosystem as well as its decision-making bodies.

Both, the ESCB and the Eurosystem have no legal personality and are parts of the institutional structure of the EU and the EMU. Whereas the ESCB consists of the national central banks (NCBs) of all 27 Member States, the Eurosystem comprises only those of the euro area.[1] According to a geometric model, the ESCB forms the outer circle, the Eurosystem the inner one, both with the ECB as the common circle centre which is granted leadership power over these systems.[2] However, the ECB can act in a legally binding manner only pertaining to the euro area Member States which results from the inapplicability of numerous provisions of monetary law to Member States with a derogation pursuant to Art. 139(2) TFEU.[3]

The implementation of the single currency has gone hand in hand with a single monetary policy leading to a system in which the NCBs are strictly subordinate to the ECB. This is highlighted in Art. 14.3. ESCB/ECB Statute qualifying the NCBs as an integral part of the ESCB which shall act in accordance with the guidelines and instructions of the ECB.

The ECB which has legal personality according to Art. 282(3) s. 1 TFEU has two decision-making bodies, the Governing Council and the Executive Board.[4] The Governing Council, which comprises the members of the ECB's Executive Board

---

[1]Art. 282(1) TFEU.

[2]Arts. 129(1), 282(2) s. 1 TFEU, Art. 8 ESCB/ECB Statute; for further details see Manger-Nestler (2020), para. 8.10.

[3]Smits (1997), pp. 103 and 135; Herrmann (2013), para. 15.

[4]Art. 9.3. ESCB/ECB Statute.

C. Manger-Nestler, M. Gentzsch, *Democratic Legitimation of Central Bank Independence in the European Union*, https://doi.org/10.1007/978-3-030-75115-9_2

and the governors of the NCBs of the Member States whose currency is the euro,[5] can be characterised as the ECB's legislative body which takes the relevant decisions on the monetary policy stance of the Eurosystem.[6] The Executive Board, which consists of the President, the Vice-President and four other members,[7] is responsible for implementing monetary policy and especially giving instructions to the NCBs.[8]

2.2 Dimensions of Independence Within the ESCB

The independence of central banks, primarily stated in Arts. 130, 131 TFEU, is an essential principle of monetary integration within the EU completing the primacy of price stability,[9] the single currency[10] as well as the conditionality[11] and irreversibility[12] of Monetary Union. This term generally comprises a non-instructed and uninfluenced performance of tasks and powers by the ECB and the NCBs and can be divided into certain constituent elements that are classified in different ways.[13] Following the classification developed by the European Monetary Institute (EMI) in its convergence reports,[14] it shall be differentiated hereafter between institutional, personal, financial and functional independence.

2.2.1 Institutional Independence

Institutional independence implies the existence of an unmodifiable legal framework ensuring the existence of central banks and preventing the European as well as the national legislator from changing organisation and competences.[15] Thus, the provisions relating to monetary policy (Arts. 127–133 TFEU) as well as those about

[5]Art. 283(1) TFEU, Art. 10.1. ESCB/ECB Statute.

[6]Art. 12.1. sub-para. 1 ESCB/ECB Statute.

[7]Art. 283(2) TFEU, Art. 11.1. sub-para. 1 ESCB/ECB Statute.

[8]Art. 12.1. sub-para. 2 ESCB/ECB Statute.

[9]See infra Sect. 2.2.4.2.

[10]See for differentiated integration Zilioli and Selmayr (2001), pp. 134–142; Manger-Nestler (2020), paras. 8.11–8.14.

[11]For details concerning legal and economic conditionalities that find their basis in the convergence criteria laid down in Art. 140 TFEU see Manger-Nestler (2020), paras. 8.31–8.56; Herrmann and Dornacher (2017), pp. 84–85.

[12]See Athanassiou (2009); Manger-Nestler (2020), paras. 8.4–8.6.; Herrmann and Dornacher (2017), pp. 87–88.

[13]See Smits (1997), pp. 155–158, 162–168; Zilioli (2016), pp. 143–155; concerning central bank independence in general Lastra (2015), paras. 2.124–2.132.

[14]See EMI (1995), pp. 91–93; (1998), p. 291.

[15]Hahn and Häde (2010), § 20 paras. 11–25.

institutional aspects (Arts. 282–284 TFEU), contain a constitutional guaranty of the ECB and the NCBs. Apart from that, the ECB's legal personality enshrined in Art. 282(3) s. 1 TFEU may also be considered as an institutional aspect.[16] As a result of being anchored in primary law, changes generally require a revision of the Treaties (Art. 48 TEU).[17]

2.2.2 *Personal Independence*

The dimension of personal independence addresses the members of the central banks' decision-making bodies and shall ensure their integrity.[18] Regarding the ECB's decision-making bodies, the Treaties and the ESCB/ECB Statute contain provisions which primarily guarantee long-term mandates and prohibit re-election.[19] Thus, the term of office of the members of the Executive Board shall be eight years and shall not be renewable.[20] These rules shall ensure that the persons responsible for performing the duties just focus on decisions instead of potential sanctions or merits. Furthermore, there are high requirements for dismissal being only possible on the grounds of serious matters[21] and incompatibility regulations throughout the membership period[22] ("professional independence"[23]).

Competence for a dismissal lies with the Court of Justice (ECJ),[24] which may, on application by the Governing Council or the Executive Board, enforce compulsory retirement of the member in question, if they no longer fulfil the conditions required for the performance of their duties or if they have been found guilty of serious misconduct.[25]

[16]Smits (1997), p. 155.

[17]See Art. 129(3) TFEU with regard to certain provisions of the ESCB/ECB Statute which may be amended by the European Parliament and the Council acting in accordance with the ordinary legislative procedure.

[18]See for details Smits (1997), pp. 156 and 157, 162–167; Zilioli (2016), pp. 145–152; in general Lastra (2015), para. 2.126 ("organic guarantees").

[19]For example Art. 283(2) sub-para. 3 TFEU, Art. 14.2. sub-para. 1 ESCB/ECB Statute.

[20]Art. 11.2. sub-para. 2 ESCB/ECB Statute.

[21]Art. 11.4. ESCB/ECB Statute.

[22]Art. 11.1. sub-para. 2 ESCB/ECB Statute.

[23]Cf. Goodhart and Lastra (2017), pp. 56 et seq.

[24]According to Art. 19(1) sub-para. 1 s. 1 TEU the Court of Justice of the European Union (CJEU) shall include the Court of Justice (ECJ), the General Court (EGC) and specialised courts.

[25]Art. 11.4. ESCB/ECB Statute; for the release of a Governor of a NCB according to Art. 14.2. sub-para. 2 ESCB/ECB Statute see ECJ, Rimšēvičs, 26.2.2019, ECLI:EU:C:2019:139.

Personal independence can also be attributed to rules that impose confidentiality of meetings as well as secret ballots,[26] as the publication of minutes, in particular, has the potential to exert specific pressure on members.[27]

2.2.3 *Financial Independence*

Moreover, exercising powers predominantly regarding monetary policy requires financial independence. Under Art. 282(3) s. 3 TFEU the ECB shall be independent in the exercise of its powers and in the management of its finance.[28] This is intended to prevent the ECB from becoming dependent on third parties for the use of monetary policy instruments.

2.2.4 *Functional Independence*

The core of independence is formed by functional independence which is classified in the literature in different ways.[29] In this analysis, it shall be understood as task-related[30] freedom from instructions and any other influence.[31]

2.2.4.1 Prohibition of Instructions and Influence

Being part of the chapter relating to monetary policy, Art. 130 TFEU, which is assigned to the institutional dimension of independence by some authors without substantive differences,[32] says:

> When exercising the powers and carrying out the tasks and duties conferred upon them by the Treaties and the Statute of the ESCB and of the ECB, neither the European Central Bank, nor a national central bank, nor any member of their decision-making bodies shall seek or

---

[26]Art. 10.4. ESCB/ECB Statute, Arts. 4.6. s. 1, 23 Decision 2004/257/EC of the European Central Bank of 19 February 2004 adopting the Rules of Procedure of the European Central Bank (ECB/2004/2), OJ 18.3.2004, L 80, p. 33.

[27]Hahn (1999), p. 957.

[28]See for details Smits (1997), pp. 157, 167–168; Zilioli (2016), pp. 153 and 154.

[29]Similarly Hahn and Häde (2010), § 20 paras. 26–41; according to Zilioli (2016), p. 152, this aspect only relates to the rationale of the independency principle whereas Art. 130 TFEU belongs to the institutional independence; Smits (1997), pp. 157, 167, focuses on the autonomous decision-making in respect of instruments whereas the prohibition of instructions and influence does not seem to be an element in the narrow sense.

[30]For details see Chap. 3.

[31]See also Vos (2016), p. 222.

[32]See Selmayr (2015), paras. 111, 218; Zilioli (2016), pp. 152–153.

take instructions from Union institutions, bodies, offices or agencies, from any government of a Member State or from any other body. The Union institutions, bodies, offices or agencies and the governments of the Member States undertake to respect this principle and not to seek to influence the members of the decision-making bodies of the European Central Bank or of the national central banks in the performance of their tasks.

This provision protects independence in two ways: whereas Art. 130 s. 1 TFEU addresses the entities within the ESCB as well as the members of the decision-making bodies who are not allowed to seek or take any instructions from any body including private persons and entities, Art. 130 s. 2 TFEU obliges the EU institutions and the member states' governments to abstain from any influence on the members of the ESCB's decision-making bodies. This provision, repeated in Art. 7 ESCB/ ECB Statute, creates material independence addressing especially all public authorities within the multi-level EU system. The wording "influence" in Art. 130 s. 2 TFEU implies that all interferences notwithstanding a binding character and the prospect of facing sanctions shall be forbidden except persuasion dominated by expert discussion or a mere expression of opinion.[33]

This view of a widely understood prohibition with regard to the quality of influence has been shared by the ECJ in its judgment of 10 July 2003 concerning the establishment of the European Anti-Fraud Office (OLAF) and its powers towards the ECB.[34] Whereas the Advocate General opined that the principle of independence aims at shielding the decision-making process of the ECB from short-term political pressures,[35] the ECJ did not reiterate the short-term nature and therefore hold that the ECB shall be shielded from all political pressure.[36]

Privileges and immunities of the ECB[37] also have a functional character, as the ECJ has recently ruled, "inasmuch as they are intended to avoid any interference with the functioning and independence of the European Union".[38,39] In particular, the ECB's archives are addressed, which prevent the seizure of documents related to the performance of ESCB/Eurosystem tasks without the ECB's authorisation.[40]

---

33 Siekmann (2013), para. 117.

34 ECJ, OLAF, 10.7.2003, ECLI:EU:C:2003:395.

35 Advocate General Jacobs, OLAF, 3.10.2002, ECLI:EU:C:2002:556, para. 150.

36 ECJ, OLAF, 10.7.2003, ECLI:EU:C:2003:395, para. 134; recently repeated in ECJ, Rimšēvičs, 26.2.2019, ECLI:EU:C:2019:139, para. 47.

37 Art. 343 TFEU, Art. 39 ESCB/ECB Statute.

38 ECJ, Commission/Republic of Slovenia, 17.12.2020, ECLI:EU:C:2020:1030, para. 73.

39 ECJ, Commission/Republic of Slovenia, 17.12.2020, ECLI:EU:C:2020:1030, para. 100.

40 ECJ, Commission/Republic of Slovenia, 17.12.2020, ECLI:EU:C:2020:1030, paras. 102 et seq.

2.2.4.2 Correlation Between Independence and the Maintenance of Price Stability

Functional independence also relates to the reasons for implementing this *modus operandi* which was discussed extensively in the economic and legal literature long before the Maastricht Treaty. It has been stressed, that there is a positive correlation between central bank measures free from political influence and their success in stabilising the currency's internal value.[41] This finding is based on empirical evidence.[42] The substantial reasoning for this lies in the fact that political bodies are unimmunised against short-term results and interested in electoral success, thus not stringently prioritising the stability of money.[43] This leads to the result that a public good, like price stability, can be safeguarded best by entrusting its maintenance to an independent authority.[44] It should also be mentioned at this point, that the diminution of external, mainly political influence is a necessary, but not a sufficient condition of effective monetary policy. *Inter alia*, the scope of the mandate as well as the quality of further objectives and the order of priority between them may affect the effectiveness of central bank operations.[45] However, this issue which also addresses the legal embedment of central bank independence shall be dealt with later.[46]

These findings which have been affirmed by the historic experiences with high inflation rates in the 1960s and 1970s resulted in granting more autonomy to central banks worldwide.[47] Especially, the German Central Bank (Deutsche Bundesbank) provided with independence under §§ 12 s. 2, 29(1) s. 1 Gesetz über die Deutsche Bundesbank (BBankG) (old version) was a role model for the conception of the ESCB.[48] However, the wording of Art. 130 TFEU as well as Art. 7 ESCB/ECB Statute does not necessarily lead to a restrictive understanding of the prohibition being limited to monetary policy functions or, even narrower, the pursuit of its primary objective.[49] Art. 130 s. 1 TFEU comprises "exercising the powers and carrying out the tasks and duties conferred upon them by the Treaties and the Statute of the ESCB and of the ECB". The wording of Article 130 s. 2 TFEU seems to be even wider referring to "the performance of their [viz. the members' of the

---

[41]Lastra (2015), para. 2.117; Smits (1997), p. 152.

[42]See for instance Swinburne and Castello-Branco (1991); de Haan and Sturm (1992); for further references see Lastra (2015), para. 2.116.

[43]See for details Smits (1997), p. 153; Zilioli (2016), pp. 128–130.

[44]Swinburne and Castello-Branco (1991), p. 5; Lastra (2015), para. 2.117.

[45]Smits (1997), p. 153 with further references.

[46]See infra Sect. 5.3.

[47]Smits (1997), p. 159.

[48]For details see Lastra (2015), paras. 2.148–2.158.

[49]In contrast, some German scholars argue that the independence granted under primary law only relates to monetary policy or the objective of maintaining price stability, see Häde (2016), para. 7; Kämmerer and Starski (2013), p. 328; Gören (2019), p. 234.

decision-making bodies of the ECB or NCBs] tasks". Art. 7 ESCB/ECB Statute contains similar provisions.

The interpretation of Art. 108 TEC, the provision previous to Art. 130 TFEU, has been a main part of the beforehand mentioned OLAF decision. The ECJ stated that "the draftsmen of the EC Treaty clearly intended to ensure that the ECB should be in a position to carry out independently the tasks conferred upon it by the Treaty".[50] However, the Advocate General pointed out the following in his opinion:

> That provision establishes, according to its wording, a principle of central bank independence. It is, as the ECB itself points out, clear that the independence thus established is not an end in itself; it serves a specific purpose. By shielding the decision-making process of the ECB from short-term political pressures the principle of independence aims to enable the ECB effectively to pursue the aim of price stability and, without prejudice to that aim, support the economic policies of the Community as required by Article 105(1) EC.[51]

He also emphasised that the "Treaty prohibits only influence which is liable to undermine the ability of the ECB to carry out its tasks effectively with a view to price stability, and which must therefore be regarded as undue".[52]

This opinion, primarily focusing on maintaining price stability and, apart from that, the support of general economic policies, has not been shared by the ECJ deciding that the provision points to influences which are "likely to interfere with the performance of the tasks which the EC Treaty and the ESCB Statute assign to the ECB".[53] According to the ECJ, the provision "seeks, in essence, to shield the ECB from all political pressure in order to enable it effectively to pursue the objectives attributed to its tasks, through the independent exercise of the specific powers conferred on it for that purpose by the EC Treaty and the ESCB Statute".[54] This interpretation only excludes assignments of tasks and powers beyond the Treaties and the ESCB/ECB Statute. This raises the challenging question whether tasks and powers conferred on the ECB by secondary law, especially the involvement in micro-prudential supervision on the basis of Art. 127(6) TFEU, would be tasks and powers "by the EC Treaty and the ESCB Statute".[55] Furthermore, it remains open up to this point whether and to what extent guarantees of independence can be implemented by secondary law as in the case of Art. 19(1) s. 2 SSMR granting independence to the members of the Supervisory Board established within the ECB for the exercise of banking supervision. These questions shall be answered in the context of specific central bank tasks.[56]

Nevertheless, the ECJ's judgment, although extending independence to all tasks and powers attributed by the Treaties and the Statute, is not opposed to a concept of

---

[50]ECJ, OLAF, 10.7.2003, ECLI:EU:C:2003:395, para. 130.

[51]Advocate General Jacobs, OLAF, 3.10.2002, ECLI:EU:C:2002:556, para. 150.

[52]Advocate General Jacobs, OLAF, 3.10.2002, ECLI:EU:C:2002:556, para. 155.

[53]ECJ, OLAF, 10.7.2003, ECLI:EU:C:2003:395, para. 134.

[54]ECJ, OLAF, 10.7.2003, ECLI:EU:C:2003:395, para. 134.

[55]ECJ, OLAF, 10.7.2003, ECLI:EU:C:2003:395, para. 134.

[56]See infra Sect. 3.2.

functional distinction. Regarding legislative measures applying to the ECB, the ECJ outlined that the compliance with Art. 130 TFEU depends on whether, and to what extent, such measures undermine independent task performance.[57] This underlines that the specific nature of tasks cannot be neglected when carving out the scope of independence in detail.[58]

2.3 Relationship to the Principle of Democracy

2.3.1 Democracy in the European Union

Democracy is one of the core values upon which the EU is founded together with human dignity, freedom, equality, the rule of law and respect for human rights, including the rights of persons belonging to minorities (Art. 2 s. 1 TEU). Besides, this principle is a requirement for the Member States (Art. 2 s. 2 TEU), even prospective ones (Art. 49(1) s. 1 TEU) whereas its compliance is procedurally secured by Art. 7 TEU. This commitment to democracy is further elaborated by the "provisions on democratic principles" summarised in Title II (Arts. 9-12 TEU). In defining a European concept of democracy, it is important to identify the intersection of national legal traditions, which prove to be extremely heterogeneous, and to reconcile this with the autonomy of the Union legal order and its constitution as an association of sovereign states (*"Staatenverbund"*[59]).[60]

A cornerstone of the Union's concept of democracy is the principle of representative democracy according to Art. 10 TEU which means that citizens are directly represented at the Union level in the European Parliament (Art. 10(2) sub-para. 1 TEU) and the Member States are represented in the European Council by their Heads of State or Government and in the Council by members of their governments, themselves democratically accountable either to their national parliaments, or to their citizens (Art. 10(2) sub-para. 2 TEU). This creates a dual legitimation structure consisting of a Union and a Member State pillar of legitimation (*"Legitimationsstrang"*).[61] Both pillars thus co-constitute the level of legitimation (*"Legitimationsniveau"*), without any precedence given to one of them in the design of the Treaties.[62]

---

[57]ECJ, OLAF, 10.7.2003, ECLI:EU:C:2003:395, paras. 136–137.

[58]Concisely Mersch (2017), according to whom "institutional independence should be subject to a functional analysis of the need for those new tasks to benefit from the same broad independence framework".

[59]FCC, Maastricht, 12.10.1993 = BVerfGE 89, 155 (p. 186).

[60]See Manger-Nestler (2015), pp. 319-320 with further references.

[61]See Calliess (2010), pp. 167–168.

[62]Nevertheless, the ECJ emphasises the importance of the European Parliament more strongly, see ECJ, Roquette Frères, 29.10.1980, ECLI:EU:C:1980:249, para. 33; Maizena, 29.10.1980, ECLI:EU:C:1980:250, para. 34; Titandioxid, 11.6.1991, ECLI:EU:C:1991:244, para. 20. In

This concept codified by the Lisbon Treaty has nevertheless been and continues to be subject to the reproach of a "democratic deficit", criticising the Union's decision-making process from various angles.[63] Granting independence to authorities, in particular central banks, is one of the criticisms because this may entail a loss of control by the representatives and thus the people. According to *Abraham Lincoln* who defined democracy as "government of the people, by the people, for the people",[64] it becomes clear that government action must be traceable to individuals. In polities, based on the principle of representative democracy, this connection is established mainly, but not exclusively, through parliaments.[65] Typically, parliaments determine government action by setting up general abstract provisions (legislative power) and electing the performing individuals (power of appointment and dismissal), supplemented by the right to decide on the budget (budgetary power).[66] Moreover, parliaments are typically responsible for scrutinising the executive (monitoring power).[67] With regard to the European Parliament, these functions are enshrined in Art. 14(1) TEU, according to which it shall exercise legislative and budgetary functions jointly with the Council (s. 1), exercise functions of political control and consultation as laid down in the Treaties (s. 2) and elect the President of the Commission (s. 3).[68]

These particular functions seem to be disturbed and affected by "drops of influence" (*"Einflussknicke"*[69]) in case of a prohibition of instructions and influence which prevents the representatives as well as the people from determining decisions, even though these can be of major importance to the general public. Similarly, the provisions granting personal and financial independence decrease parliamentary and thus democratic control because the representatives can neither dismiss the respective actors by their own decision nor can they influence the fulfilment via budgetary control. Solely, the dimension of institutional independence does not seem to create tensions because it is limited to maintaining the constitutional framework and thus carrying out the intention of the draftsmen.

This finding calls for an analysis of the existing democratic mechanisms to determine whether, and to what extent, central bank action requires and bears

---

contrast, the FCC focuses significantly on the national parliaments providing legitimation, see FCC, Maastricht, 12.10.1993 = BVerfGE 89, 155 (pp. 184–186); Lisbon, 30.6.2009, 2 BvE 2/08 et al., paras. 262–264.

[63] See Craig and de Búrca (2015), pp. 151–152; Nettesheim (2020), para. 115–121.

[64] Gettysburg Address, 1863.

[65] For the powers of the European Parliament see Craig and de Búrca (2015), pp. 53–56; cornerning the tasks of the Bundestag see Klein (2019), paras. 47–56.

[66] Cf. Repasi (2020), paras. 17.7–17.8.

[67] Ibid.

[68] For details see Repasi (2020), paras. 17.19 et seq.

[69] FCC, PSPP (order for reference), 18.7.2017, 2 BvR 859/15 et al., para. 103; Banking Union, 30.7.2019, 2 BvR 1685/14 et al., para. 126.

democratic reconnection and responsibility. In this context, the other democratic principles set out in Arts. 9-12 TEU will also be brought to the fore.[70]

2.3.2 *The Concept of Legitimation*

2.3.2.1 Legitimacy and Legitimation

To capture the tension between democracy and independence, literature predominantly uses the term democratic legitimacy. Yet irrespective of the requirements this concept places on the establishment and performance of independent central banks, legitimacy can be considered from two perspectives. On the one hand, it addresses a normative category that imposes conditions on the justification of government action.[71] On the other hand, it also refers to the acceptance of government action or, at least, its worthiness of recognition,[72] which primarily requires verification by empirical studies and is therefore not a viable model for a legal analysis.

In contrast, the concept of democratic legitimation, which is found primarily in the FCC's case law on the principle of democracy enshrined in Art. 20(1), (2) Grundgesetz (GG) addresses only the normative component and derives from this, *inter alia*, requirements for administrative organisation.[73] In this study, we use an approach of examining the extent to which government action is enabled and limited by legal rules which ensure that it is linked to the subject of legitimation, i.e. the citizens of the Union or the citizens resp. the people of the Member States. As already described, this does not say anything about the specific requirements that go with that. Therefore, the concept of democratic accountability to be discussed below also has potential for providing democratic legitimation.[74]

2.3.2.2 Input and Output Legitimation

Not only in political science,[75] but also in jurisprudence[76] a distinction is made between input and output legitimation, which to a certain extent reflects the approaches to democracy emphasised by Lincoln.

---

[70]See infra Sect. 5.1.

[71]Schmidt-Aßmann (1991), pp. 330–331.

[72]Amtenbrink and Lastra (2008), p. 121 ("Democratic legitimacy is not only an issue of legally binding rules, but also an issue of perception."); Ritleng (2016), p. 83; for the different concepts of legitimacy see Peuker (2011), pp. 96–122.

[73]See infra Sect. 5.2.

[74]For example, the term democratic legitimation is also used by Amtenbrink (2019), pp. 305–306 and 315–316. In contrast, Zilioli (2016), p. 178, addresses democratic legitimacy.

[75]See Scharpf (1970), pp. 21–28; (1999), pp. 16–28.

[76]See for example Craig and de Búrca (2015), pp. 157–158; Peters (2001), pp. 521–524.

Input legitimation is linked to the "government by the people, of the people" and includes all requirements that control governmental action *ex ante* and that are derived from regularly held elections and forms of direct democracy.[77] This justification of state action is contrasted with output legitimation, which is described and understood in very different ways in the literature. Many voices focus on the element of promoting the public good and thus, in the sense of a "government for the people", the benefits of governmental action.[78] Important parameters of such legitimation are therefore the expertise of the actors, the efficiency of the processes and the quality of the results.[79] The importance of such a concept, especially concerning governance in the EU, was impressively demonstrated by *Scharpf*. The structural characteristic elements of the supranationally constituted EU, in particular the participation of government representatives in EU legislation, the possibility of majority decisions in the Council and the election of the European Parliament, which is not characterised by strict equality, pose considerable challenges to input legitimation tailored to the nation-state.[80] This can be overcome by seeking legitimation – not exclusively, but additionally—in other normatively tangible mechanisms that establish a control and responsibility relationship for achieving the public good. Legitimation is thus provided by legally aligning decision-making processes in such a way that the common good is achieved or at least promoted.[81]

2.3.3 *The Concept of Democratic Accountability and Its Application to the ECB*

An important mechanism anchored in primary law and controlling central bank action is accountability.[82] This source of legitimation requires, first, that the establishment of central banks as autonomous authorities is based on a democratic act, by constitution or by legislation, constituting the legal basis.[83]

After their establishment, however, sovereign authorities also require on-going legitimation with regard to the exercise of powers. This justification is described by the term accountability, which is aptly defined by Lastra:

[77]See Scharpf (1999), p. 17; Petersen (2010), p. 145.

[78]Scharpf (1999), pp. 16, 20–28; Calliess (2005), p. 298; for a critical view regarding the lack of measurability of the output see Gärditz (2010), pp. 278–279.

[79]Schmitter (2001), pp. 2, 7–8; Menon and Weatherill (2007), p. 3.

[80]See Scharpf (1999), pp. 17–18; Menon and Weatherill (2007), pp. 4–5, 20–22, 24.

[81]See the concept of output legitimation formulated by Schliesky (2004), p. 666; Trute (2012), para. 53.

[82]See for this concept in general Harlow (2002); Mulgan (2003); concerning delegation Lupia (2006), p. 35; Strøm (2006), pp. 61–64.

[83]Lastra (2015), para 2.163; see also De Boer and van 't Klooster (2020), p. 1698, who differentiate between authorisation and accountability.

> [A]ccountability is thus the process of bringing back (by giving account, explaining, justifying, or taking measures of amendment or redress) that independent entity to the procedures and processes of a democratic society.[84]

The purpose of such a concept is to prevent the abuse of power by deconcentrating decision-making power and establishing checks and balances.[85]

This concept, whose standards admittedly depend on legal norms, can generally be depicted as a three-stage process that characterises the relationship between the person who is accountable (hereinafter: the actor) and the person to whom accountability is due (hereinafter: forum).[86] The first step is for the actor to provide the forum with *ex post* information about its actions. In the second step, the forum can initiate a debate on the basis of the information obtained, in which the actor must justify its actions when asked to do so, so that the forum may evaluate its actions. In the third step, the forum can draw conclusions based on his evaluation and within the scope of his decision-making powers. In this respect, soft control mechanisms, such as the pronouncement of disapproval, can be considered as well as disciplinary measures or the overruling of the actor's decisions.

In the following, the control mechanisms which serve to hold the ECB accountable will be briefly presented. Here the concept of accountability is divided into three aspects, namely political, administrative and judicial, of which all are characterised by elements of explanation and justification by the actor and possible sanctions by the forum.[87] These mechanisms, which limit and at the same time safeguard central bank independence, are essential elements of democratic legitimation, but need not be exhaustive as will be shown later.

2.3.3.1 Political Accountability

An important part of the concept is marked by accountability and reporting obligations imposed on the ECB by the Treaties. According to Art. 284(1) TFEU, the President of the Council and a Member of the Commission may participate in meetings of the Governing Council of the ECB. According to Art. 284(3) TFEU the ECB shall deliver an annual report on the activities of the ESCB and on the monetary policy of both the previous and current year to the European Parliament, the Council and the Commission, and also to the European Council.[88] In addition to

---

[84] Lastra (2015), para 2.163; on the other hand, Zilioli (2016), pp. 178–179, considers accountability to be "an important complement to the exercise of power by an independent institution in a democratic society", but sees no need for "ongoing legitimation" because "[i]ndependence and legitimacy are located at two different levels".

[85] Amtenbrink and Lastra (2008), p. 121.

[86] For further details on the process described below see Bovens (2007), pp. 451–452; Busuioc (2010), pp. 33–34.

[87] For a similar approach see ter Kuile et al. (2015), p. 156; Lamandini and Ramos Muñoz (2020), pp. 12–13.

[88] Further reporting commitments can be found in Art. 15 ESCB/ECB Statute.

this, the President of the ECB shall present this report to the Council and to the European Parliament, which may hold a general debate on that basis.[89] Moreover, the President of the ECB and the other members of the Executive Board may, at the request of the European Parliament or on their own initiative, be heard by the competent committees of the European Parliament.[90] This hearing established the so-called monetary dialogue between the European Parliament and the ECB, which in practice is held in a meeting of the European Parliament's Economic and Monetary Affairs committee (ECON committee) and addresses not only monetary but also economic policy issues.[91]

This mechanism seems to be accountability in the strictest sense, whereby the ECB justifies its actions *ex post* to the EU institutions and the latter evaluate these actions on an informed basis. With regard to the instruments to which the forum is entitled, it can be observed that the concept of central bank independence generally prohibits harsh sanctions, such as disciplinary measures or the overruling of central bank decisions. However, the annulment of measures in the case of illegality of Union law is reserved for the CJEU. Therefore, the legislative bodies are constrained to steer the ECB's action in abstract and general terms within the framework set by the Treaties.

At this point it should already be pointed out that the transfer of further tasks to the ECB by secondary law has not only been rounded off by specific independence standards, but also by accountability and reporting obligations, in particular for the members of the Supervisory Board within the SSM[92] as well as for the ESRB and its Chair, i.e. the President of the ECB.[93]

2.3.3.2 Administrative Accountability

Although the Union's institutional organisation is characterised less by the separation of powers and more by the division of functions, there are administrative entities that exercise specific control instruments. To be mentioned here are the Commission, which has both governmental and administrative functions, but also the European Court of Auditors (ECA), which shall carry out the Union's audit according to Art. 285(1) TFEU. According to Art. 287(1) s. 1, (2) s. 1 TFEU, the ECA examines the accounts of all revenue and expenditure of the Union which includes checking whether all revenue has been received and all expenditure incurred in a lawful and regular manner and whether the financial management has been sound. However, with regard to the ECB, Art. 27 ESCB/ECB Statute introduces an important modification. Hereafter, the accounts of the ECB shall be audited by independent

[89] Art. 284(3) sub-para. 1 s. 2 TFEU.

[90] Art. 284(3) sub-para. 2 TFEU.

[91] See Repasi (2020), paras. 17.48–17.50.

[92] Arts. 20, 21 SSMR.

[93] Art. 19 ESRBR.

external auditors to be recommended by the Governing Council and approved by the Council having full power to examine all books and accounts and obtaining full information about their transactions.[94] However, the ECA's control is limited to examining the operational efficiency of the management of the ECB.[95]

It should be noted that, by transferring tasks of banking supervision in the SSM context to the ECB, further control mechanisms have been established or extended. This pertains firstly to the internal administrative control of supervisory decisions by the Administrative Board of Review (ABoR).[96] In addition, the ECB has also been integrated into the ESFS as a supervisory authority and is thus also subject to the specific control mechanisms of the EBA, especially Arts. 17 to 20 EBAR.

2.3.3.3 Judicial Accountability

Judicial review and interpretation of acts and omissions of the ECB is generally carried out by the CJEU.[97] According to Art. 263 sub-para. s. 1 TFEU the CJEU reviews the legality of acts of the ECB, other than recommendations and opinions. According to Art. 263 sub-para. 2 TFEU, the court shall for this purpose have jurisdiction upon actions brought by a Member State, the European Parliament, the Council or the Commission on grounds of lack of competence, infringement of an essential procedural requirement, infringement of the Treaties or of any rule of law relating to their application, or misuse of powers. According to Art. 263 sub-para. 4 TFEU, any natural or legal person may also institute proceedings against an act addressed to that person or which is of direct and individual concern to them, and against a regulatory act which is of direct concern to them and does not entail implementing measures. Omissions of the ECB which are an infringement of the Treaties may be subject to legal proceedings under the conditions laid down in Art. 265 TFEU. These provisions also apply to banking supervision, which is clarified by Art. 24(11) SSMR.

With regard to damages, it should be noted that the ECB is subject to the liability regime of Art. 340 TFEU.[98] Being the only institution of the EU with legal personality although it is a Union's institution, the ECB itself makes good any damage caused by it or by its servants in the performance of their duties.[99] According to the ECJ, non-contractual liability requires that "the rule of law infringed must be intended to confer rights on individuals; the breach must be

---

[94] Art. 27.1. ESCB/ECB Statute.

[95] Art. 27.2. ESCB/ECB Statute.

[96] Art. 24 SSMR.

[97] Art. 35.1. ESCB/ECB Statute. However, disputes between the ECB, on the one hand, and its creditors, debtors or any other person, on the other, shall be decided by the competent national courts, save where jurisdiction has been conferred upon the CJEU (Art. 35.2. ESCB/ECB Statute).

[98] Art. 35.3. s. 1 ESCB/ECB Statute.

[99] Art. 340(3) TFEU.

sufficiently serious; and there must be a direct causal link between the breach of the obligation resting on the State and the damage sustained by the injured parties".[100] Concerning the requirement of a sufficiently serious infringement the courts must test "whether the Member State or the Community institution concerned manifestly and gravely disregarded the limits of its discretion".[101]

As far as the ECB is concerned, liability may also be envisaged in the fulfilment of its monetary policy mandate, for example with regard to infringements by the determination of minimum reserves. Nevertheless, the liability of the ECB has come to the fore, particularly with regard to the tasks it has assumed during the financial and sovereign debt crisis. This applies in particular to its joint task with the Commission, the International Monetary Fund (IMF) and the ESM of advising and monitoring euro area Member States affected by crises in the implementation of reform programmes if they have received assistance from the EFSF or the ESM.[102] Moreover, SSM supervision, which includes the adoption of ECB supervisory decisions, in particular imposing sanctions, on individual market participants, bears potential liability risks.[103]

2.3.4 *Democratic Safeguarding of Independence in the Case Law of the ECJ*

In infringement proceedings initiated by the Commission against Germany, the ECJ was given the opportunity to deliver an opinion on the compatibility of independent authorities with the principle of democracy in the field of data protection supervision. Art. 28(1) sub-para. 2 Data Protection Directive[104] provided that the supervisory authorities to be established by the Member States shall act with complete independence in exercising the functions entrusted to them. When implemented into German law, however, the laws of the German federal states *("Länder")* expressly provided that the bodies entrusted with the control of data processing in the non-public sector were subject to state supervision.

Germany justified the rule that the legality of the actions of the data protection supervisory authorities is ensured by means of instruments for monitoring legality or substance *("Rechts- und Fachaufsicht")* primarily on the basis of the principle of

[100]ECJ, Brasserie du pêcheur, 5.3.1996, ECLI:EU:C:1996:79, para. 51.

[101]ECJ, Brasserie du pêcheur, 5.3.1996, ECLI:EU:C:1996:79, para. 55.

[102]Cf. ECJ, Ledra Advertising, 20.9.2016, ECLI:EU:C:2016:701, para. 55.

[103]For details see Almhofer (2018).

[104]Directive 95/46/EC of the European Parliament and of the Council of 24 December 1995 on the protection of individuals with regard to the processing of personal data and on the free movement of such data, OJ 23.11.1995, L 281, p. 31; now Art. 52(1) Regulation (EU) 2016/679 of the European Parliament and of the Council of 27 April 2016 on the protection of natural persons with regard to the processing of personal data and on the free movement of such data, and repealing Directive 95/46/EC (General Data Protection Regulation), OJ 4.5.2016, L 119, p. 1.

democracy, which ensures the democratic legitimation of the administration being subject to the instructions of the government which is accountable to its parliament.[105]

The ECJ clearly rejected this argument:

> That principle [viz. of democracy] does not preclude the existence of public authorities outside the classic hierarchical administration and more or less independent of the government. The existence and conditions of operation of such authorities are, in the Member States, regulated by the law or even, in certain States, by the Constitution and those authorities are required to comply with the law subject to the review of the competent courts. Such independent administrative authorities, as exist moreover in the German judicial system, often have regulatory functions or carry out tasks which must be free from political influence, whilst still being required to comply with the law subject to the review of the competent courts. That is precisely the case with regard to the tasks of the supervisory authorities relating to the protection of data.[106]

The ECJ thus does not regard the government's power to issue instructions as a mandatory democratic element. Instead, democratic embedment is created on the one hand by the binding effect of law and on the other hand by judicial control.

The binding effect of law upon executive powers, which is also found in the German concept of democratic legitimation,[107] ensures that the representatives' will expressed in abstract and general rules is transported to individual cases regulated by administrative decisions. Judicial control should also develop democratic effectiveness. This may seem surprising from a German perspective, since judicial control is primarily anchored in the rule of law (Art. 20(3) GG, *"Rechtsstaatsprinzip"*). However, judicial review also develops democratic effectiveness to the extent that it ensures compliance with the decisions made by the legislature. Seen in this light, the courts, although being independent bodies themselves, also serve democracy through generating output legitimation. It should be pointed out here, that in its Banking Union decision, the FCC *inter alia* referred to the ECJ's decision on data protection authorities and the instruments of democratic control mentioned therein when ultimately accepting independent bodies required by European Union law under certain conditions.[108]

The ECJ, although rejecting the necessity of governmental oversight to ensure democratic legitimation, nevertheless stressed that "the absence of any parliamentary influence over those authorities is inconceivable".[109] As channels of influence, also provided for in the Data Protection Directive, the ECJ identified the appointment of the management of the supervisory authorities by the parliament or the government

---

[105]See ECJ, Data Protection Authorities, 9.3.2010, ECLI:EU:C:2010:125, paras. 39–40; for details concerning the requirements of the principle of democracy enshrined in Art. 20(1), (2) GG see infra Sect. 5.2.

[106]ECJ, Data Protection Authorities, 9.3.2010, ECLI:EU:C:2010:125, para. 42.

[107]See infra Sect. 5.2.1.

[108]FCC, Banking Union, 30.7.2019, 2 BvR 1685/14 et al., paras. 130, 136; see infra Sect. 5.2.2.

[109]ECJ, Data Protection Authorities, 9.3.2010, ECLI:EU:C:2010:125, para. 43.

and the legislator's power to define the powers of those authorities.[110] Furthermore, the legislator may impose an obligation on the supervisory authorities to report their activities to the parliament.[111] Thereby, the ECJ demonstrated how democratic legitimation can be established beyond the government's power to issue instructions, in particular by emphasising accountability mechanisms. However, this does not mean that such a concept necessarily fulfils the requirements of the principle of democracy enshrined in the Grundgesetz whose fundamentals must neither be affected in the context of the European integration.[112] Nevertheless, the advance of Union law concepts of independence should not only be accompanied by critical voices,[113] but also lead to an open-minded approach to European accountability concepts.

The ECJ not only highlighted options for establishing democratic legitimation, but also referred to the regulatory function of authorities as well as the need to exempt them from political influence.[114] Thus, the court underlined the function of the specific task to be performed and placed this aspect in the context of independence. By no means, such a functional approach must be restricted to certain authorities, but may be made productive for the ECB's various tasks, as the following analysis will show.

References

Almhofer M (2018) Die Haftung der Europäischen Zentralbank für rechtswidrige Bankenaufsicht. Mohr Siebeck, Tübingen

Amtenbrink F (2019b) Independence and accountability in the new age of European central banking – revisiting Gormely and de Haan's 'The democratic deficit of the European Central Bank'. In: Amtenbrink F, Davies G, Kochenov D, Lindeboom J (eds) The internal market and the future of European integration – essays in honour of Laurence W. Gormley. Cambridge University Press, Cambridge, pp 305–321

Amtenbrink F, Lastra RM (2008) Securing democratic accountability of financial regulatory agencies – a theoretical framework. In: de Mulder RV (ed) Mitigating risk in the context of safety and security – how relevant is a rational approach? Erasmus University Rotterdam, Rotterdam, pp 115–135

Athanassiou P (2009) Withdrawal and expulsion from the EU and EMU – some reflections, ECB Legal Working Paper Series No. 10. https://www.ecb.europa.eu/pub/pdf/scplps/ecblwp10.pdf (26 February 2021)

Bovens M (2007) Analysing and assessing accountability – a conceptual framework. Eur Law J 13:447–468

Bull HP (2010) Die "völlig unabhängige" Aufsichtsbehörde – Zum Urteil des EuGH vom 9.3.2010 in Sachen Datenschutzaufsicht. Europäische Zeitschrift für Wirtschaftsrecht, pp 488–494

[110]ECJ, Data Protection Authorities, 9.3.2010, ECLI:EU:C:2010:125, para. 44.

[111]ECJ, Data Protection Authorities, 9.3.2010, ECLI:EU:C:2010:125, para. 45.

[112]Art. 23(1) s. 3 GG in conjunction with Arts. 79(3), 20(1)(2) GG.

[113]For a critical view of independent regulatory authorities see Gärditz (2010), pp. 251 et seq.; of independent data protection Bull (2010), pp. 488 et seq.

[114]ECJ, Data Protection Authorities, 9.3.2010, ECLI:EU:C:2010:125, para. 42.

Busuioc EM (2010) The accountability of European agencies – legal provisions and ongoing practices. Eburon, Delft
Calliess C (2005) Optionen zur Demokratisierung der Europäischen Union. In: Bauer H, Huber PM, Sommermann K-P (eds) Demokratie in Europa. Mohr Siebeck, Tübingen, pp 281–317
Calliess C (2010) Die neue Europäische Union nach dem Vertrag von Lissabon – Ein Überblick über die Reformen unter Berücksichtigung ihrer Implikationen für das deutsche Recht. Mohr Siebeck, Tübingen
Craig P, de Búrca G (2015) EU law – text, cases, and materials, 6th edn. Oxford University Press, Oxford
De Boer N, van 't Klooster J (2020) The ECB, the courts and the issue of democratic legitimacy after Weiss. Common Mark Law Rev 57:1689–1724
De Haan J, Sturm JE (1992) The case for central bank independence. Banco Nazionale del Lavoro Quarterly Review 45(182):305–327
European Monetary Institute (1995) Progress towards convergence – report prepared in accordance with Article 7 of the EMI Statute. https://www.ecb.europa.eu/pub/pdf/other/emiprogresstowardsconvergence199511en.pdf?b4ddfeeb739e28100d355807d3e2a510 (26 February 2021)
European Monetary Institute (1998) Convergence report – report required by Article 109j of the Treaty establishing the European Community. https://www.ecb.europa.eu/pub/pdf/conrep/cr1998en.pdf (26 February 2021)
Gärditz KF (2010) Europäisches Regulierungsverwaltungsrecht auf Abwegen. Archiv des öffentlichen Rechts 135:251–288
Goodhart C, Lastra RM (2017) Populism and central bank independence. Open Econ Rev 29:49–68
Gören E (2019) Der Einheitliche Aufsichtsmechanismus bei der Europäischen Zentralbank (Single Supervisory Mechanism). Nomos, Baden-Baden
Häde U (2016) Kommentierung zu Art. 130 AEUV. In: Calliess C, Ruffert M (eds) EUV/AEUV, 5th edn. Beck, Munich
Hahn HJ (1999) Berichtspflichten und Informationsmöglichkeiten der Europäischen Zentralbank. Juristenzeitung, pp 957–963
Hahn HJ, Häde U (2010) Währungsrecht, 2nd edn. Beck, Munich
Harlow C (2002) Accountability in the European Union. Oxford University Press, Oxford
Herrmann C (2013) Kommentierung zu Art. 139 AEUV. In: Siekmann H (ed) EWU – Kommentar zur Europäischen Währungsunion. Mohr Siebeck, Tübingen
Herrmann C, Dornacher C (2017) International and European monetary law – an introduction. Springer, Heidelberg
Kämmerer JA, Starski P (2013) Die Europäische Zentralbank in der Bankenunion oder: Vor Risiken und Nebenwirkungen wird gewarnt. Zeitschrift für Gesetzgebung, pp 318–338
Klein HH (2019) Kommentierung zu Art. 38 GG. In: Maunz T, Dürig G (eds) GG, 88th edn. Beck, Munich
Lamandini M, Ramos Muñoz D (2020) SSM and SRB accountability at European level – what room for improvements? https://www.europarl.europa.eu/RegData/etudes/STUD/2020/645711/IPOL_STU(2020)645711_EN.pdf (26 February 2021)
Lastra RM (2015) International financial and monetary law, 2nd edn. Oxford University Press, Oxford
Lupia A (2006) Delegation and its perils. In: Strøm K, Müller WC, Bergman T (eds) Delegation and accountability in parliamentary democracies, 2nd edn. Oxford University Press, Oxford, pp 33–54
Manger-Nestler C (2015) EU-Agenturen als Ausdruck des europäischen Demokratiemangels? Zeitschrift für Europäische Studien, pp 315–346
Manger-Nestler C (2020b) Chapter 8: The architecture of EMU. In: Amtenbrink F, Herrmann C (eds) The EU law of Economic and Monetary Union. Oxford University Press, Oxford, pp 191–213
Menon A, Weatherill S (2007) Democratic politics in a globalising world – supranationalism and legitimacy in the European Union, LSE Law, Society and Economy Working Papers 13. https://www.lse.ac.uk/law/working-paper-series/2007-08/WPS13-2007MenonandWeatherill.pdf (26 February 2021)

Mersch Y (2017b) Central bank independence revisited, Keynote at the "Symposium on Building the Financial System of the 21st Century: An Agenda for Europe and the United States", Frankfurt a.M., 30 March 2017. https://www.ecb.europa.eu/press/key/date/2017/html/sp170330.en.html (26 February 2021)
Mulgan R (2003) Holding power to account – accountability in modern democracies. Palgrave Macmillan, Hampshire
Nettesheim M (2020) Kommentierung zu Art. 10 EUV. In: Grabitz E, Hilf M, Nettesheim M (eds) Das Recht der Europäischen Union, 70th edn. Beck, Munich
Peters A (2001) Elemente einer Theorie der Verfassung Europas. Duncker & Humblot, Berlin
Petersen N (2010) Demokratie und Grundgesetz – Veränderungen des Demokratieprinzips in Art. 20 Abs. 2 GG angesichts der Herausforderungen moderner Staatlichkeit. Jahrbuch desöffentlichen Rechts 58:137–171
Peuker E (2011) Bürokratie und Demokratie in Europa – Legitimität im Europäischen Verwaltungsverbund. Mohr Siebeck, Tübingen
Repasi R (2020) 17 European Parliament and national parliaments. In: Amtenbrink F, Herrmann C (eds) The EU law of Economic and Monetary Union. Oxford University Press, Oxford
Ritleng D (2016) The independence and legitimacy of the European Court of Justice. In: Ritleng D (ed) Independence and legitimacy in the institutional system of the European Union. Oxford University Press, Oxford, pp 83–124
Scharpf FW (1970) Demokratietheorie zwischen Utopie und Anpassung. Konstanz University Press, Konstanz
Scharpf FW (1999) Regieren in Europa. Effektiv und demokratisch? Campus, Frankfurt a.M./New York
Schliesky U (2004) Souveränität und Legitimität von Herrschaftsgewalt – Die Weiterentwicklung von Begriffen der Staatslehre und des Staatsrechts im europäischen Mehrebenensystem. Mohr Siebeck, Tübingen
Schmidt-Aßmann E (1991) Verwaltungslegitimation als Rechtsbegriff. Archiv des öffentlichen Rechts 116:329–390
Schmitter PC (2001) What is there to legitimize in the European Union… and how might this be accomplished?, Political Science Series No. 75. Institute for Advanced Studies, Vienna. https://nbn-resolving.org/urn:nbn:de:0168-ssoar-246372 (26 February 2021)
Selmayr M (2015) § 23 Das Recht der Europäischen Währungsunion. In: Müller-Graff P-C (ed) Europäisches Wirtschaftsordnungsrecht (Enzyklopädie Europarecht, Vol. 4), 1st edn. Nomos, Baden-Baden
Siekmann H (2013) Kommentierung zu Art. 130 AEUV. In: Siekmann H (ed) EWU – Kommentar zur Europäischen Währungsunion. Mohr Siebeck, Tübingen
Smits R (1997) The European Central Bank – institutional aspects. Kluwer Law International, The Hague
Strøm K (2006) Parliamentary democracy and delegation. In: Strøm K, Müller WC, Bergman T (eds) Delegation and accountability in parliamentary democracies, 2nd edn. Oxford University Press, Oxford, pp 55–106
Swinburne M, Castello-Branco M (1991) Central bank independence: issues and experience, IMF Working Paper No. 91/58. https://ssrn.com/abstract=884870 (26 February 2021)
ter Kuile G, Wissink L, Bovenschen W (2015) Tailor-made accountability within the single supervisory mechanism. Common Mark Law Rev 52:155–190
Trute H-H (2012) § 6 Die demokratische Legitimation der Verwaltung. In: Hoffmann-Riem W, Schmidt-Aßmann E, Voßkuhle A (eds) Grundlagen des Verwaltungsrechts, vol 1, 2nd edn. Beck, Munich
Vos E (2016) EU agencies and independence. In: Ritleng D (ed) Independence and legitimacy in the institutional system of the European Union. Oxford University Press, Oxford, pp 206–227
Zilioli C (2016) The independence of the European Central Bank and its new banking supervisory competences. In: Ritleng D (ed) Independence and legitimacy in the institutional system of the European Union. Oxford University Press, Oxford, pp 125–179
Zilioli C, Selmayr M (2001) The law of the European Central Bank. Hart Publishing, Oxford

Chapter 3
Dimensions of Independence in the Various Tasks of the ECB

Since the specific function, i.e. the tasks to be performed, is a key factor in determining the degree of independence as well as the nature and scope of legitimation and control, the ECB's various tasks and related powers shall now be analysed. Here, not only the basic tasks (core mandates[1]), enshrined in Art. 127(2) TFEU, but also the functions conferred on the ECB on the basis of European legislation or international treaties are taken into account.

In this context, characteristic elements of independence and relevant provisions are to be discussed and, at the same time, function-related peculiarities are to be identified in the framework of accountability.

3.1 Monetary Policy

According to Art. 127(2) 1st indent TFEU defining and implementing the monetary policy of the Union is one of the basic tasks carried out through the ESCB. Art. 282 (1) s. 2 TFEU constitutes the Eurosystem and entrusts it with conducting the monetary policy of the Union. This field of tasks is closely interlinked with the primacy of price stability and to a great extent characterised by the monetary instruments which are provided by the ESCB/ECB Statute.[2] At the same time, monetary policy is part of economic policy in a broader sense, which requires a conceptual demarcation of competences, especially with regard to independence.

[1]Lamandini et al. (2017), p. 5.
[2]Smits (1997), p. 196.

C. Manger-Nestler, M. Gentzsch, *Democratic Legitimation of Central Bank Independence in the European Union*, https://doi.org/10.1007/978-3-030-75115-9_3

3.1.1 Objectives and Means

In 1998, the ECB adopted a definition of price stability within its powers to conduct monetary policy according to which price stability is defined as a year-on-year increase in the Harmonised Index of Consumer Prices (HICP) for the euro area of below 2%.[3] To achieve this goal, primary law provides the ECB with various instruments. According to chapter IV of the ESCB/ECB Statute, the ECB and the NCBs especially may open accounts for credit institutions, public entities and other market participants (Art. 17), conduct open market and credit operations (Art. 18) and require credit institutions to hold minimum reserves (Art. 19). Of particular importance are the so-called key interest rates (Art. 12.1 sub-para. 1 s. 2 ESCB/ECB Statute), which include the interest rate on the main refinancing operations (MRO), the rate on the deposit facility and the rate on the marginal lending facility[4] and signal the ECB's general monetary policy stance. With the help of monetary policy, the ECB aims to influence the so-called transmission mechanism, which describes how monetary policy measures are transmitted to economic variables (such as price levels, output and employment).[5] The transmission of monetary policy measures mainly, although not exclusively, takes place via commercial banks by refinancing, although the effects of monetary policy operations can vary considerably over time. *Inter alia*, main or longer-term refinancing, and their impact on the primary objective of price stability are not fully predictable.

The constitutional framework, which outlines the instruments rather generally and leaves the concretisation of the stability objective to the ECB itself, can certainly be classified as broad and allows for flexible action towards new challenges, which, however, leaves certain gaps with regard to democratic authorisation.[6] An important limit for the use of monetary policy instruments is, however, set by the prohibition of monetary financing laid down in Art. 123 TFEU, which, although it does not permit justifiable interferences,[7] nevertheless depends, to a considerable extent, on market expectations when determining whether the requirements resulting from this have been complied with.[8]

---

[3]ECB, Press Release of 13 October 1998.

[4]See ECB, Key ECB interest rates.

[5]For details see ECB (2000), pp. 43–58.

[6]De Boer and van 't Klooster (2020), pp. 1701–1703.

[7]FCC, PSPP, 5.5.2020, 2 BvR 859/15 et al., para. 196.

[8]See infra Sect. 5.1.3.2.

3.1.2 Demarcation and Interaction Between Economic and Monetary Policy

3.1.2.1 Crisis-Induced Non-Standard Measures

In the course of the financial and sovereign debt crisis, the ECB used instruments that were (resp. are) characterised by exceptionality and temporariness and are therefore referred to as non-standard measures. This dichotomy (standard/non-standard measures) is only of a linguistic and factual nature, as EU law does not contain specific emergency powers. Therefore, from a legal point of view, the non-standard measures are standard instruments which the ECB used in an environment not provided for.[9] In this context, the ECB combined traditional interest rate policy and liquidity-providing measures, which are complementary due to their different objectives. These measures included the provision of additional liquidity in the context of expanded open market operations and several interest rate cuts, supplemented by a communication policy geared to the management of expectations (forward guidance).

In concrete terms, a number of interest rate reduction steps towards an interest rate on deposit facility of −0.5%[10] have been supported by an extension of open market operations to provide supplementary liquidity,[11] especially the Outright Monetary Transactions (OMT) Programme (announced in 2012, but never put into practise)[12] and the Expanded Asset Purchase Programme (EAPP) including the Public Sector Purchase Programme (PSPP)[13] (2014–2018, resumed in 2019[14]).

Further liquidity was provided by the so-called Enhanced Credit Support, comprising fixed rate tender with full allotment, long term refinancing operations (LTRO) as well as targeted longer term refinancing operations (TLTRO).[15] This was supplemented by the extension of repayment terms and the temporary lowering of the requirements for accepted collateral.[16]

---

[9]See also Advocate General Cruz Villalón, Gauweiler, 14.1.2015, ECLI:EU:C:2015:7, paras. 119–122; for a definition of conventional/unconventional measures translated from economic to legal terms see Bassan (2017), pp. 236–237.

[10]ECB, Press Release of 12 September 2019; Press Release of 21 January 2021.

[11]For details Steinbach (2016), pp. 367–368.

[12]See ECB, Press Release of 6 September 2012.

[13]See ECB, Press Release of 22 January 2015, subsequently Decision (EU) 2015/774 of the European Central Bank of 4 March 2015 on a secondary markets public sector asset purchase programme (ECB/2015/10), OJ 14.5.2015, L 121, p. 20.

[14]ECB, Press Release of 12 September 2019.

[15]Herrmann and Dornacher (2017), pp. 130–131; Bassan (2017), pp. 239, 241, 247.

[16]See Regulation (EC) No 1053/2008 of the European Central Bank of 23 October 2008 on temporary changes to the rules relating to eligibility of collateral (ECB/2008/11), OJ 25.10.2008, L 282, p. 17; Decision (2009/522/EC) of the European Central Bank of 2 July 2009 on the implementation of the covered bond purchase programme (ECB/2009/16), OJ 4.7.2009, L 175, p. 18.

Also, among the unconventional, crisis-induced measures is the so-called Emergency Liquidity Assistance (ELA), which can be granted by the central banks as emergency loans to distressed credit institutions and which can be assigned to the emergency function of central banks in their role as lender of last resort (LoLR).[17]

3.1.2.2 Proceedings Before the FCC and the ECJ: OMT/PSPP

In its proceedings on the OMT programme and the PSPP, the FCC, which was charged with the verification of constitutional compliance of announced or even implemented bond purchase programmes, referred several questions to the ECJ for a preliminary ruling under Art. 267 TFEU.[18] One of the central questions proved to be whether these measures could (still) be classified as monetary policy at all in view of their strong economic policy effects.[19] The need for such a demarcation of competences, which are blurred due to the economic entanglements, results from the asymmetrical structure of the EMU as expressed in Arts. 3(1)(c), 5, 119(1), (2) TFEU. Whereas monetary policy falls within the exclusive competence of the Union, the responsibility for economic policy has largely remained with the Member States. With regard to the latter, the Treaties only provide for a support function of the ECB according to Arts. 127(1) s. 2, 282(2) s. 3 TFEU and Art. 2 s. 2 ESCB/ECB Statute.[20]

Nevertheless, the attempt to separate monetary and economic policy from each other meets the challenge that the former forms a part of the latter.[21] The interdependencies between the two areas are particularly evident in the PSPP. In this respect, the ECB makes use of non-standard monetary policy measures known as

[17]For details see Steinbach (2016), pp. 369 et seq.

[18]For in-depth analysis see for example Borger (2016), pp. 139 et seq.; Baroncelli (2016), pp. 79 et seq.; Cafaro (2017), pp. 224–228; Lamandini et al. (2017), pp. 6–19 (OMT/Gauweiler proceedings); Gentzsch (2019), pp. 279 et seq.; Dawson and Bobić (2019), pp. 1005 et seq.; Gentzsch (2020), pp. 576 et seq.; Bobić and Dawson (2020), pp. 1953 et seq. (PSPP/Weiss proceedings).

[19]Moreover, both proceedings involved the compatibility with Art. 123(1) TFEU (prohibition of monetary budget financing), ECJ, Gauweiler, 16.6.2015, ECLI:EU:C:2015:400, paras. 93–127; Weiss, 11.12.2018, ECLI:EU:C:2018:1000, paras. 101–158; FCC, OMT, 21.6.2016, 2 BvR 2728/13 et al., paras 197 et seq.; PSPP, 5.5.2020, 2 BvR 859/15 et al., paras 180 et seq. The PSPP proceedings also raised the question whether, "based on this risk sharing, the Bundestag's right to decide on the budget (Budgetrecht), protected under Art. 20(1) and (2) GG in conjunction with Art. 79(3) GG, as well as its overall budgetary responsibility could be affected by the PSPP Decision and its implementation in terms of potential losses to be borne by the Bundesbank", FCC, PSPP (order for reference), 18.7.2017, 2 BvR 859/15 et al., paras. 124–134. The ECJ classified the question concerning unlimited risk sharing as hypothetical and therefore inadmissible, ECJ, Weiss, 11.12.2018, ECLI:EU:C:2018:1000, paras. 159–167.

[20]See for coordination of economic policy within the EMU Craig and de Búrca (2015), pp. 735–741.

[21]Cf. Lamandini et al. (2017), p. 18.

quantitative easing (QE), by which it provides the market with additional liquidity through the purchase of debt instruments, thereby facilitating the supply of credit in the euro area and easing borrowing conditions for households and firms.[22] As in the case of the main and longer-term refinancing operations, monetary policy effects are transmitted to the real economy, with the expectation that the provision of liquidity to the interbank market and credit to the euro area economy will increase.[23] The achievement of monetary policy objectives, especially returning to inflation levels below, but close to, 2%, is therefore to a large extent dependent on certain economic effects.

3.1.2.3 Demarcation as a Matter of Competence and Independence

This issue concerns not only the competence of the ECB but also the relevant degree of independence. In the view of the FCC, the constitutional approval of a central bank endowed with independence requires that its mandate must be interpreted restrictively. According to the court, the ECB's mandate is primarily limited to matters of monetary policy serving the aim of stability and cannot be extended to other areas of policy.[24] This opinion has been upheld by the court in its *Banking Union decision*,[25] though considering the independence of the ECB and the national supervisory authorities in the area of SSM supervision to be constitutional in the end.[26]

In the *Gauweiler decision*, the ECJ referred to its ruling in the Pringle/ESM case which also dealt with the distinction between economic and monetary policy and stressed that "the FEU Treaty contains no precise definition of monetary policy but defines both the objectives of monetary policy and the instruments which are available to the ESCB for the purpose of implementing that policy".[27] Further, the court held "that in order to determine whether a measure falls within the area of monetary policy it is appropriate to refer principally to the objectives of that measure. The instruments which the measure employs in order to attain those objectives are also relevant".[28] The mere fact, that a monetary policy measure may have indirect effects on the economic stability of the euro area, does not create an equivalent to an economic policy measure.[29]

---

[22]Recital 2 Decision (EU) 2015/774.

[23]Recital 4 Decision (EU) 2015/774.

[24]FCC, Maastricht, 12.10.1993 = BVerfGE 89, 155 (pp. 208–209); PSPP (order for reference), 18.7.2017, 2 BvR 859/15 et al., para. 103.

[25]FCC, Banking Union, 30.7.2019, 2 BvR 1685/14 et al., para. 210.

[26]FCC, Banking Union, 30.7.2019, 2 BvR 1685/14 et al., 3rd headnote.

[27]ECJ, Pringle, 27.11.2012, ECLI:EU:C:2012:756, para. 53; Gauweiler, 16.6.2015, ECLI:EU:C:2015:400, para. 42.

[28]ECJ, Pringle, 27.11.2012, ECLI:EU:C:2012:756, paras. 53 and 55; Gauweiler, 16.6.2015, ECLI:EU:C:2015:400, para. 46.

[29]ECJ, Gauweiler, 16.6.2015, ECLI:EU:C:2015:400, para. 52; see, by analogy, Pringle, 27.11.2012, ECLI:EU:C:2012:756, para. 56.

In its subsequent *OMT decision*, the FCC criticised this control approach of the ECJ with regard to compliance with the monetary policy mandate:

> Generously accepting as fact asserted aims while at the same time granting wide margins of assessment to bodies of the European Union and considerably decreasing the intensity of judicial review is well-suited to enable institutions, bodies, offices, and agencies of the European Union to autonomously decide upon the scope of the competences that the Member States have attributed to them. Such an understanding of competences does not sufficiently take into account the constitutional dimension of the principle of conferral.[30]

This criticism finally resulted in the *PSPP decision*, in which the FCC essentially reproaches the ECJ for nevertheless classifying effects intended or at least consciously accepted by the ECB as indirect effects and taking over the alleged monetary policy objectives of the ECB without further examination.[31] The FCC sees in this the danger that "the purported monetary policy objective is possibly only invoked to disguise what essentially constitutes an economic and fiscal policy agenda".[32] Ultimately, the FCC states:

> [W]hat this reasoning entails is that it would not be possible to prevent such purchases even if they constituted an abuse of law.[33]

Even if the ECJ's access to control, i.e. the delimitation according to the objective and means of the respective measures, appears unsatisfactory at first sight, the FCC's view must however be countered by the fact that it does not allow a positive interpretation of the monetary policy mandate. The ECJ therefore has rightly used an *argumentum ad absurdum* that even the FCC could not convincingly refute:

> [I]f the ESCB were precluded altogether from adopting such measures when their effects are foreseeable and knowingly accepted, that would, in practice, prevent it from using the means made available to it by the Treaties for the purpose of achieving monetary policy objectives and might – in particular in the context of an economic crisis entailing a risk of deflation – represent an insurmountable obstacle to its accomplishing the task assigned to it by primary law.[34]

In so far as the FCC insists on a delimitation of competences in order to ensure a judicially verifiable compliance with the principle of conferral (Art. 4(1) TEU), it finds approval here. However, it is not convincing that the court justifies such a separation unexpectedly with the protection of central bank independence. In the *PSPP decision* within the examination of a structurally significant transfer of competencies, the court states that an approach that prevents distinction between economic and monetary policy to a large extent "jeopardises the independence of the ECB guaranteed in Art. 130 TFEU, as it possibly exposes the ECB to political

[30] FCC, OMT, 21.6.2016, 2 BvR 2728/13 et al., para. 184.

[31] FCC, PSPP, 5.5.2020, 2 BvR 859/15 et al., paras. 135 and 136.

[32] FCC, PSPP, 5.5.2020, 2 BvR 859/15 et al., para. 137.

[33] FCC, PSPP, 5.5.2020, 2 BvR 859/15 et al., para. 137.

[34] ECJ, Weiss, 11.12.2018, ECLI:EU:C:2018:1000, para. 67.

pressure that it make use of the leeway afforded it by the CJEU".[35] From this the FCC concludes:

> The broader the scope of the ECB's mandate, and the further it reaches into areas reserved to economic and fiscal policy, the greater the risk that interested parties try to influence the ECB's decision-making.[36]

This suggests a little-reasoned link between the range of tasks and the potential for influence, which assumes that the ECB, on the one hand, and the Union, the Member States or private actors, on the other, are willing to violate the principle of independence. Equally unconvincing would be an argument which counters the extension or reinterpretation of judicial control powers by arguing that this poses the risk of influence violating judicial independence.

3.1.2.4 The Competence-Related Principle of Proportionality as a Delimitation Criterion

In order to resolve these shortcomings of such a dichotomy, the FCC finally makes use of the principle of proportionality, which is laid down in Art. 5(1) s. 2, (4) TEU and addresses the Union, in particular its institutions and thus also the ECB. The FCC sees this principle as a limitation of competences, which is intended to ward off encroachments on the competences of the Member States:

> Relying on the principle of proportionality to distinguish between monetary policy and economic policy (Art. 5(1) s. 2 and Art. 5(4) TEU) implies that a programme's effects can render it disproportionate. Thus, assessing the consequences of such a programme is a necessary step in the delimitation of competences.[37]

Considering the ECB's PSPP decision to be disproportionate, the FCC based its opinion mainly on the fact that neither the ECJ nor the ECB have sufficiently taken into account the economic policy effects of the programmes although the core of the principle of proportionality shall be formed by the balancing of conflicting interests.[38] The FCC therefore criticises both the ECB and the ECJ particularly severely to the extent that they do not weigh the "effects that a programme for the purchase of government bonds has on, for example, public debt, personal savings, pension and retirement schemes, real estate prices and the keeping afloat of economically unviable companies".[39] In the FCC's view, the ECB is obliged to "weigh these effects and balance them, based on proportionality considerations, against the expected positive contributions to achieving the monetary policy objective the ECB itself has set".[40]

---

[35]FCC, PSPP, 5.5.2020, 2 BvR 859/15 et al., para. 161.

[36]FCC, PSPP, 5.5.2020, 2 BvR 859/15 et al., para. 161.

[37]FCC, PSPP, 5.5.2020, 2 BvR 859/15 et al., para. 139.

[38]Cf. FCC, PSPP, 5.5.2020, 2 BvR 859/15 et al., paras. 138 and 139.

[39]FCC, PSPP, 5.5.2020, 2 BvR 859/15 et al., paras. 139 and 173.

[40]FCC, PSPP, 5.5.2020, 2 BvR 859/15 et al., paras. 139 and 173.

As a result, the FCC held that the European institutions had obviously exceeded their competences in a structurally significant way.[41] In the view of the FCC, the prerequisites of its *ultra vires* control reserve were thus fulfilled, so that the challenged decisions as far as found to be *ultra vires* acts do not partake in the precedence of application of EU law *("Anwendungsvorrang")*.[42]

Following a systematic and historic interpretation of Art. 5(4) TEU, it is admittedly convincing that the FCC takes a competence dimension from the provision that distinguishes it from the principle of proportionality developed in the case law of the CJEU, especially pertaining individual rights.[43] This also implies that the ECB's actions as a Union institution may in principle be subject to different, possibly stricter control than was the case with the actions of the Deutsche Bundesbank prior to entry into the third stage of monetary union.[44]

However, the question arises whether structuring the principle of proportionality like the FCC is, in fact, so compelling that the decision of the ECJ turns out to be "not comprehensible and [...] arbitrary from an objective perspective".[45,46] The FCC has been well aware of the demanding prerequisites of such a reproach. Therefore, the court carefully reflected the case law of the CJEU especially regarding fundamental rights, freedoms of the single market, the principle of effectiveness and the principle of equivalence where the CJEU weighs conflicting interests that go beyond a necessity test.[47]

The FCC considers such a weighing to be necessary not only inasmuch as individual rights are affected but also in order to protect the competences of the Member States. The principle of conferral may be convincing in its approach. However, the FCC largely equates economic effects and economic policy effects without making clear enough the effects on the Member State's power to shape policy.[48] This is probably the greatest weakness of the decision, which attempts to avoid legal and factual deficits in the delimitation of economic and monetary policy by referring to the Member States' competences without filling these in a demanding manner.

This has also led to uncertainty about which concerns should be included in this balancing act. In the account of the monetary policy meeting of the ECB's

---

[41]FCC, PSPP, 5.5.2020, 2 BvR 859/15 et al., paras. 157–161 and 178.

[42]FCC, PSPP, 5.5.2020, 2 BvR 859/15 et al., para. 234.

[43]Competence dimension also underlined by German scholars, for example Streinz (2018), paras. 43 and 44; Calliess (2016), para. 45; for another view see Bobić and Dawson (2020), pp. 1974–1975.

[44]See also Zilioli (2017), p. 96.

[45]FCC, PSPP, 5.5.2020, 2 BvR 859/15 et al., 2nd headnote and paras. 123 and 153.

[46]Cf. Brade and Gentzsch (2020), who emphasise that the FCC tends to force the domestic standards of one constitutional system upon the ECJ not only in the *PSPP decision*; see also Bobić and Dawson (2020), p. 1978 ("colonization").

[47]FCC, PSPP, 5.5.2020, 2 BvR 859/15 et al., paras. 146–153; see also Craig and de Búrca (2015), pp. 552–558.

[48]Cf. Marzal (2020), Gentzsch (2020), p. 579.

Governing Council held in June 2020,[49] which was published on 25 June 2020 and can be understood as an element of the balancing process required of the ECB according to the *PSPP Decision*, it became clear that the ECB primarily weighs the "unintended effects" and the "positive effects" and that it is seen as important "to continuously assess the effectiveness and efficiency of the monetary policy measures, their transmission channels and their benefits and costs". However, this is unlikely to meet standards set by the FCC, according to which the ECB's action could also prove to be an *ultra vires* act even if the positive economic effects outweigh the negative effects, because any disproportionate encroachment on the Member States' spheres of competence is prohibited.[50]

The FCC's control approach also gives rise to concerns with regard to the EU concept of central bank independence, as will become clear in the following.

3.1.3 Functional Characteristics of Monetary Policy

It has already been shown that in the field of monetary policy there is a strong need to ward off particular political influences for the purpose of making decisions for the general interest. However, this does not exempt the central bank from control, in particular from its political, administrative and judicial accountability. However, these control mechanisms, understood as limitations to independence, encounter functional characteristics that impose restrictions on the nature and extent of the control itself. In contrast, these characteristics can also place high demands on the nature and extent of control.

3.1.3.1 Capacity of Control Institutions

Functionally structured systems are characterised by the fact that the allocation of tasks to specific institutions depends on which institution fulfils the task in a successful manner in terms of equipment, expertise and resources.[51] This concept, which is expressed in the case law of the FCC under the term organ adequacy (*"Organadäquanz"*)[52] is all the more important for the EU as an association of sovereign states. On the basis of an output-oriented concept of legitimation, the way in which the public good, which is constituted by the objectives previously laid

---

[49]Available at https://www.ecb.europa.eu/press/accounts/2020/html/ecb.mg200625~fd97330d5f.en.html (26 February 2021).

[50]De Boer and van't Klooster (2020), p. 1714, n. 100. This is sometimes misunderstood, see for example Maduro (2020), who criticised the fact that the FCC's proportionality test does not consider the economic, fiscal and political benefits.

[51]Cf. Steinbach (2017), p. 512; fundamentally Ossenbühl (1980), pp. 548–549, 555.

[52]FCC, Atomwaffenstationierung, 18.12.1984 = BVerfGE 68, 1 (p. 86).

down in the constitutions and laws, can best be achieved is important in the exercise of the tasks by the acting institutions (organs), but also in their control.

In the field of monetary policy, the issue of efficiency is reflected above all in judicial control.[53] At first glance, strict judicial control seems to be necessary to enforce the binding effect of law in the service of democracy. Already in its *OMT decision*, the FCC has therefore explained the following on the independence of the ECB:

> This limitation on the democratic legitimation emanating from the electorate is as such one of the modifications of the principle of democracy envisaged in Art. 88 sec. 2 GG that is justified on the grounds of the specific framework conditions of monetary policy. However, by way of compensation, the principles of democracy and the sovereignty of the people require that the monetary policy mandate of the European Central Bank be interpreted restrictively and that its observance be subject to strict judicial review in order to at least limit the decrease in the level of democratic legitimation of the Bank's actions to what is absolutely necessary.[54]

This approach of control is fundamentally different from that of the ECJ, which exercises judicial self-restraint. The latter therefore examined in the *Weiss case* whether "the specification of the objective of maintaining price stability as the maintenance of inflation rates at levels below, but close to, 2% over the medium term, [...] is vitiated by a manifest error of assessment and goes beyond the framework established by the FEU Treaty"[55] and whether "the PSPP does not go manifestly beyond what is necessary to achieve that objective".[56] Also, with regard to the weighing of conflicting interests, the ECJ reduces its control density by finding that "the ESCB weighed up the various interests involved so as effectively to prevent disadvantages which are manifestly disproportionate to the PSPP's objective from arising on implementation of the programme".[57]

The ECJ bases this approach mainly on the fact that "the ESCB must be allowed a broad discretion since, when it prepares and implements an open market operations programme, it is required to make choices of a technical nature and to undertake complex forecasts and assessments".[58] The ECJ thus addresses a characteristic of monetary policy which justifies independence not only because of the danger of political influence but also because of the specific efficiency of a monetary authority.[59] The decision-making process is mainly characterised by the fact that the economic concepts differ from one another and that forecast elements also play an important role. A strict judicial control, i.e. a comprehensive review of the suitability, necessity and appropriateness (proportionality *stricto sensu*), seems not possible

---

[53]See for details Gentzsch (2019), pp. 284–286, 291–293.

[54]FCC, OMT, 21.6.2016, 2 BvR 2728/13 et al., para. 189.

[55]ECJ, Weiss, 11.12.2018, ECLI:EU:C:2018:1000, para. 56.

[56]ECJ, Weiss, 11.12.2018, ECLI:EU:C:2018:1000, para. 79.

[57]ECJ, Weiss, 11.12.2018, ECLI:EU:C:2018:1000, para. 93.

[58]ECJ, Weiss, 11.12.2018, ECLI:EU:C:2018:1000, para. 24.

[59]For this connection see Baroncelli (2016), pp. 91–92.

from the outset. Assigning special resources and expertise to the ESCB in the pursuit of monetary policy creates knowledge asymmetries towards other institutions, in particular the courts, which cannot be easily resolved.[60] A closer look reveals that this reasoning, which is linked to the complexity of issues and the resulting asymmetries in knowledge, need by no means be limited to monetary policy measures or even the control of central bank actions.

Moreover, judicial control in the context of monetary policy cannot sufficiently fulfil the democratic function described above. The very term "monetary policy" makes it clear that this area, attributed to administration, is not characterised by a statutory steering in the sense of a verifiable conditional programme.[61] If one looks at the monetary provisions of the Treaties, including the ESCB/ECB Statute, it becomes clear that there is a widespread lack of concrete stipulations.[62] Therefore, such a concept, which formulates objectives of administrative authorities and provides them with the means to achieve them, entails primarily a reduction of judicial control,[63] but also of control by parliaments as well as the courts of auditors.

3.1.3.2 Fundamental Rights and Essentiality

Independent administrative action may also collide with the principle of democracy when it leads to decisions that affect fundamental rights. According to the case law of the ECJ, the density of judicial control is intensified when fundamental rights are affected.[64] However, this is only exceptionally the case for monetary policy measures, because these typically do not have the quality of an intervention by the state due to their market-conform design.[65] Admittedly, the maintenance of price stability influences economic fundamental rights, in particular the freedom to choose an occupation and right to engage in work (Art. 15 CFR), the freedom to conduct a business (Art. 16 CFR) and the right to property (Art. 17 CFR). Nevertheless, monetary policy measures typically do not interfere with these rights, but rather provide the economic framework for their exercise. This may be different for certain tasks, such as taking specific and individual decisions as determining minimum reserve requirements towards credit institutions as far as they have fundamental rights.[66]

---

[60]Cf. Steinbach (2017), pp. 512–513; regarding PSPP see also Pliakos and Anagnostaras (2010), pp. 143–144.

[61]Cf. Lehmann (2017), pp. 118–119; Zilioli (2017), pp. 99–100.

[62]Cf. De Boer and van 't Klooster (2020), pp. 1718–1719.

[63]Cf. Steinbach (2017), pp. 510 and 519.

[64]Cf. ECJ, Biovilac, 6.12.1984, ECLI:EU:C:1984:380, para. 22; Springer, 23.9.2004, ECLI:EU:C:2004:552, para. 49; Digital Rights, 8.4.2014, ECLI:EU:C:2014:238, paras. 47–48.

[65]Cf. Gentzsch (2019), p. 287.

[66]The applicability of fundamental rights to legal persons is only partly explicitly stipulated in the CFR, e.g. in Art. 42 CFR.

The FCC has so far left open "[w]hether, and if so in what more detailed circumstances, the purchasing power of money is included in the area of protection of the fundamental right to property of Article 14.1 of the Basic Law".[67] In this respect, it stresses that "the value of money is community-related and community-dependent in a specific way".[68] A form of review only comes into consideration in cases "where there is a manifest decrease of monetary value as a result of state measures".[69] Although money, given its role as a store of value and a medium of exchange, can be assigned to the scope of protection of the property guarantee, a certain intensity of intervention must be assessed, for example in the case of measures that evidently endanger price stability.[70]

Beyond the concern for fundamental rights, a stronger need for democratic legitimation could arise from the fact that monetary policy affects an essential policy area as the *Maastricht decision* also indicates.[71] In other decisions in the area of national law, too, the FCC has taken into account the political scope of a decision *("politische Tragweite")* with regard to the need for legitimation.[72] Comparable to this is the FCC's doctrine of essentiality *("Wesentlichkeitslehre")*, which attempts to distribute powers between the legislative and executive branches on the basis of the principle of democracy and the rule of law.[73] However, it must be pointed out that a determination of the need for legitimation via essentiality does not reveal sufficiently clear contours.

Therefore, instead of focusing on essentiality, it seems more convincing to look at the extent to which the decisions to be taken are characterised by a balance of competing interests. The specific performance potential of expert authorities ends where conflicting values and interests must be brought into balance by making fundamental value decisions.[74] These are genuine political decisions to be assigned to democratically legitimated representative institutions and not to technocratic authorities.[75] For the actions of central banks, this means that while monetary policy, which is guided by the idea of long-term neutrality, is a predominantly technical issue, the legal mandate must be drafted by the legislator enjoying a high level of

[67]FCC, Greece/EFSF, 7.9.2011, 2 BvR 987/10 et al., para. 111 with reference to FCC, Euro, 31.3.1998, 2 BvR 1877/97 et al., para. 88.

[68]FCC, Euro, 31.3.1998, 2 BvR 1877/97 et al., para. 87; cf. FCC, Greece/EFSF, 7.9.2011, 2 BvR 987/10 et al., para. 112.

[69]FCC, Greece/EFSF, 7.9.2011, 2 BvR 987/10 et al., para. 112; Banking Union, 30.7.2019, 2 BvR 1685/14 et al., para. 97.

[70]For further details see Gentzsch and Brade (2019), pp. 613–616.

[71]Cf. FCC, Maastricht, 12.10.1993 = BVerfGE 89, 155 (p. 207).

[72]FCC, Bremer Personalvertretung, 27.4.1959 = BVerfGE 9, 268 (p. 282).

[73]See for example FCC, Kalkar I, 8.8.1978 = BVerfGE 49, 89 (pp. 139–140); concise criticism at Herzog (1999), p. 26.

[74]Cf. Nettesheim (2005), p. 182; with regard to agencies Craig (2018), pp. 192 et seq.; see further Majone (1998), p. 14.

[75]For a different conceptual approach Cafaro (2017), pp. 231–232 accepting political central banks.

democratic legitimation.[76] As it shall detailed below, the FCC's decision on the PSPP exposes another field of problems concerning the relationship between the ECB's mandate and the degree of independence provided and imposed on it.

3.1.3.3 Embedment of Independence through Clear Commitment to the Aim of Stability

On the one hand, central bank independence, as enshrined in the Treaties, constitutes a *modus operandi* for the performance of the tasks covered by it. On the other hand, the performance of these tasks is characterised by a commitment to objectives among which price stability has priority. This entails that the pursuit of other objectives, such as the support of general economic policies, is allowed only to the extent that this can be achieved without prejudice to the objective of price stability.

Beyond a strict primacy in the Treaties, the stability objective is also characterised by the fact that the achievement of this aim can be quantified and concretely measured.[77] In addition, the strict hierarchy of objectives provides the ECB with clear priorities where the pursuit of different, colliding objectives is envisaged.[78] Both, the implementation of one-target mandates and a hierarchy of objectives have a decisive influence on the central bank's actions, because they enable effective democratic and judicial control and ultimately justify the high degree of independence.[79] This creates the normative conditions for legitimation by its outcome, which justifies the independence of the ECB since its establishment.[80]

The FCC emphasised in its *PSPP decision* that the ECB must, on the basis of Art. 5(4) TEU, make a balancing act that takes into account not only the appropriateness and necessity of the considered measures for achieving the stability objective, but also the economic effects. Contrary to the criticism sometimes voiced,[81] this does not require the ECB to conduct economic policy, because it is not the intended achievement of economic policy objectives that is at stake, but only a weighing of consequences. Nevertheless, such a balancing act, especially if it is subject to strict judicial control, is suitable for weakening the strict commitment of central banks which is a democratic justification for independence. Weighing consequences, actually, requires the making of assessments which must be subject to democratic debate or, at least, democratic control. This applies not only to the consideration of economic effects, but also other ones, for example environmental and social policy,[82] although the Union's shared competence (Art. 4(2)(b), (e) TFEU) for those

[76] De Boer and van't Klooster (2020), p. 1698.
[77] Cf. Kern (2015), p. 170; Zilioli (2016), p. 162.
[78] Cf. Steinbach (2017), p. 522.
[79] See also Mersch (2017).
[80] Cf. De Boer and van 't Klooster (2020), p. 1696.
[81] Goldmann (2020); Möllers (2020), p. 503.
[82] Cf. Marzal (2020).

lead to the consequence, that the competences of the Member States are not affected to the same extent.[83] However, these considerations on the justification of a monetary policy mandate that is rounded off with independence must therefore also find their way into the current debate on whether and to what extent the ECB can actively pursue climate[84] and social policy objectives *de constitutione lata* or *de constitutione ferenda*.

As regards the relationship between the primacy of stability and the principle of proportionality, it can be stated that Art. 127(1) TFEU is to be classified as an absolutely conceived mandate,[85] which is limited by Art. 5(4) TEU only to the extent that the measures do not go beyond what is necessary to achieve the objectives of the Treaties. At most, it seems to be conceivable that the ECB, when implementing monetary policy measures, weighs up the functioning of central banks, because this is a precondition for the pursuit of the stability objective. In this respect, the ECJ in the *Weiss decision* had also examined whether "the ESCB weighed up the various interests involved so as effectively to prevent disadvantages which are manifestly disproportionate to the PSPP's objective from arising on implementation of the programme"[86] and reviewed the programme to ensure that "the risks to which the substantial volume of asset purchases under the PSPP might possibly expose the central banks of the Member States".[87] In this respect, the ECJ's assessment of the ECB's submissions takes into account the concern to "prevent the position of a central bank of one Member State from being weakened in the event of an issuer in another Member State failing to make a repayment".[88] This interpretation of the relationship between the monetary policy mandate and the principle of proportionality is convincing.

3.2 Other Traditional Central Bank Functions

Although defining and implementing the monetary policy of the Union is the most important function of the ECB/Eurosystem, the Treaties provide for further tasks. Unlike the tasks assigned to the ECB during the financial and sovereign debt crisis in the area of financial supervision and fiscal policy, these can be regarded as traditional central bank functions.

---

[83]Gentzsch (2020), p. 583.

[84]See infra Sect. 5.3.4.

[85]See also Bobić and Dawson (2020), p. 1979 ("[. . .] Article 127 TFEU tips the scales of balancing from the outset"); Mooij (2020), p. 723.

[86]ECJ, Weiss, 11.12.2018, ECLI:EU:C:2018:1000, para. 93.

[87]ECJ, Weiss, 11.12.2018, ECLI:EU:C:2018:1000, para. 98.

[88]ECJ, Weiss, 11.12.2018, ECLI:EU:C:2018:1000, para. 96.

3.2.1 *Issuance of Banknotes*

The traditional central bank tasks include the monopoly for issuing banknotes, understood as the power of the issue (so-called monetisation) and the withdrawal (so-called demonetisation) of banknotes and coins.[89] In the EMU, the issue of euro banknotes and coins is subject to a strict ESCB/Eurosystem monopoly, with competences shared between the ECB and the NCBs.[90] While the monopoly to issue banknotes belongs to the ECB according to Art. 128(1) TFEU, the right to issue euro coins belongs to the Member States, though being subject to the ECB's approval, according to Art. 128(2) TFEU. The issue of banknotes covers every act relevant to the circulation of banknotes, i.e. all activities relating to the nature and design, the production, transport and delivery process and the denominations of the banknotes. However, it is only the act of issue, the putting into circulation that creates a liability of the issuer (the ECB) vis-à-vis the holder for the nominal value.

3.2.1.1 Division of Competences Regarding Monetary Law

Although the independence of the ESCB/ECB also extends to the field of banknote and coin issuance, the central banks in this field are governed to a large extent by Union legislation, based on primary law enabling provisions. This applies first of all to the measures adopted by the Council, acting on a proposal from the Commission and after consulting the European Parliament and the ECB on the basis of Art. 128 (2) s. 2 TFEU, to harmonise the denominations and technical specifications of all coins intended for circulation to the extent necessary to permit their smooth circulation within the Union.[91] In addition, Art. 133 TFEU empowers the European Parliament and the Council, without prejudice to the powers of the ECB, to lay down, in accordance with the ordinary legislative procedure and after consulting the ECB, the measures necessary for the use of the euro as the single currency. This provision succeeds Art. 109l(4) s. 3 TEC-Maastricht and finally Art. 123(4) s. 3 TEC-Nice, according to which the Council could take "all other measures necessary for the rapid introduction of the ECU [viz. European Currency Unit] as the single currency of these Member States". This previous provision was already seen as the legal basis for euro-related provisions, which Art. 133 TFEU removes from the situational context and generalises.[92]

[89]See for details Smits (1997), pp. 203–210.

[90]Art. 128 TFEU, Art. 16 ESCB/ECB Statute.

[91]This was made use of by Council Regulation (EU) No 729/2014 of 24 June 2014 on denominations and technical specifications of euro coins intended for circulation (Recast), OJ 2.7.2014, L 194, p. 1.

[92]Häde (2016), Art. 133 TFEU para. 1.

Art. 109l(4) s. 3 TEC-Maastricht was used as a basis in particular for Regulation (EC) No. 974/98 on the introduction of the euro,[93] which also addresses the limitations on payments in notes and coins established by the Member States for public reasons and their compatibility with the status of legal tender of euro banknotes and coins.[94] Art. 10 s. 2 Regulation (EC) No 974/98 is related to Art. 128 (1) s. 3 TFEU and provides that euro banknotes put into circulation by the ECB and the NCBs of the participating Member States shall be the only banknotes which have the status of legal tender in the participating Member States.[95] Also, regulations concerning measures against counterfeiting[96] and authentication of euro coins[97] find their legal basis in Art. 123(4) s. 3 TEC-Nice resp. Art. 133 TFEU.[98]

This horizontal division of competences which is expressed hereby has also been implicitly taken up by the ECJ in the *case Dietrich (vs. Hessischer Rundfunk)* concerning the limitation on payment of radio and television licence fees *("Rundfunkbeiträge")* in cash.[99] With regard to the concept of monetary policy in Art. 3(1)(c) TFEU, the ECJ, following the opinion of the Advocate General, ruled that "[...] the concept of 'monetary policy' is not limited to its operational implementation, which, under the first indent of Article 127(2) TFEU, is one of the basic tasks of the ESCB, but also entails a regulatory dimension intended to guarantee the status of the euro as the single currency".[100]

At the same time, the ECJ pointed out that monetary law and monetary policy are not loosely related:

> Such an interpretation of the concept of 'monetary policy' is supported by the primary objective of that policy, as set out in Article 127(1) and Article 282(2) TFEU, that is, to maintain price stability. As the Advocate General noted, in essence, in point 66 of his Opinion, if the status of the euro as the single currency could be understood differently and governed by different rules in the Member States whose currency is the euro, the singleness

---

[93]Council Regulation (EC) No 974/98 of 3 May 1998 on the introduction of the euro, OJ 11.5.1998, L 139, p. 1.

[94]Recital 19 s. 2 Council Regulation (EC) No 974/98.

[95]For euro coins a similar provision has been laid down in Art. 11 s. 2 Regulation (EC) No 974/98.

[96]Council Regulation (EC) No 1338/2001 of 28 June 2001 laying down measures necessary for the protection of the euro against counterfeiting, OJ 4.7.2001, L 181, p. 6, as amended by Council Regulation (EC) No 44/2009 of 18 December 2008 amending Regulation (EC) No 1338/2001 laying down measures necessary for the protection of the euro against counterfeiting, OJ 22.1.2009, L 17, p. 1.

[97]Regulation (EU) No 1210/2010 of the European Parliament and of the Council of 15 December 2010 concerning authentication of euro coins and handling of euro coins unfit for circulation, OJ 22.12.2010, L 339, p. 1.

[98]See also Advocate General Pitruzzella, Dietrich, 29.9.2020, ECLI:EU:C:2020:756, para. 63.

[99]For details see Manger-Nestler and Gramlich (2019), pp. 1949 et seq., 1997 et seq.

[100]ECJ, Dietrich, 26.1.2021, ECLI:EU:C:2021:63, para. 38; previously Advocate General Pitruzzella, Dietrich, 29.9.2020, ECLI:EU:C:2020:756, para. 57; see also paras. 59–60 and 70. It has to be noted, that the ECJ does not distinct between these dimensions when, in its Pringle decision, assigning the issue of euro currency to monetary policy without reasons, ECJ, Pringle, 27.11.2012, ECLI:EU:C:2012:756, para. 96.

> of the single currency would be called into question and that objective of maintaining price stability would thereby be seriously jeopardised.[101]

In this context, the ECJ's reasoning, insofar as it refers to Art. 128 TFEU and Art. 133 TFEU, clearly shows that at the Union level,[102] the ECB is not solely responsible for enacting monetary law provisions, but that, in particular pursuant to Art. 133 TFEU, the Union legislator also has certain competences.

In addition to the horizontal distribution of competences, the vertical distribution of competences must also be taken into account. Although the ECJ made clear in the *Dietrich case* that "[...], where competence is conferred exclusively on the European Union, the loss of competence by the Member States occurs immediately and, unlike in the case of areas falling within a shared competence, it does not matter, for the purposes of that loss, whether or not the European Union has exercised its competence",[103] it nevertheless highlights areas of competence of the Member States with regard to regulating the use of cash:

> It follows that the European Union's exclusive competence in matters of monetary policy is, as the Advocate General noted in point 98 of his Opinion, without prejudice to the competence of the Member States whose currency is the euro to regulate the procedures for settling pecuniary obligations, whether under public law or private law, provided, in particular, that the legislation does not affect the principle that, as a general rule, it must be possible to discharge a payment obligation in cash. [...][104]

With regard to monetary policy or monetary law measures, which are in the context of cash regulation, a careful delimitation of competences is required, which also relates to central bank independence.

3.2.1.2 Functional Characteristics of Banknote and Coin Issuance

Where the monetary policy dimension of banknote or coin issuance is involved, it is part of the ECB's mandate. The ECB's competence also includes provisions that do not relate to the use of the euro under Art. 133 TFEU, but to primarily technical

---

[101]ECJ, Dietrich, 26.1.2021, ECLI:EU:C:2021:63, para. 39.

[102]ECJ, Dietrich, 26.1.2021, ECLI:EU:C:2021:63, paras. 40–43, 51.

[103]ECJ, Dietrich, 26.1.2021, ECLI:EU:C:2021:63, para. 54; previously Advocate General Pitruzzella, Dietrich, 29.9.2020, ECLI:EU:C:2020:756, paras. 38 and 39.

[104]ECJ, Dietrich, 26.1.2021, ECLI:EU:C:2021:63, para. 56; see also Advocate General Pitruzzella, Dietrich, 29.9.2020, ECLI:EU:C:2020:756, para. 98, who outlined the competences of the Member States in more detail: "Accordingly, there is a need to coordinate [...] the European Union's exclusive competence for the definition of legal tender with that of the Member States, both in civil law, with regard to the settlement of monetary debts of a private nature, the organisation and functioning of public and tax administrations, and the discharge of pecuniary obligations of a public nature, and in criminal law, with regard to the interrelationship between the circulation of money and the fight against crime".

decisions concerning the issuance, i.e. decisions on the denominations,[105] design[106] and technical specifications of banknotes.[107] However, the situation is different if the ECB or the NCBs take measures that interfere with fundamental rights or are at least essential for the exercise of those. This concerns in particular the possible, sometimes passionately debated, abolition of cash, understood as a decision by the Eurosystem to stop producing and monetising banknotes and coins and, if necessary, to withdraw and dismantle any banknotes and coins in circulation.[108] In the *Dietrich case*, the Advocate General considered that "legislation that could lead, in law or in fact, to the complete abolition of euro banknotes or which could render ineffective the status of legal tender of euro banknotes must be regarded as incompatible with the third sentence of Article 128(1) TFEU".[109] If one does not share this view,[110] a careful analysis must be made of whether, and if so to what extent, such measures interfere with fundamental rights.[111] The same applies, moreover, to measures limiting the use of cash, although here the Member State's powers must be respected.[112] This then has an impact on accountability, i.e. in particular on parliamentary and judicial control. These issues have particular relevance in the context of the introduction of a digital euro, which will receive special attention as a future challenge.[113]

---

[105] Regarding the end of production and issuance of EUR 500 banknote by the ECB see ECB, Press Release of 4 May 2016.

[106] See Art. 1 Decision 2013/211/EU of the European Central Bank of 19 April 2013 on the denominations, specifications, reproduction, exchange and withdrawal of euro banknotes (recast), OJ 30.4.2013, L 188, p. 37.

[107] See Freimuth (2013), para. 18.

[108] See the speeches and contributions to the debate on the occasion of the "4. Bargeldsymposium" organised by the Deutsche Bundesbank in 2018, available at https://www.bundesbank.de/de/service/termine/bargeldsymposium-2018-633916 (26 February 2021).

[109] Advocate General Pitruzzella, Dietrich, 29.9.2020, ECLI:EU:C:2020:756, para. 127. The ECJ followed this opinion in principle, but only envisaged an abolition of cash by the Member States, see ECJ, Dietrich, 26.1.2021, ECLI:EU:C:2021:63, paras. 59 et seq.

[110] Cf. Omlor (2015), p. 2299, who classifies Art. 128 TFEU as a rule on the allocation of powers, but currently sees an obligation to issue cash under Council Regulation (EC) No 974/98.

[111] For details see Advocate General Pitruzzella, Dietrich, 29.9.2020, ECLI:EU:C:2020:756, paras. 129 et seq.; see also Omlor (2015), p. 2301, who underlines the broad discretion of central banks, which is founded on their independence, and therefore considers the abolition of cash and its replacement by other forms of money to be largely unproblematic.

[112] See ECJ, Dietrich, 26.1.2021, ECLI:EU:C:2021:63, para. 56; Advocate General Pitruzzella, Dietrich, 29.9.2020, ECLI:EU:C:2020:756, para. 119.

[113] See infra Sect. 5.3.4.3.

3.2.2 *Foreign-Exchange Operations and Official Foreign Reserves*

The basic tasks of the ESCB also include conducting foreign exchange operations consistent with Art. 219 TFEU[114] and holding and managing the official foreign reserves of the Member States.[115] These tasks can be classified under the foreign monetary policy, which covers the external relations of a currency with other currencies and, in the form of exchange rate policy, the external value of a currency.

If and to the extent that the EU decides to pursue a specific exchange rate policy actively, Art. 219(1) TFEU provides that it is not the ECB but the Council, precisely the Economic and Financial Affairs Council (ECOFIN), which has the competence under primary law to define such a policy, including in particular formal agreements with third countries on an exchange rate system for the euro and the fixing of the central rates of the euro within such a system.[116] A formal exchange rate agreement is concluded by the Council either on a recommendation from the ECB or on a recommendation from the Commission and after consulting the ECB.[117] The same formal requirements apply to the adoption, adjustment or abandonment of the central rates of the euro within the exchange-rate system,[118] the formulation of general orientations for exchange-rate policy[119] and the negotiation and conclusion of agreements relating to monetary or foreign exchange regime matters.[120] When the Council adopts so-called common positions to safeguard the position of the euro in the international monetary system, it also consults the ECB.[121]

Such ECB involvement is necessary to counter the risk of conflicts of interest between the ECB and the Council as a result of the separation of competences between internal and external monetary stability.[122] However, this rather advisory role of the ECB, based on monetary policy expertise, must not obscure the fact that the ECB has at least a de facto right to influence the euro exchange rate, namely in the form of foreign exchange intervention,[123] at least as long as the Council does not exercise its monetary policy powers. As the acquisition and sale of foreign exchange assets, in particular foreign currencies, is identified as a monetary policy task and power in Art. 127(2) 2nd TFEU and Art. 23 ESCB/ECB Statute, the primary law guarantee of independence in the field of monetary policy as well as the primacy of

[114]Art. 127(2) 2nd indent TFEU.

[115]Art. 127(3) 3rd indent TFEU.

[116]For details see Manger-Nestler (2019), pp. 124 et seq.

[117]Art. 219(1) sub-para. 1 s. 1 TFEU.

[118]Art. 219(1) sub-para. 2 s. 1 TFEU.

[119]Art. 219(2) s. 1 TFEU.

[120]Art. 219(3) s. 1 TFEU.

[121]Art. 138(1) TFEU.

[122]Manger-Nestler (2019), p. 127.

[123]Art. 23 2nd indent ESCB/ECB Statute.

price stability in Art. 127(1) s. 1 TFEU applies to this.[124] In this respect, it must not be ignored that exchange rate fluctuations have an influence on import and export prices and thus also on the inflation rate.[125] The current surge of the euro and its contribution to the risk of deflation is therefore "carefully monitored" by the ECB.[126]

The official foreign reserves of the Member States, the holding and management of which is the responsibility of the ESCB/Eurosystem, are another instrument of foreign exchange policy.[127] Within the Eurosystem, in line with the principle of decentralisation,[128] the ECB has largely left the operational management of the transferred foreign reserves (portfolio management) to the NCBs, which carry out operations on behalf of the ECB. Art. 127(2) 3rd indent TFEU explicitly covers all foreign assets, i.e. not only those transferred to the ECB but also those remaining with the NCBs.[129] Thus, neither the ECB nor the NCB is bound by instructions from the Union institutions or the national authorities pursuant to Art. 130 TFEU.[130] Thus, for example, an instruction by a Member State government to the NCB on the sale of gold reserves is prohibited.

3.2.3 *Payment Systems*

To promote the smooth operation of payment systems is another basic task of the ESCB according to Art. 127(2) 4th indent TFEU. This task supplemented by the enabling provision of Art. 22 ESCB/ECB Statute not only aims at creating the infrastructure necessary for a stable financial system with robust payment and settlement systems, but also sets out the technical conditions for the functioning of the transmission mechanism.[131] Moreover, payment and settlement systems serve to effectively implement the free movement of capital and payments (Art. 63 TFEU) in the EU internal market for financial services.

The task assigned to the ESCB is explicitly limited to promoting the smooth operation of payment systems, so that, in particular, it is not given extensive regulatory powers. Instead, the European Parliament and the Council are responsible for regulating capital movements and payments.[132] Although functioning payment

[124]See further Art. 219(2) s. 2 TFEU.

[125]Athanassiou and Zagouras (2015), para. 9.

[126]Ewing, Surging Euro Presents E.C.B. With a Dilemma, New York Times of 10 September 2020, https://www.nytimes.com/2020/09/10/business/ecb-euro.html (26 February 2021).

[127]Art. 127(2) 3rd indent TFEU; for details see Manger-Nestler (2019), pp. 131–132.

[128]Art. 12.1. sub-para. 3 ESCB/ECB Statute.

[129]See Arts. 30, 31 ESCB/ECB Statute.

[130]Likewise Waldhoff (2013), para. 56.

[131]Cf. Kaufhold (2016), p. 203; Athanassiou (2020), para. 24.14.

[132]Arts. 63 TFEU et seq.; regarding the ECB's lack of competence to regulate central counterparties (CCP) involved in securities clearing, ECJ, CCP clearing systems, 4.3.2015, ECLI:EU:T:2015:133, paras. 85 et seq.

systems are closely linked to financial stability,[133] Art. 127(2) TFEU is merely a supporting competence, which in any case cannot be used to provide liquidity support in the event of a crisis, even if systemically relevant institutions are affected.[134]

In order to efficiently process cross-border large-value payments within the scope of monetary policy measures, the EMI first developed the Trans-European Automated Real-Time Gross Settlement Express Transfer System (TARGET), which was replaced by the second generation of the system (TARGET2) at the end of 2007.[135] TARGET2 is supplemented by another system for the settlement of securities transactions (TARGET2-Securities).[136]

From a functional perspective, it can be noted that in fulfilling this task, mainly technical decisions are made that do not interfere with the fundamental rights of market participants. The ECB, which has as a coordinating function, therefore has a broad discretion. This applies in particular to the implementation of the TARGET2 Guideline, which entails that the day-to-day netting of cross-border transactions gives rise to TARGET2 balances which constitute claims on or liabilities to the ECB.[137]

The complainants in the ESM proceedings before the FCC also challenged these measures, which are discussed in economic literature.[138] However, the FCC dismissed the constitutional complaints in so far because, above all, they lacked sufficient substantiation of the requirements of an *ultra vires* act and a violation of constitutional identity with regard to the budgetary autonomy of the Bundestag.[139] This view is shared in the literature and it is emphasised that the causes of the target balances are based on monetary policy decisions, and cannot be attributed to the operation of the payment system.[140]

---

[133]Cf. Athanassiou (2020), para. 24.14.

[134]For a different view Steinbach (2016), p. 368, according to whom, in a liquidity crisis, "the supply of liquidity may become pivotal for safeguarding of the stability of the payment system as such in order to eliminate systemic risks".

[135]See Guideline 2013/47/EU of the European Central Bank of 5 December 2012 on a Trans-European Automated Real-time Gross settlement Express Transfer system (TARGET2) (ECB/2012/27), OJ 30.1.2013, L 30, p. 1.

[136]Guideline 2012/473/EU of the European Central Bank of 18 July 2012 on TARGET-2-Securities (ECB/2012/13), OJ 11.8.2012, L 215, p. 19.

[137]For details see Sandberger (2019), pp. 600–606.

[138]For references see Sandberger (2019), p. 1, n. 1.

[139]FCC, ESM, 18.3.2014, 2 BvR 1390/12 et al., paras. 136–141.

[140]Sandberger (2019), pp. 606–607.

3.2.4 Collecting Statistical Information

Another task of the ESCB is not mentioned in the Treaties, but only in Art. 5 ESCB/ECB Statute. According to this provision, the ECB, assisted by the NCBs, collects the necessary statistical information in order to undertake the tasks of the ESCB, in cooperation with Union, national and international authorities.[141] Through its statistical activities, the ECB also contributes significantly to the macro-prudential supervision by the ESRB, which is provided with statistical information.[142] Within the ESCB system, these tasks are to be carried out by the NCBs to the extent possible, reflecting in particular the principle of decentralisation laid down in Art. 12.1. sub-para. 3 ESCB/ECB Statute.[143]

The ECB and the NCBs fulfil an essential function in the field of economic and financial statistics, whereby the statistical activities of the ESCB/ECB are explicitly linked to their tasks.[144] In this function, the ESCB complements the European Statistical System (ESS), which comprises the Community (now Union) statistical authority, which is the Commission (Eurostat), and the national statistical institutes (NSIs) and other national authorities responsible in each Member State for the development, production and dissemination of European statistics.[145] While the ESS which is grounded on Art. 338(1) TFEU is responsible for statistics which are necessary for the performance of the activities of the Union, especially general economic statistics, the ECB has primary responsibility for monetary and financial statistics, statistics on the international reserves of the Eurosystem, and statistics on the nominal and real effective exchange rates of the euro.[146] Both share responsibility for balance of payments statistics and financial and non-financial accounts broken down by institutional sector.[147]

---

[141] Art. 5.1. s. 1 ESCB/ECB Statute.

[142] Arts. 2(b), 5 ECB-ESRBR; see infra Sect. 3.3.2.

[143] Art. 5.2. ESCB/ECB Statute; for details concerning the distribution of competences see van den Berg (2004), pp. 291–292.

[144] Smits (1997), p. 215; van den Berg (2004), pp. 291–292.

[145] Art. 4 Regulation (EC) No 223/2009 of the European Parliament and of the Council of 11 March 2009 on European statistics and repealing Regulation (EC, Euratom) No 1101/2008 of the European Parliament and of the Council on the transmission of data subject to statistical confidentiality to the Statistical Office of the European Communities, Council Regulation (EC) No 322/97 on Community Statistics, and Council Decision 89/382/EEC, Euratom establishing a Committee on the Statistical Programmes of the European Communities, OJ 31.3.2009, L 87, p. 164.

[146] See *inter alia* Regulation (EU) No 1071/2013 of the European Central Bank of 24 September 2013 concerning the balance sheet of the monetary financial institutions sector (recast) (ECB/2013/33), OJ 7.11.2013, L 297, p. 1; Regulation (EU) No 1072/2013 of the European Central Bank of 24 September 2013 concerning statistics on interest rates applied by monetary financial institutions (recast) (ECB/2013/34), OJ 7.11.2013, L 297, p. 51.

[147] Memorandum of Understanding between Eurostat and the ECB/Directorate General Statistics on the quality assurance of statistics underlying the Macroeconomic Imbalances Procedure, MOU/2016/11071, p. 3.

In the context of the statistical function, the ECB also has the task, where necessary, of contributing to the harmonisation of the rules and practices governing the collection, compilation and distribution of statistics in the areas within its field of competence,[148] which the ECB has made use of mainly through regulations and guidelines.[149]

With regard to the independence of the ECB, which also applies to the task under Art. 5 ESCB/ECB, it should be noted that the ECB's actions are largely determined by provisions laid down by the Council. Although the ECB may collect the necessary statistical information either from the competent national authorities or directly from economic agents,[150] the Council defines the natural and legal persons subject to reporting requirements, the confidentiality regime and the appropriate arrangements for enforcement.[151] Thus, a scope of tasks which is relevant to fundamental rights in respect of economic burdens but also the protection of commercial data is contained by the Council, which has made use of this by adopting Regulation (EC) No 2533/98.[152] As far as fundamental rights are concerned, such involvement of the European legislator strengthens the democratic legitimation of central bank action. This applies in particular in so far as the protection and use of confidential statistical information collected by the ESCB is subject to strict and clearly defined requirements.[153] This also applies to the rather intrusive powers of the ECB resp. NCBs to verify the accuracy and quality of the statistical information and to carry out its compulsory collection as well as to impose sanctions in case of not complying with reporting obligations.[154] This degree of intervention has repercussions on parliamentary and judicial control, comparable to measures of banking supervision.[155] With regard to the EU-wide collection of statistical information for macroprudential supervision, it should also be noted that this is the responsibility of the

[148]Art. 5.3. ESCB/ECB Statute.

[149]See for example Guideline 2014/3/EU of the European Central Bank of 25 July 2013 on the statistical reporting requirements of the European Central Bank in the field of quarterly financial accounts (ECB/2013/24), OJ 7.1.2014, L 2, p. 34.

[150]Art. 5.1. s. 1 ESCB/ECB Statute.

[151]Art. 5.4. ESCB/ECB Statute in conjunction with Art. 41 ESCB/ECB Statute.

[152]Council Regulation (EC) No 2533/98 of 23 November 1998 concerning the collection of statistical information by the European Central Bank, OJ 27.11.1998, L 318, p. 8, last amended by Council Regulation (EU) 2015/373 of 5 March 2015 amending Regulation (EC) No 2533/98 concerning the collection of statistical information by the European Central Bank, OJ 7.3.2015, L 64, p. 6.

[153]Art. 8 Regulation (EC) No 2533/98. The exchange of confidential statistical information between the ESCB and the ESS is provided for in Art. 8a Regulation (EC) No 2533/98 and Art. 21 (2) Regulation (EC) No 223/2009.

[154]Arts. 6, 7 Regulation (EC) No 2533/98.

[155]See infra Sect. 3.3.1.3.2.

ESRB,[156] while the ECB collects all necessary information on behalf of the ESRB and makes it available to the ESAs as necessary.[157]

However, the statistical field of activity also has some specific features which justify the high degree of independence of the statistical authorities. This holds particularly true with regard to the fact that the knowledge generated by statistics is supposed to provide rationality to a special degree because it shall be a central basis for political, but also social and economic decision making.[158] For this reason, Art. 3a s. 1 Regulation (EC) No 2533/98 provides that the development, production and dissemination of European statistics by the ESCB shall be governed by the principles of impartiality, objectivity, professional independence, cost-effectiveness, statistical confidentiality, minimisation of the reporting burden and high output quality, including reliability and the definitions of these principles shall be adopted, elaborated on and published by the ECB.[159] It is precisely this commitment to professional or scientific independence that ensures that the collection, compilation and distribution of statistics is determined solely by scientific methodology and not by extraneous influences.[160]

Therefore, professional (also understood in the sense of functional) independence is described as a *modus operandi* for the ESCB and the ESS ensuring that the performance of tasks is free from any pressures from political or interest groups or from Union or national authorities.[161] This principle is partly supplemented by institutional arrangements, for example in regard to the Director-General of Eurostat who shall act in an independent manner and shall neither seek nor take instructions from the Union institutions or bodies, from any government or other institution, body, office or agency when carrying out statistical tasks.[162]

3.2.5 Right of Consultation, International Cooperation

The ECB has an advisory role, which gives the ECB extensive rights to be consulted and to submit opinions in both Union and national legislative procedures where

---

[156] Art. 3(2)(a) ESRBR in conjunction with Art. 5(1) s. 1 ECB-ESRBR.

[157] Art. 5(1) s. 2, (2) ECB-ESRBR; for details see Muscheler-Lorange (2013), paras. 4–8.

[158] See Kröger and Pilniok (2016), pp. 137–138, 141–143 in particular with regard to the relevance of statistics for the legal framework of the Stability and Growth Pact and the allocation of EU funds.

[159] A similar provision is found for the ESS in Art. 2 Regulation (EC) No 223/2009; see also Art. 338(2) TFEU.

[160] See Kröger and Pilniok (2016), p. 145.

[161] Art. 3a s. 2 Regulation (EC) No 2533 and 98 in conjunction with Art. 2(1)(a) Regulation (EC) No 223/2009.

[162] Art. 6a(3) Regulation (EC) No 223/2009.

these relate to its field of competence.[163] Consultation is also explicitly provided for with regard to measures laid down by the European Parliament and the Council which are necessary for the use of the euro as the single currency.[164] Further consultation rights can be found in Arts. 48(3) sub-para. 1 s. 2, (6) sub-para. 2 s. 2 TEU and Arts. 127(6), 138(1) s. 2, (2) s. 2, 283(2) sub-para. 2, 219 TFEU. Legal acts in the ECB's field of competence, which of course must not interfere with the ECB's competence to adopt its own legal acts, should benefit in substance from the ECB's expertise.[165] Thus, the ECB recently issued an opinion on the proposal of the Commission for a Regulation on Markets in Crypto-assets[166] and underlined the possible impact of crypto assets on the monetary policy transmission mechanism, the maintenance of financial stability and the smooth operation of payment systems.[167] In contrast, measures relating to the internal organisation of the ECB are not encompassed, as the ECJ has made clear in its *OLAF decision*.[168]

The ECB enjoys a high degree of independence in the exercise of its right to be consulted and to submit opinions. This is particularly true since this does not entail any binding legal consequences.

Functionally comparable to this is the role of the ECB, both in its central bank function and in its supervisory function, in international institutions and committees, especially the Bank for International Settlements (BIS) and the Basel Committee on Banking Supervision (BCBS).[169] The legal basis for such a cooperation is provided by Art. 6 ESCB/ECB Statute.

However, independence is also subject to certain concerns, particularly with regard to international institutions in the field of financial market regulation. With regard to the BCBS, for example, *Viterbo* has convincingly demonstrated that its expertise cannot be had without transparency, accountability and democratic legitimacy.[170] Although not binding, the standards developed by the BCBS in particular have a considerable influence on the regulation implemented by the legislator. In this context, it seems convincing to envisage a stronger involvement of political actors,

[163]Arts. 127(4), 282(5) TFEU, Art. 4 ESCB/ECB Statute; see also Council Decision 98/415/EC of 29 June 1998 on the consultation of the European Central Bank by national authorities regarding draft legislative provisions, OJ 3.7.1998, L 189, p. 42.

[164]Art. 133 TFEU.

[165]See Waldhoff (2013), para. 82.

[166]Proposal for a Regulation of the European Parliament and of the Council on Markets in Crypto-assets, and amending Directive (EU) 2019/1937 of 24 September 2020, COM(2020) 593 final (hereinafter: MiCAR).

[167]Opinion of the European Central Bank of 19 February 2021 on a proposal for a regulation on Markets in Crypto-assets, and amending Directive (EU) 2019/1937 (CON/2021/4), pp. 3 et seq.

[168]ECJ, OLAF, 10.7.2003, ECLI:EU:C:2003:395, paras. 106 et seq.

[169]For details see Smits (1997), pp. 422 et seq.

[170]Viterbo (2019), p. 228.

for example through consultation and hearing rights,[171] without affecting independence.

3.3 Financial Stability and Financial Supervision

In the course of the financial and sovereign debt crisis the ECB has experienced a growth in tasks and powers concerning not only depth, but also breadth. This applies in particular to the stability of the financial system and prudential supervision addressed in Art. 127(5), (6) TFEU.

Financial stability is regarded as a broad and discretionary concept that generally refers to the safety and soundness of the financial system and to the stability of payment and settlement systems.[172] Nevertheless, it is difficult to develop an operable, positive definition that allows to consistently grasp the objectives to be pursued and the means to achieve them.[173] Actually, the objective of financial stability is closely linked to the protection of institutions, investors and depositors as well as the functioning of the internal market. The instruments for achieving the stability objective include regulation, supervision, crisis management, fiscal support as well as providing liquidity to financial institutions.[174] Thus, the safeguarding of financial stability is fundamentally different from the area of monetary policy, which is committed to a priority objective and rounded off by specific powers.

Financial stability was an important directive of the European Union in the reforms of financial supervision beginning in 2009, enshrining it as an objective of both, macro-prudential supervision, understood as supervision of the financial system as a whole, especially with regard to systemic risks, and micro-prudential supervision, i.e. supervision of individual institutions.[175] The measures taken to grant financial assistance to Member States, especially stability support provided by the ESM, also aim at preserving fiscal and hence financial stability.[176]

This triad of fiscal, price and financial stability also determines the ECB's post-crisis orientation, which will be explored here with regard to central bank independence.

[171]For enhancing democratic legitimacy of the BCBS by improving the role of the European Parliament see Viterbo (2019), pp. 222 et seq.

[172]Lastra (2015), para. 3.60; see also Bauerschmidt (2019), p. 476.

[173]For details see Lastra (2015), paras. 3.61–3.70.

[174]Cf. Garicano and Lastra (2010), pp. 597 et seq.

[175]Cf. High-Level Group on Financial Supervision in the EU (2009), pp. 38–39. See also ECJ, Kotnik, 19.7.2016, ECLI:EU:C:2016:570, paras. 88, 91.

[176]Cf. Recital 6 TESM.

3.3.1 *Banking Supervision Within the SSM*

3.3.1.1 Micro-Prudential Supervision by the ECB

In course of the financial crisis, the Commission entrusted the High-Level Group on Financial Supervision in the EU chaired by former IMF Director *Jacques de Larosière* to develop proposals to make European financial market regulation and supervision more efficient. In 2009, this committee launched the *de Larosière* Report which revealed the deficiencies of supervision by the national authorities.[177] On the one hand, there is a risk that institutions operating across borders will exploit the varying degrees of strictness in the application of standards. On the other hand, there is a fear that national supervisors will take particular account of the interests of their Member States. The reason for the unionisation of micro-prudential supervision was the crisis in the Spanish real estate market in 2012, which also threatened the existence of the country's fourth largest institution (Bankia).[178] After a summit statement by the euro area Member States[179] and a "Roadmap towards a Banking Union" by the Commission,[180] and after long political discourse, a Single Supervisory Mechanism (SSM) has been established comprising all euro area Member States with an opt-in clause for non-euro Member States.[181] By the SSMR based on Art. 127(6) TFEU, the Council conferred specific tasks upon the ECB concerning policies relating to the prudential supervision of credit institutions. Within the SSM, which is composed of the ECB and the national competent authorities (NCAs),[182] the ECB carries out tasks of micro-prudential supervision[183] laid down in Art. 4 (1) SSMR. This is in principle organised in such a way that the ECB exercises direct supervision only over significant institutions (SIs), while less significant institutions (LSIs) are in principle supervised by the NCAs in accordance with Art. 6 SSMR.[184] However, with regard to all institutions, the ECB is exclusively responsible for authorising credit institutions and withdrawing authorisations as well as assessing notifications of the acquisition and disposal of qualifying holdings in credit institutions.[185] In order to carry out its tasks, the ECB has also been granted investigatory

[177] High-Level Group on Financial Supervision in the EU (2009), pp. 40–41.

[178] For details Tröger (2013), pp. 9–11.

[179] Euro Area Summit Statement of 29 June 2012.

[180] Communication from the Commission to the European Parliament and the Council of 12 September 2012, COM(2012) 510 final.

[181] Art. 7 SSMR; for details see Dumitrescu-Pasecinic (2019), pp. 359 et seq. In 2020, the Republic of Bulgaria and the Republic of Croatia also joined the SSM, see ECB, Press Releases of 10 July 2020.

[182] Art. 6(1) SSMR.

[183] By Art. 5 SSMR, the ECB has also been entrusted with limited macro-prudential tasks. For details see for example Bassani (2019), pp. 53–55.

[184] For details see for example Schuster (2014), pp. 4–6.

[185] Art. 6(4) s. 1 SSMR in conjunction with Art. 4(1)(a), (c) SSMR.

powers[186] and special supervisory powers,[187] which include the imposing of administrative pecuniary penalties.[188]

Moreover, the ECB is responsible for the effective and consistent functioning of the SSM,[189] which is why it is granted indirect supervision over LSIs with powers towards the NCAs, *inter alia* the power to issue regulations, guidelines or general instructions.[190] The relationship between the ECB and NCAs is also characterised by the fact that NCAs assist the ECB with the preparation and implementation of any acts relating to the supervisory tasks following the instructions given by the ECB.[191]

However, the conferral of banking supervision on the ECB was accompanied by concerns about a trade-off between price stability on the one hand and financial stability on the other.[192] For this reason, the Supervisory Board was established as an internal body of the ECB, composed of its Chair and Vice-Chair, four representatives of the ECB, and one representative of the NCA in each participating Member State.[193] According to Art. 26(8) SSMR the Supervisory Board shall carry out preparatory works regarding the supervisory tasks and proposes to the ECB's Governing Council complete draft decisions to be adopted by the latter. This decision-making modus, together with the separation of supervisory function from monetary policy function according to Art. 25 SSMR, shall prevent trade-offs within the institutional framework set by the Treaties.

3.3.1.2 Dimensions of Supervisory Independence

The legislator supplemented the transfer of supervisory tasks by organisational and procedural arrangements, including the guarantee of independence. Subsequently, this mode of supervisory independence shall also be measured in dimensions in order to identify similarities and differences to the independence laid down in primary law. In this respect, it is necessary to differentiate between the Governing Council as the decision-making body of the ECB and the supervisory body as an operational actor in banking supervision.

[186] Arts. 10–13 SSMR.

[187] Arts. 14–16 SSMR.

[188] Art. 18 SSMR; for details see Schneider (2014), pp. 18 et seq.

[189] Art. 6(1) s. 2 SSMR.

[190] Art. 6(5) SSMR; on the question whether the NCAs also act in the field of indirect supervision on the basis of an original Member State competence or a derivative union competence see Karagianni and Scholten (2018), pp. 191–193; Gentzsch and Brade (2019), pp. 618–620.

[191] Art. 6(3) SSMR.

[192] For details see Ferran and Babis (2013), pp. 12–16; a more holistic approach discussed at Goldmann (2018), pp. 283 et seq.

[193] Art. 26(1) sub-para. 1 s. 1 SSMR.

Institutional Independence

If institutional independence is not only interpreted as legal personality but also of organisational and competence resilience against change, this constitutional guarantee must be ensured by the legislator when implementing a supervisory body as a new body and allocating banking supervision.

With regard to the Supervisory Body, however, it should be noted that it is a preparatory body which, while having a significant operational role, does not affect the ultimate decision-making powers of the Governing Council.[194] Concerning changes of competence, Art. 127(6) TFEU provides a sufficient basis for the conferral of supervisory tasks which has been approved by the FCC contrary to critical voices in German literature.[195] A conferral of banking supervisory tasks together with organisational arrangements for their exercise thus does not affect the institutional independence of the ECB. However, it should be noted that the institutional independence of the supervisory function is not very resistant to change, bearing in mind that the Union legislator can change the legal basis of the SSMR, in particular by withdrawing tasks or changing organisation.

Personal Independence

It is a recurring demand that an effective, independent supervisory authority must ensure that the acting supervisors cannot be dismissed without sufficient reason.[196] In the SSM, with regard to personal independence, it should first be noted that the members of the Governing Council and the Executive Board derive their independence from primary law. However, there are special provisions for the members of the Supervisory Board.

The personal independence of the Supervisory Board is, first of all, ensured by the fact that the Chair may not hold any other office at any NCAs.[197] Their term of office is limited to five years and is non-renewable.[198] If the Chair no longer fulfils the conditions required for the performance of their duties or has been guilty of serious misconduct, the Council, on a proposal from the ECB and with the approval of the European Parliament, may adopt an implementing decision to remove the Chair from office.[199] To this end, the Parliament and the Council have the power to inform the ECB that the conditions are fulfilled leading to the ECB responding.[200]

---

[194] Cf. FCC, Banking Union, 30.7.2019, 2 BvR 1685/14 et al., paras. 199–201.

[195] FCC, Banking Union, 30.7.2019, 2 BvR 1685/14 et al., paras. 199–201; for an overview of critical voices see Gentzsch and Brade (2019), p. 616, n. 78.

[196] Cf. Quintyn and Taylor (2007), p. 21.

[197] Art. 26(3) sub-para. 2 s. 1 SSMR.

[198] Art. 26(3) sub-para. 2 s. 2 SSMR.

[199] Art. 26(4) sub-para. 1 s. 1 SSMR.

[200] Art. 26(4) sub-para. 3 SSMR.

These rules are comparable to those concerning the members of the Governing Council and the Executive Board, in particular as regards the term length of office of the President—albeit five years instead of eight—, the prohibition of reappointment and high material conditions for removal. However, the power to decide on dismissal is assigned to the Council rather than to the ECJ, thus replacing judicial review by more political control. Therefore, the personal independence of the Chair is weaker than that of the members of the Governing Council and the Executive Board.[201]

With regard to the Vice-Chair, due to simultaneously being a member of the Executive Board,[202] the primary law provisions remain in place, which may also cover supervisory deficits in view of incapacity or serious misconduct. If the Vice-Chair is removed from office as a member of the Executive Board,[203] they no longer fulfil the conditions set out in Art. 26(3) s. 4 SSMR. Although the relevant provision on removal from office[204] appears optional ("may") from a grammatical point of view, the Vice-Chair is to be removed from office by the Council.[205]

For the other members of the Supervisory Board, i.e. the four representatives of the ECB and the representatives of the NCAs, there are no comparable arrangements. This absence of EU legislation which makes the dismissal of NCA representatives subject to certain requirements also reduces the level of material protection.[206] A limit is, however, set by Art. 19(1), (2) SSMR, with the consequence that the removal of NCA representatives must at least not impair their independence.[207] However, such an impairment is probable if the reason for dismissal is related to concrete supervisory decisions.[208]

Financial Independence

The fact that supervisory authorities should also have budgetary independence from the government and parliaments is justified above all by the financial and fiscal policy influence of governments and parliaments, which can be supported by austerity considerations, especially in times of crisis.[209] In the SSM, financial

---

[201] Similarly Zilioli (2016), p. 170.

[202] Art. 26(3) s. 4 SSMR.

[203] Art. 11.4. ESCB/ECB Statute.

[204] Art. 26(4) sub-para. 2 s. 1 SSMR.

[205] Cf. Zilioli (2016), p. 171.

[206] Cf. Zilioli (2016), p. 169, however, more emphasising the representative status of these members; Lambrinoc (2016), p. 236.

[207] The EMI argued accordingly with regard to provisions on the personal independence of members of the NCBs' decision-making bodies, cf. EMI, Convergence Report 1998, p. 311.

[208] According to Hahn and Häde (2010), § 20 para. 101 for the members of the decision-making bodies of the NCBs.

[209] Quintyn and Taylor (2007), p. 24.

independence is established by Arts. 28, 30 SSMR.[210] According to Art. 28 SSMR, the ECB is responsible for devoting the necessary financial and human resources to carry out the tasks assigned to it by the SSMR. Art. 30(1) SSMR empowers the ECB to levy an annual supervisory fee on supervised institutions, subject to the cost recovery principle. The calculation and collection of the supervisory fees have been further specified by the ECB in a regulation.[211]

Functional Independence

Prohibition of Instructions and Influence

According to Art. 19(1) s. 1 SSMR the ECB and the NCAs acting within the SSM shall act independently when carrying out the tasks conferred by the SSMR. Pursuant to Art. 19(1) s. 2 SSMR, the members of the Supervisory Board "shall act independently and objectively in the interest of the Union as a whole and shall neither seek nor take instructions from the institutions or bodies of the Union, from any government of a Member State or from any other public or private body". In addition, the institutions, bodies, offices and agencies of the Union and the governments of the Members States and any other bodies shall respect that independence according to Art. 19(2) SSMR.

Contrary to what is partly claimed in the literature,[212] this independence provision not only has a clarifying function in relation to Art. 130 TFEU, because independence is explicitly extended to the Supervisory Board and the NCAs.[213] In this context, however, the question arises whether central bank independence enshrined in primary law applies to the exercise of SSM supervision at all.[214] This is particularly relevant in the light of possible amendments to secondary law that would limit supervisory independence, for example by implementing further control and maybe overruling mechanisms. In German literature in particular, there are numerous voices according to which the guarantee of independence under primary law does not extend to the performance of supervisory tasks.[215] Admittedly, it can be argued that SSM supervision is based on secondary legislation, which means that the activation of Art. 127(6) TFEU *prima facie* proves to be a conferral of tasks *in regard to* the Treaties, but not *by* the Treaties.[216]

210For details see Wolfers and Voland (2014), p. 1479; Wymeersch (2014), p. 56.

211Regulation (EU) No 1163/2014 of the European Central Bank of 22 October 2014 on supervisory fees (ECB/2014/41), OJ 31.10.2014, L 311, p. 23.

212See for example Peuker (2014), p. 770; Gören (2019), p. 236.

213Cf. ter Kuile et al. (2015), pp. 165–166; Ohler (2015), § 5 paras. 82, 90.

214Cf. Zilioli (2016), pp. 157, 158, 164–165.

215See for example Siekmann (2013), para. 110; Häde (2016), Art. 130 TFEU para. 18; see also Mersch (2017); Repasi (2020), para. 17.78.

216In this direction Kämmerer and Starski (2013), p. 327.

However, such differentiation would unduly equate a conferral of supervisory tasks on the ECB in accordance with Art. 127(6) TFEU with a conferral of competences on the Union under the principle of conferral (Art. 5(2) s. 1 TEU). Indeed, the transfer of supervisory competence to the Union has already taken place through the Maastricht Treaty or its ratification in the Member States, although its activation was made conditional on a unanimous decision of the Council by way of a regulation.[217] The SSMR does not, however, imply any transfer of sovereign rights as confirmed by the FCC in its *Banking Union decision*.[218]

It cannot be argued either that the exercise of the competence requires the adoption of a regulation which ultimately assigns tasks relating to the supervision of credit institutions to the ECB. Even if the tasks to be performed are not transferred to the ECB by primary law alone, but finally by an additional secondary legal act, these are nevertheless tasks originally conferred by the Treaties.[219] The SSM supervision therefore participates in the primary law guarantee of independence, without prejudice to possible functional differentiation.[220]

Correlation Between Independence and Financial Stability

The parallels between central bank independence in general and supervisory independence in particular, which have just become clear, lead to the question whether this also holds true from a functional point of view, i.e. whether a correlation between independence and supervisory action, in particular with regard to the financial stability objective, can also be observed.

Approaching supervisory independence from an international perspective, the so-called Core Principles for Effective Banking Supervision, developed by the BCBS, established at the BIS, contain global, albeit non-binding minimum standards ("soft law") for sound supervisory and regulatory practice.[221] Core Principle 2, which is entitled "Independence, accountability, resourcing and legal protection for supervisors", states that supervisors possess operational independence, transparent processes, sound governance and adequate resources, and are accountable for the discharge of its duties.[222] A more concrete specification can be found in No. 1 of the essential criteria relating to Principle 2 which prohibits government and industry interference which compromises the independence of the supervisor.[223]

---

[217]Mayer and Kollmeyer (2013), pp. 1159–1160.

[218]FCC, Banking Union, 30.7.2019, 2 BvR 1685/14 et al., para. 311.

[219]Cf. Ohler (2015), § 5 para. 82.

[220]Likewise, for example, Herdegen (2012), p. 1894; Wolfers and Voland (2014), p. 1487; Lambrinoc (2016), pp. 224–225; left open by Amtenbrink (2019), p. 315, who, however, argues that, should Art. 130 TFEU not be applicable, independent SSM supervision by the ECB can only be established by amending the Treaty.

[221]Cf. BCBS (2012), p. 1.

[222]BCBS (2012), p. 22.

[223]BCBS (2012), pp. 22–23.

These principles have been adapted in the SSM, as can be seen in Recital 75 SSMR. According to that, the ECB should exercise the supervisory tasks conferred on it in full independence, in particular free from undue political influence and from industry interference which would affect its operational independence.

Comparable to monetary policy, this addresses the danger that state and private actors, i.e. above all governments and supervised institutions, exert influence on the supervisory authority which, thus, do not make decisions based only on the objectives of the regulatory framework. While in the area of monetary policy there may be an incentive for political actors to move towards monetary stability in favour of short-term growth, in the area of supervision there is a risk that supervisors may be induced to be lenient towards institutions in the long run (so-called supervisory forbearance) in order to reduce settlement costs in the short term and accept higher costs especially for the budget.[224] Indeed, there may be political reasons for maintaining certain institutions, although such measures may have a negative impact on the functioning of the financial system or on financial stability.[225] The crises of the 1990s impressively demonstrate the fact that not only weak and ineffective regulatory and supervisory structures, but above all political influence vis-à-vis supervisory authorities contribute to financial crises.[226]

Moreover, the separation of government and supervision is sometimes argued for because, in the field of financial supervision, political actors themselves are affected by the consequences of supervisory decisions, because they regularly require capital and take on the role of borrower, in particular by taking out loans.[227]

In summary, it can be said that there are some connections between a supervision free of influences and an optimal achievement of objectives. This must always be borne in mind when trying to determine the democratic legitimation of central bank action in the field of banking supervision. In this respect, the *Banking Union decision* of the FCC is partly not convincing in its reasoning. Although the FCC had already emphasised in its *Maastricht decision* that the independence of monetary policy in the sovereign competence of the ECB could not be applied to other policy areas,[228] it considered the independent SSM supervision by the NCAs to be materially justified only by reference to Recital 75 SSMR.[229] In so doing, however, the FCC omitted to examine in greater detail the functional reasons for guaranteeing independence.[230]

[224]Cf. Bini Smaghi (2007), pp. 46, 48; more reserved Wolfers and Voland (2014), p. 1492.

[225]Quintyn and Taylor (2007), p. 23; Zilioli (2016), p. 158.

[226]Cf. Quintyn and Taylor (2007), pp. 7–8.

[227]Forkel (2011), p. 101; German Council of Economic Experts (2012/13), p. 173.

[228]FCC, Maastricht, 12.10.1993 = BVerfGE 89, 155 (pp. 207 et seq.).

[229]FCC, Banking Union, 30.7.2019, 2 BvR 1685/14 et al., para. 219.

[230]See infra Sect. 5.2.2.

3.3.1.3 Functional Characteristics of Banking Supervision and Their Impact on Democratic Legitimation

As in the field of monetary policy, further functional specificities are now to be identified, which argue for and against extensive independence and thus determine the necessary level of legitimation. These particularly affect the accountability which shall be described afterwards.

Capacity of Control Institutions

Compared to monetary policy, banking supervision has similarities and differences. Financial supervision is also significantly influenced by the dynamics of financial markets, which requires a continuous state of knowledge update. Risks can typically not be adequately determined and regulated in advance, so that the corresponding assessments require a certain degree of flexibility.[231]

In addition to the dynamics, the complexity of this field is another functional aspect. In the field of financial market regulation and supervision, where the activities are becoming demanding in view of increasing globalisation and fast progress, specialised units are required to develop and implement the relevant standards and to adapt them continuously to changing conditions.[232] Not only the implementation of abstract and general standards, but also their enforcement requires the integration and concentration of expertise that can ensure effective and efficient decision-making.[233]

The efficiency of the legislator, but also of the controlling institutions, especially courts and auditors, is greater than in the field of monetary policy, because here the abstract and general programme, which can be traced back to the legislator, has a far greater significance. It should be noted that, unlike monetary policy, banking supervision is not concentrated at the ECB but, as part of the competence for the internal market,[234] is also subject to more far-reaching regulation by the Council and the Parliament.

At the same time, this legal control through the provision of concrete conditions and consequences allows for improved control by other institutions, in particular the CJEU and the ECA, which can more closely examine the compatibility of action with prior-ranking law.

---

[231] Cf. Thiele (2014), p. 425.

[232] Cf. Quintyn and Taylor (2007), p. 9; Armour et al. (2016), p. 91; Viterbo (2019), p. 208.

[233] Zilioli (2016), p. 158.

[234] The FCC has not made any further specification here, but has, however, explicitly referred to the internal market concerning bank resolution; see FCC, Banking Union, 30.7.2019, 2 BvR 1685/14 et al., paras 248–252; for a shared competence over banking prudential regulation Viterbo (2019), pp. 217–218.

Fundamental Rights and Essentiality

Furthermore, SSM supervision is more characterised by individual enforcement than other central banking activities, in particular through the adoption of supervisory decisions by the ECB vis-à-vis market participants, especially credit institutions.[235] This requires in principle a high level of legitimation, as supervisory measures are typically part of public commercial law and thus interfere with fundamental rights.[236] Especially measures with a high degree of intensity of intervention, e.g., the withdrawal of authorisations or the imposition of sanctions, must therefore be secured by adequate control mechanisms.

Another characteristic element of financial supervision is that economic fundamental rights are not restricted by supervisory measures alone. Rather, the protection of trade secrets under fundamental rights requires confidentiality, so that control by other institutions may be restricted. With regard to business relevant information, Arts. 16, 17 CFR but also Art. 8 CFR (protection of personal data), whose relationship to one another has not yet been fully explored,[237] are relevant.

How much fundamental rights are actually affected, has a particular impact on the intensity of judicial control.[238] In its *Banking Union decision*, the FCC assumed that the ECB, to the extent that it is granted discretion in certain cases,[239] uses broad, albeit not unlimited discretion.[240]

In this respect, the FCC refers to the decision of the ECJ in the *L-Bank case*, which dealt with the classification of an institution as significant and thus subject to direct ECB supervision. In that decision, the ECJ had pointed out, following the EGC, that "the assessment of the proportionality of a measure must be reconciled with compliance with the discretion that may have been conferred on the EU institutions at the time it was adopted".[241]

In any event, it will be necessary in the future to give greater emphasis to the density of judicial control, particularly with regard to proportionality. A mere adoption of the standards set for monetary policy is not convincing because of the functional differences. In this respect, the specific performance potential of the courts as well as the degree of fundamental rights involved are important factors for judicial control.

[235]Cf. Lehmann (2017), p. 119; Bauerschmidt (2019), p. 492.

[236]For an in-depth analysis see Almhofer (2018), pp. 229 et seq.

[237]See for details Almhofer (2018), p. 241.

[238]Zilioli (2017), p. 100.

[239]The FCC refers to the classification of credit institutions as less significant under Art. 6 (4) sub-para. 2 SSMR in conjunction with Arts. 70, 71 SSMFR or the imposition of additional capital requirements under Art. 16(1)(c) SSMR.

[240]FCC, Banking Union, 30.7.2019, 2 BvR 1685/14 et al., para. 212.

[241]ECJ, L-Bank, 8.5.2019, ECLI:EU:C:2019:372, para. 53.

Multi-Target Mandate Without Sufficiently Clear Parameters

While monetary policy in the ESCB/Eurosystem with the stability primacy is committed to a clear primary objective, whose achievement is measurable in concrete terms, banking supervision in the SSM is characterised by a multi-target mandate without sufficiently clear measurement criteria.[242]

This becomes particularly apparent in Recital 30 SSMR, according to that "[t]he ECB should carry out the tasks conferred on it with a view to ensuring the safety and soundness of credit institutions and the stability of the financial system of the Union as well as of individual participating Member States and the unity and integrity of the internal market, thereby ensuring also the protection of depositors and improving the functioning of the internal market [. . .]".

Thus, the concept of financial stability encompasses a variety of objectives which may well conflict with each other.[243] For example, in certain cases, rigid measures toward institutions may be necessary to protect the stability of the financial system, but this may have significant negative consequences for depositors.

In contrast to monetary policy, where concrete technical parameters, such as the inflation rate, provide information on the achievement of objectives, there is no such benchmark in SSM supervision.[244] However, this also leaves unclear what is actually needed to achieve the objectives. This has a decisive impact on the determination of the level of legitimation, as it makes *ex post* control of the extent to which the supervisory authority actually commits itself to these objectives and resolves the conflicting objectives much more difficult.[245] In its Special Report on the establishment of the SSM, the ECA has also emphasised, as a prerequisite for accountability, that the actions of supervisors should be assessed in light of certain standards and with respect to defined objectives.[246] With regard to transparency and accountability, it deplored "lack of a proper mechanism for assessing and then reporting on supervisory effectiveness".[247] However, the report does identify performance indicators and related measures, such bankruptcies and losses, or public confidence in the banking sector or supervisor.[248] To strengthen the democratic legitimation of prudential supervision, it would certainly be useful to develop such criteria in line with advancing supervisory practice and, where appropriate, to enshrine them in law.

---

242 Cf. Kern (2015), p. 170.

243 Cf. Amtenbrink and Markakis (2019), p. 12.

244 ter Kuile et al. (2015), pp. 167–168; Mersch (2017); in general Quintyn and Taylor (2003), p. 280; Bini Smaghi (2007), pp. 49 and 52.

245 ter Kuile et al. (2015), p. 168; Amtenbrink and Markakis (2019), p. 12.

246 ECA (2016), p. 46.

247 ECA (2016), p. 10.

248 For further examples see ECA (2016), p. 47.

3.3.1.4 Accountability

The functional features presented have an influence on how the ECB is ultimately held accountable for its actions. In the area of banking supervision, accountability is also the necessary democratic counterpart to independence, which already emerges in the Basel Principles stating that the supervisor "is accountable for the discharge of its duties and use of its resources".[249]

In the following, the different accountability mechanisms shall be elaborated in an SSM-specific manner.

Political Accountability

Of crucial importance for political accountability are the reporting and accountability obligations set out in Arts. 20, 21 SSMR, which have been further specified in an Interinstitutional Agreement between the European Parliament and the ECB, in particular as regards access to information and confidentiality.[250]

These provisions require the ECB to submit an annual report to the European Parliament, the Council, the Commission and the Eurogroup on the execution of the tasks conferred upon it by the SSMR.[251] That report has to be presented in public to the European Parliament and to the Eurogroup by the Chair of the Supervisory Board.[252] The Chair of the Supervisory Board may also be heard by the Eurogroup.[253] At the request of the European Parliament, they shall participate in hearings carried out by the competent committees.[254] The ECB is also obliged to reply to questions from the European Parliament and the Eurogroup.[255] Upon request, the Chair of the Supervisory Board "shall hold confidential oral discussions behind closed doors with the Chair and Vice-Chairs of the competent committee of the European Parliament concerning its supervisory tasks".[256]

Furthermore, Art. 21 SSMR explicitly grants rights to the national parliaments of the participating Member States. In addition to reporting obligations of the ECB,[257] the national parliaments may request the ECB to reply in writing to any observations

[249] BCBS (2012), p. 22.

[250] Interinstitutional Agreement between the European Parliament and the European Central Bank on the practical modalities of the exercise of democratic accountability and oversight over the exercise of the tasks conferred on the ECB within the framework of the Single Supervisory Mechanism (2013/694/EU), OJ 30.11.2013, L 320, p. 1.

[251] Art. 20(2) SSMR.

[252] Art. 20(3) SSMR.

[253] Art. 20(4) SSMR.

[254] Art. 20(5) SSMR.

[255] Art. 20(6) SSMR.

[256] Art. 20(8) s. 1 SSMR.

[257] Art. 21(1) SSMR.

or questions submitted by them concerning SSM supervision.[258] Furthermore, they may invite the Chair or a member of the Supervisory Board to participate in an exchange of views in relation to the supervision of credit institutions in that Member State together with a representative of the NCA.[259]

Although this form of democratic control has encountered criticism in the literature precisely because of the lack of overriding and sanctioning powers,[260] the FCC has classified the reporting and accountability obligations as (still) sufficient compensation for the "drops of influence" it has identified.[261] This is because these obligations facilitate political governance and enable the competent authorities to assess the ECB's actions, to review their legality and to enforce compliance with Union law, if necessary, through the courts.[262] They also enable the SSM to be kept under constant review so that it can be amended or removed.[263]

Nevertheless, it should be noted that the effectiveness of such parliamentary control powers depends on the frequency and intensity with which they are exercised.[264] With regard to the SSM, *Amtenbrink* and *Markakis* have analysed practical challenges for effective control.[265] Especially the multitude of European institutions in the field of financial regulation and supervision (especially the ECB, including its Supervisory Board, the Commission, and the EBA, all participating in the BCBS,[266] but also the SRB) as well as the multi-level structure mean that questions regarding certain actions are not always precisely addressed and thus threaten to blur the lines of responsibility.[267]

Administrative Accountability

Classifying interinstitutional control between the Union's institutions according to specific functions, the audit of the ECB by the ECA can be seen as administrative control. According to Art. 20(7) SSMR, the ECA also examines the operational efficiency of the management of the ECB under Art. 27.2. ESCB/ECB Statute concerning supervisory tasks.[268]

---

[258]Art. 21(2) SSMR.

[259]Art. 21(3) SSMR.

[260]See for example Peuker (2014), p. 768.

[261]Cf. FCC, Banking Union, 30.7.2019, 2 BvR 1685/14 et al., para. 217; see infra Sect. 5.2.2.

[262]Ibid.

[263]Ibid.

[264]Cf. Dawson et al. (2019), pp. 85–88.

[265]See Amtenbrink and Markakis (2019), pp. 16–22; see also Maricut-Akbik (2020), pp. 1199 et seq.

[266]For details see Viterbo (2019), pp. 211–214.

[267]Cf. Amtenbrink and Markakis (2019), p. 23.

[268]Moreover, the supervisory section of the annual accounts shall be audited by independent external auditors according to Art. 29(3) SSMR in conjunction with Art. 27.1. ESCB/ECB Statute.

However, similar to the relationship between the ECB and the European Parliament, it is important to bear in mind that access to documents and information must be reconciled with the interest in confidentiality.[269] In order to further specify the mutual rights and obligations, the ECB and the ECJ agreed on a Memorandum of Understanding in October 2019, which in principle grants the ECJ a right of access and in return regulates the handling of highly confidential documents and information.[270] This takes account of Art. 287(3) sub-para. 2 TFEU imposing particularly on other Union institutions to forward to the ECA, at its request, any document or information necessary to carry out its task.

Administrative control also includes the Administrative Board of Review under Art. 24 SSMR,[271] carrying out internal administrative reviews of the decisions taken by the ECB in the exercise of SSM supervision. As the ABoR is composed of reputable supervisors "having a proven record of relevant knowledge and professional experience, including supervisory experience, to a sufficiently high level in the fields of banking or other financial services",[272] it provides output legitimation in view of the expertise guaranteed by legal conditions. In addition, the requirement that members are not part of the current staff of the ECB, NCAs or other Union and Member State bodies related to SSM tasks[273] ensures a quasi-judicial impartiality that enables objective decision-making.

As an internal body of the ECB, the ABoR reviews supervisory decisions for procedural and substantive conformity with the SSMR.[274] Eligible applicants are—comparable to an action for annulment – natural or legal persons, to whom decisions are addressed or who are directly and individually concerned by decisions.[275] If the ABoR considers that the review is admissible, it issues an opinion and refers the case to the Supervisory Body for a new draft decision.[276] Taking account of the opinion, the Supervisory Board shall adopt a new draft decision abrogating the original decision or replacing it with a decision of the same content or an amended decision.[277] This new draft decision will be submitted to the Governing Council and will be deemed to be adopted unless the Governing Council objects within a maximum period of ten working days.[278]

---

[269] Cf. Amtenbrink and Markakis (2019), pp. 15–16.

[270] ECA/ECB, Memorandum of Understanding, 9.10.2019, pp. 3–4.

[271] In conjunction with Decision 2014/360/EU of the European Central Bank of 14 April 2014 concerning the establishment of an Administrative Board of Review and its Operating Rules (ECB/2014/16), OJ 14.6.2014, L 175, p. 47.

[272] Art. 24(2) s. 1 SSMR.

[273] Art. 24(2) s. 1 SSMR.

[274] Art. 24(1) SSMR.

[275] Art. 24(5) s. 1 SSMR.

[276] Art. 24(7) s. 1 SSMR.

[277] Art. 24(7) ss. 2, 3 SSMR.

[278] Art. 24(7) s. 4 SSMR.

The potential of the ABoR's control should not be underestimated, as it provides an additional administrative remedy that not only safeguards the credit institutions' interest in confidentiality but can also relieve pressure on the courts.[279] However, the fact that the ABoR's decisions are not binding seems worthy of criticism. Due to the institutional constitution of the ECB, which is laid down in primary law, only an amendment to the Treaty (Art. 48 TEU) could improve the situation.

Judicial Accountability

The fact that supervisory decisions of the ECB are subject to judicial review is clarified by Art. 24(11) TFEU. In addition to the density of control, the cooperation between the ECB and NCAs in the multi-leveled SSM poses a particular challenge, which may diffuse the spheres of responsibility.

Specific problem areas have already become apparent in the case law of the ECJ. This concerns first of all the control of NCAs' actions. As NCAs are established under the law of their Member States, legal protection against their actions must in principle be sought before the national courts. In direct supervision, however, NCAs are subject to the ECB's power of instruction—comparable to the NCBs in the Eurosystem—so that they become an integral part of a specific cooperation mechanism. In the event that the activities of NCAs are limited to mere preparatory acts or proposals, whereas the ECB has an exclusive decision-making power, the ECJ has decided, for reasons of procedural economy and in order to avoid divergent assessments, that the Union Courts should also review these national measures.[280] This is, of course, not without its problems, as it means that the Union Courts also have to examine the conformity with national law. The assumption of an exclusive competence of the CJEU to review national acts also carries the risk of blurring the conceptually separate spheres of Union law and national law, in which conflicts between legal norms are resolved by giving EU law precedence, in its application, over national law.[281]

A further challenge for legal protection and judicial review is posed by the fact that the ECB also applies national law to a certain extent.[282] Under Art. 4 (3) sub-para. 1 s. 1 SSMR, the ECB shall apply all relevant Union law, and where

---

[279] Cf. Thiele (2015), p. 159.

[280] ECJ, Berlusconi/Fininvest, 19.12.2018, ECLI:EU:C:2018:1023, paras. 43–51; see also Brito Bastos (2019), pp. 1355 et seq. These principles have been applied to the SRM concerning the SRB's decision setting the amount of the individual *ex ante* contribution to the SRF, see ECJ, Iccrea Banca, 3.12.2019, ECLI:EU:C:2019:1036, paras. 47 et seq.

[281] See also the similar problem concerning the legal nature of the action under Art. 14.2. sub-para. 2 ESCB/ECB Statute, ECJ, Rimšēvičs, 26.2.2019, ECLI:EU:C:2019:139, paras. 64–77; Advocate General Kokott, 19.12.2018, ECLI:EU:C:2018:1030, paras. 36–68; Weinzierl (2019), pp. 440 et seq.

[282] For an in-depth analysis see Bassani (2019), pp. 73 et seq.

this Union law is composed of directives, the national legislation transposing those directives. In addition, Art. 4(3) sub-para. 1 s. 2 SSMR provides for the application of national legislation exercising options explicitly granted for the Member States by regulations.

Since the ECJ has exclusive jurisdiction over the Union institutions, including the ECB, it must also decide on the correct application of law, where necessary, even if it is based on national law transforming directives or exercising options granted by regulations.[283] This applies in particular to actions for annulment of ECB measures. However, in the case of preliminary rulings, for example, where legal protection is sought against the actions of NCAs and the interpretation and validity of ECB measures is at stake, the national courts are responsible for interpreting and applying national law.

In the *Caisse régionale de crédit agricole mutuel Alpes Provence case*, the EGC also applied national law on which the ECB relied when conducting fit and proper assessments, according to the French monetary and financial code which transposed the CRD.[284] However, in this respect the EGC referred to the interpretation given by the national courts.[285] Although practical legal difficulties seem manageable in this context, questions of competence still remain. Ultimately, however, considerations based on the need to ensure effective legal protection are likely to underpin this extraordinary concept of Union law enforcement laid down in Art. 4(3) sub-para. 1 SSMR, also with a view to judicial review.

Although the FCC, in contrast, did not reflect legal protection and thus legitimation problems in its *Banking Union decision*,[286] it remains a task of the multi-level governance and jurisdictional system of the EU *("Verwaltungs- und Rechtsprechungsverbund")* to embed SSM supervision into legal certainty and thus to establish clear lines of responsibility.

3.3.2 Macro-Prudential Supervision Within the ESRB

3.3.2.1 The ECB Within the Mandate of the ESRB

The High-Level Group on Financial Supervision in the EU had stressed the key role of central banks in a sound macro-prudential system.[287] The committee therefore suggested that the ESCB/ECB should particularly receive an explicit formal mandate

[283] For a critical view see Peuker (2014), p. 768; Thiele (2015), pp. 159–160; Martini and Weinzierl (2017), p. 181; largely uncritical Lo Schiavo (2019), pp. 117 et seq.

[284] EGC, Caisse régionale de crédit agricole mutuel Alpes Provence, 24.4.2018, ECLI:EU:T:2018:219.

[285] EGC, Caisse régionale de crédit agricole mutuel Alpes Provence, 24.4.2018, ECLI:EU:T:2018:219, paras. 84 et seq.

[286] See FCC, Banking Union, 30.7.2019, 2 BvR 1685/14 et al., para. 212.

[287] High-Level Group on Financial Supervision in the EU (2009), p. 44.

to assess high-level macro-financial risks to the system and to issue warnings where required.[288]

The subsequently established ESFS therefore consists not only of the European and national supervisory authorities but also of the newly established ESRB, which is responsible for the macro-prudential oversight of the financial system within the Union in order to contribute to the prevention or mitigation of systemic risks to financial stability in the Union.[289] The range of tasks encompass *inter alia* determining, collecting and analysing information, identifying and prioritising systemic risks, issuing warnings and recommendations as well as monitoring the follow-up to these.[290]

In performing the tasks of the ESRB, which has no legal personality,[291] the ECB plays a central role by giving analytical, logistical and administrative support and ensuring the Secretariat.[292] In addition, the President and Vice-President of the ECB and the governors of the NCBs are members of the ESRB's General Board with voting rights.[293] Furthermore, the ESRB and the ECB are institutionally interlinked because of the ECB's President chairing the ESRB.[294]

In order to anchor the activities related to the support of the ESRB in the ECB's portfolio of tasks, the European legislator made use of Art. 127(6) TFEU.

3.3.2.2 Impartiality According to Art. 7 ESRBR

Art. 7 ESRBR contains provisions on impartiality. According to Art. 7(1) s. 1 ESRBR, when participating in the activities of the General Board or when conducting any other activity relating to the ESRB, the members of the ESRB shall perform their duties impartially and solely in the interest of the Union as a whole. Pursuant to Art. 7(1) s. 2 ESRBR, they shall not seek nor take instructions from any government, the Union institutions or any other public or private body. In

[288] High-Level Group on Financial Supervision in the EU (2009), p. 44.

[289] Art. 3(1) s. 1 ESRBR.

[290] Arts. 3(2), 15–18 ESRBR.

[291] Recital 15 ESRBR.

[292] Art. 2 ECB-ESRBR.

[293] Art. 6(1)(a), (b) ESRBR. Since the ESA reform (2019), the Chair of the Supervisory Board of the ECB and the Chair of the SRB are also non-voting members, Art. 6(2)(c) and (d) of Regulation (EU) 1092/2010 as amended by Regulation (EU) 2019/2175 of the European Parliament and of the Council of 18 December 2019 amending Regulation (EU) No 1093/2010 establishing a European Supervisory Authority (European Banking Authority), Regulation (EU) No 1094/2010 establishing a European Supervisory Authority (European Insurance and Occupational Pensions Authority), Regulation (EU) No 1095/2010 establishing a European Supervisory Authority (European Securities and Markets Authority), Regulation (EU) No 600/2014 on markets in financial instruments, Regulation (EU) 2016/1011 on indices used as benchmarks in financial instruments and financial contracts or to measure the performance of investment funds, and Regulation (EU) 2015/847 on information accompanying transfers of funds, OJ 27.12.2019, L 334, p. 1.

[294] Art. 5(1) ESRBR as amended by Regulation (EU) 2019/2175.

addition, neither the Member States, the Union institutions nor any other public or private body shall seek to influence the members of the ESRB in the performance of their tasks according to Art. 7(3) ESRBR. These provisions are supplemented by incompatibility rules concerning functions in the financial industry and the central government of a Member State.[295]

These rules need to be looked at more closely. At first glance, clear parallels with the central bank independence enshrined in Art. 130 TFEU are apparent. This applies in particular to the freedom from instructions granted to and required of the members of the General Board on the one hand and the prohibition of influence addressed to certain bodies on the other. However, clear differences are also noticeable. In particular, Art. 7(1) ESRBR uses the term impartiality instead of independence to describe the mode of operation, complemented by the obligation to act solely in the interest of the Union. While the prohibition of seeking instructions in Art. 7(1) s. 2 ESRBR resembles Art. 130 s. 1 TFEU, the prohibition of influence addressed to third parties in Art. 7(3) ESRBR does not only include Union bodies and Member State governments like Art. 130 s. 2 TFEU, but all bodies, public and private.

According to *Zilioli*, the use of the term "impartiality" makes a significant difference to the concept of central bank independence, although the resulting obligations are essentially similar.[296] The conceptual difference shall imply a different interpretation of impartiality "meaning prohibition of interference by national and private interests rather than political interference".[297] Although the influence of private individuals is more strongly prohibited in Art. 7(1) s. 2 ESRBR than in Art. 130 S. 2 TFEU, it should nevertheless be noted that political influence, for example by the governments of the Member States, is also not allowed. Therefore, there is a strong case for assuming a similarly strong protection of independence by law.[298]

Nevertheless, the question arises as to whether the ECB and its bodies or members of its bodies are covered by the primary law guarantee of independence when they perform tasks related to the ESRB. These tasks have been conferred by the ECB-ESRBR based on Art. 127(6) TFEU. If one transfers the argumentation made with regard to SSM supervision to the ECB's activities in the ESRB, it can be argued that the primary law guarantee of independence also applies here due to the fact that supervision of credit institutions is anchored in primary law. Another opinion is at least not convincing on the grounds that macro-prudential supervision is not mentioned among the basic tasks in Art. 127(2) TFEU and that Art. 127 (5) TFEU only provides for a supporting role of the ESCB. The provision of Art. 127 (6) TFEU, which allows for the conferral of specific tasks concerning policies relating to the prudential supervision of credit institutions and other financial

[295] Art. 7(2), (4) ESRBR.

[296] Zilioli (2016), p. 158, n. 143.

[297] Zilioli (2016), p. 158, n. 143.

[298] Likewise Selmayr (2015), para. 48, n. 81.

institutions by means of regulations, has anticipated further tasks, so that macro-prudential supervision, like micro-prudential supervision, falls not exclusively within the competence of the Member States.[299]

However, Art. 7 ESRBR is not a redundant provision because it extends a comparably high standard of independence to all members of the ESRB's General Board. This extension of the independence granted to the ECB to other members may also prevent other channels of influence from being activated, which could ultimately undermine central bank independence.

3.3.2.3 Functional Characteristics of the ESRB's Action

The main characteristic of the ESRB's activities is that they are analytical. This can be seen, for example, in the collection and exchange of information in support of the ESAs under Art. 15(1) ESRBR. As the ESRB requests as a rule information in summary or aggregated form,[300] this task does not regularly involve interference with fundamental rights, such as the protection of business-related data. The collection of information concerning individual institutions is subject to strict procedural and substantive requirements under Art. 15(6), (7) ESRBR. The warnings and recommendations issued by the ESRB[301] are characterised by the fact that they are not binding. With regard to the implementation of recommendations, there is only a "comply or explain" mechanism, which requires the addressees to provide a reasoned explanation in the event of non-compliance.[302] With regard to the publication of warnings and recommendations,[303] it should be noted that these mainly concern systemic risks[304] and thus fundamental issues of financial stability, which is unlikely to affect the legal interests of certain financial market participants.[305]

Although this macro-prudential supervision is of enormous importance for financial stability, it is an overall analytical activity that is not characterised by binding action vis-à-vis third parties or by the collection, processing and analysis of business or personal data. Thus, the level of legitimation is not too high, both in terms of the fundamental rights involved and the content of decisions, but also in terms of the absence of fundamental balancing decisions.

This also and especially applies to the participation of the ECB, which, according to Art. 2 ECB-ESRBR, will mainly act in a supportive role by providing analytical, statistical, logistical and administrative resources. In so far as the ECB acquires

[299]For a different view Mersch (2017).

[300]Art. 15(3) ESRBR.

[301]Arts. 16–18 ESRBR.

[302]Art. 17(1) ESRBR.

[303]Art. 18 ESRBR.

[304]Art. 3(2)(c) ESRBR.

[305]Gurlit (2013), p. 890.

confidential information and data in the course of its activities, it is subject to strict rules on confidentiality in accordance with Art. 6 ECB-ESRBR.

3.3.2.4 Accountability

Independence in the ESRB is also safeguarded by accountability arrangements. Concerning political accountability, Art. 19 ESRBR provides accountability and reporting obligations. These comprise the invitation of the Chair of the ESRB to hearings in the European Parliament (paras. 1, 4), the annual report which has to be made public (para. 2), confidential oral discussion between the Chair of the ESRB and the Chair and Vice-Chairs of the ECON committee of the European Parliament (para. 5) and the ESRB's obligation to reply orally or in writing to questions put to it by the European Parliament or by the Council (para. 6). It should also be noted that the European Parliament, the Council or the Commission can invite the ESRB to examine specific issues.[306] In this advisory role, the ESRB can provide qualitative support for decisions of the respective Union institutions and deliver an appropriate output through its expertise.

Beyond that political accountability, however, there is neither administrative nor judicial accountability. Only for the request for information that is not summarised or aggregated, an integration of the ESAs holding the information is provided for. Judicial control by means of an action for annulment is regularly ruled out because recommendations and opinions do not constitute admissible subjects of legal action according to Art. 263 sub-para. 1 s. 1 TFEU. This also applies to other non-binding statements,[307] including warnings issued by the ESRB.

3.3.3 *Financial Assistance Under the ESM*

3.3.3.1 The ESM: Tasks and Institutional Aspects

In the context of crisis management, stabilisation mechanisms were set up to provide conditional loans to ailing Member States. The initially provisional measures, namely the European Financial Stabilisation Mechanism (EFSM) and subsequently the EFSF, were consolidated in the ESM in 2012. Like the EFSF,[308] the ESM is based on an international treaty between the euro area Member States and thus constitutes an independent institution in the structure of Union law, although it was

[306] Art. 19(3) ESRBR.

[307] Cremer (2016), para. 15.

[308] However, the EFSM was established by Council Regulation (EU) No 407/2010 of 11 May 2010, OJ 12.5.2010, L 118, p. 1, which based on Art. 122(2) TFEU.

legitimised by Art. 136(3) TFEU.[309] On 30 November 2020, the Eurogroup reached an agreement completing the Treaty reform process that was preceded by many years of political discourse.[310] In January and February 2021, ESM Members signed a revised Treaty, entrusting the institution with new tasks.[311]

According to Art. 3 TESM the purpose of the ESM is mobilise funding and provide stability support under strict conditionality, appropriate to the financial assistance instrument chosen, to the benefit of ESM Members which are experiencing, or are threatened by, severe financing problems, if indispensable to safeguard the financial stability of the euro area as a whole and of its Member States.[312] For this purpose, the ESM can raise funds by issuing financial instruments or by entering into financial or other agreements or arrangements with ESM Members, financial institutions or other third parties.[313]

The solidarity between Member States expressed in the granting of financial aid is inseparable from responsibility, which means that beneficiaries must undertake the necessary reforms to restabilise the financing situation. This is illustrated by the fact that all financial assistance instruments available to the ESM[314] may only be granted under Art. 12 TESM if the basic conditions of Art. 3 TESM, namely strict conditionality and indispensability to safeguard the financial stability of the euro area, are met.

In regard of institutional aspects, the ESM, which is an international financial institution under Luxembourg law and has an authorised capital stock of more than EUR 700 billion,[315] is in essence headed by the Board of Governors (BoG), which is composed of the national Finance Ministers.[316] This board takes central decisions, especially to provide stability support by the ESM, including the economic policy conditionality and to establish the choice of instruments and the financial terms and conditions.[317] Other bodies mentioned in the Treaty are the Board of Directors[318] and the Managing Director.[319]

---

[309] For details concerning the ESM's position within the EU legal framework see Forsthoff and Lauer (2020), paras. 30.9 et seq.

[310] See also infra Sect. 5.3.3.

[311] Hereinafter: TESM new version.

[312] Art. 3(1) TESM new version.

[313] Art. 3(3) TESM new version.

[314] See for details Arts. 14–18 TESM.

[315] Arts. 1(1), 8(1) TESM; see amended Annexes I and II, effective from 1 January 2021, available at https://www.esm.europa.eu/legal-documents/esm-treaty (26 February 2021).

[316] Art. 5(1) TESM.

[317] Art. 5(6)(f) TESM new version.

[318] Art. 6 TESM.

[319] Art. 7 TESM.

3.3.3.2 Involvement of the ECB in the Procedure for Granting Financial Assistance

The decision of the BoG to grant stability support depends not only on substantive, but also on formal requirements. According to Art. 13(2) TESM the BoG decides on the basis of the request of the ESM Member and the assessment in Art. 13(1) TESM. This assessment includes an analysis and evaluation of risks to the financial stability of the euro area, the debt sustainability of the requesting member and its actual or potential financing needs.[320] With regard to the competence for this assessment, it should be noted that according to Art. 13(1) s. 3 TESM new version the Chairperson of the BoG shall entrust both, the Managing Director and the Commission in liaison with the ECB with these tasks. This integrates the economic, financial and monetary policy expertise of these EU institutions into the decision-making process of the ESM. This is complemented by the IMF's participation in the debt sustainability assessment "[w]herever appropriate and possible" as envisaged in Art. 13(1) s. 3 (b) TESM. With regard to the instrument of secondary market interventions, Art. 18 (2) TESM states that the ECB is exclusively competent for recognising the existence of exceptional financial market circumstances and risks to financial stability.[321]

If the BoG adopts a decision to grant financial assistance, it shall entrust the Managing Director, the Commission—in liaison with the ECB and, wherever possible, together with the IMF—with the task of negotiating, with the ESM Member concerned, a Memorandum of Understanding (MoU)[322] detailing the conditionality attached to the financial assistance facility.[323] Finally, the BoG shall approve the MoU and the Commission (and the Managing Director) shall sign it on behalf of the ESM.[324] The Managing Director, the Commission, the ECB and the IMF not only assess the conditions for granting financial assistance and negotiate a MoU, but also monitor compliance.[325]

In general, it becomes clear that the ECB as well as the Commission, the IMF and, after the ESM reform, also the Managing Director play an important role in the assessment, granting and enforcement of financial assistance.[326] The required cooperation is institutionally referred to as the "Troika" or (adhering the ESM) "Quadriga", although this term is not mentioned in the Treaties or in the TESM.

[320] Art. 13(1) s. 3(a-c) TESM new version.

[321] See Art. 13(1) s. 3(a) TESM.

[322] See also the definition of the ECJ, Florescu, 13.7.2017, ECLI:EU:C:2017:448, para. 34, concerning assistance under Art. 143 TFEU.

[323] Arts. 13(3) s. 1, 5(6)(g) TESM new version. A proposal for a financial assistance facility agreement, including the financial terms and conditions and the choice of instruments, is prepared by the Managing Director of the ESM and adopted by the BoG according to Art. 13(3) s. 3 TESM new version.

[324] Art. 13(4) TESM new version.

[325] Art. 13(7) TESM new version.

[326] Cf. Lettanie (2019), p. 326.

In addition, the Commission and the ECB play a special role in the application of the voting rules. While a decision by the BoG to provide stability support and to mandate the Managing Director and the Commission in liaison with the ECB is in principle adopted by mutual agreement, i.e. unanimously, adoption under the so-called emergency voting procedure requires a qualified majority of 85%.[327] Such emergency procedure shall be applied in accordance with Art. 4(4) TESM new version in conjunction with Art. 4(3) s. 1 "where the Commission and the ECB both conclude that a failure to urgently adopt a decision to grant or implement financial assistance, as defined in Articles 13 to 18, would threaten the economic and financial sustainability of the euro area".

3.3.3.3 Classification Within the ECB's Field of Tasks and Determination of Independence

In order to determine the level of independence of the ECB in the field of ESM action, it is necessary to locate the tasks to be performed here within the ECB's mandate.

In the Pringle ruling, the ECJ was given the opportunity to rule on whether Decision 2011/199,[328] amending Art. 136 TFEU, and the conclusion and ratification of the ESM Treaty by the euro Member States is in conformity with primary law.[329] Of central importance was the question of whether this affected the Union's exclusive competence for monetary policy. Since the Treaties do not provide for a definition of monetary policy, the ECJ examined the objectives to be attained by a measure and the instruments provided to that end.[330] With regard to the establishment of the ESM, the ECJ rejected any monetary affiliation for both aspects:

> As regards, first, the objective pursued by that mechanism, which is to safeguard the stability of the euro area as a whole, that is clearly distinct from the objective of maintaining price stability, which is the primary objective of the Union's monetary policy. Even though the stability of the euro area may have repercussions on the stability of the currency used within that area, an economic policy measure cannot be treated as equivalent to a monetary policy measure for the sole reason that it may have indirect effects on the stability of the euro.
>
> As regards, secondly, the instruments envisaged in order to attain the objective concerned, Decision 2011/199 states only that the stability mechanism will grant any required financial assistance; it contains no other information on the operation of that mechanism. The grant of financial assistance to a Member State however clearly does not fall within monetary policy.[331]

---

[327] Arts. 4(4) sub-para. 1 s. 2, 5(6)(f)(g) TESM in conjunction with Art. 4(3) s. 1 TESM.

[328] European Council Decision 2011/199/EU of 25 March 2011 amending Article 136 of the Treaty on the Functioning of the European Union with regard to a stability mechanism for Member States whose currency is the euro, OJ 6.4.2011, L 91, p. 1.

[329] ECJ, Pringle, 27.11.2012, ECLI:EU:C:2012:756.

[330] ECJ, Pringle, 27.11.2012, ECLI:EU:C:2012:756, paras. 53–55.

[331] ECJ, Pringle, 27.11.2012, ECLI:EU:C:2012:756, paras. 56–57.

Instead, the ECJ explicitly assigns the establishment of the ESM and its activities to economic policy.[332] With regard to the functions allocated to the ECB by the TESM, the ECJ finds that "they are in line with the various tasks which the FEU Treaty and the Statute of the ESCB [and of the ECB] confer on that institution",[333] because "[b]y virtue of its duties within the ESM Treaty, the ECB supports the general economic policies in the Union, in accordance with Article 282 (2) TFEU".[334]

Although economic and monetary policy are, as seen, characterised by mutual interference, this interpretation raises some concerns. The ECB is allowed to support "general economic policies in the Union", which conceptually includes all non-specific measures to steer the economic process, economic structure and economic order.[335] However, it does not include specific financial stimuli geared to the national economic framework of the individual Member State.[336]

Although the ECB only performs auxiliary tasks in the ESM due to its concentrated expertise, while the Member States, represented in the BoG, have the final decision-making power, specific financial assistance to certain Member States goes beyond the scope of general economic policies.[337] Another possible legal basis could be Art. 127(5) TFEU, according to which the ESCB, and hence the ECB, also contributes to the smooth conduct of policies pursued by the competent authorities relating to the stability of the financial system. However, this mandate should be seen in conjunction with the tasks of financial supervision, which, in its micro- and macro-prudential aspects, focuses on the stability of individual, particularly systemically relevant institutions, but also of the financial system as a whole.[338]

With regard to the institutional independence of the ECB, the question arises whether the ECB can be involved in the performance of a treaty under international law, albeit concluded by EU Member States. In the Pringle decision, the ECJ referred to its case law, pointing out, "that the Member States are entitled, in areas which do not fall under the exclusive competence of the Union, to entrust tasks to the institutions, outside the framework of the Union, such as the task of coordinating a collective action undertaken by the Member States or managing financial assistance,

[332] ECJ, Pringle, 27.11.2012, ECLI:EU:C:2012:756, paras. 60, 160; previously Advocate General Kokott, Pringle, 26.10.2012, ECLI:EU:C:2012:675, para. 180.

[333] ECJ, Pringle, 27.11.2012, ECLI:EU:C:2012:756, paras. 165.

[334] ECJ, Pringle, 27.11.2012, ECLI:EU:C:2012:756, paras. 165; approving Mersch (2017).

[335] See definition by Nettesheim (2018), § 18 para. 15.

[336] Pilz (2017), pp. 642–643.

[337] Manger-Nestler and Böttner (2019), p. 79; see also Advocate General Cruz Villalón, Gauweiler, 14.1.2015, ECLI:EU:C:2015:7, para. 143, according to whom "the ECB, in participating in the assistance programmes concerned, has been actively involved in measures which, in certain circumstances, might be perceived as going beyond 'support' for economic policy".

[338] Manger-Nestler and Böttner (2019), p. 80.

provided that those tasks do not alter the essential character of the powers conferred on those institutions by the EU and FEU Treaties".[339]

This does not indicate the extent to which the ECB acts independently in the performance of ESM activities. However, it is important to determine this, even though the ECB may not have decision-making powers.[340]

In contrast to primary law and the secondary legislation already mentioned, there is no provision in the TESM, with the exception of the external auditors and the Board of Auditors,[341] to establish the independence of the acting bodies. As already seen, the ECB does not conduct any monetary policy in this area, so it does not benefit from the independence associated with it from the outset. Moreover, the ECB's activities are not sufficiently supported by its competence to provide support for economic policies and financial stability. Unlike in the case of SSM and ESRB, the ESM activity is not linked to a primary law empowerment, but is derived from an international treaty. This leads to the conclusion that the ECB's actions are not protected by a guarantee of independence under primary law, at least not under Art. 130 TFEU.[342] Nevertheless, it should be stressed that all measures taken in the context of the ESM must be compatible with Union law and thus with the primacy of price stability and the guarantee of independence under primary law.[343] Therefore, measures must not interfere with central bank independence, in particular with regard to monetary policy.

3.3.3.4 Functional Characteristics Regarding the Granting of Financial Assistance

When looking from a functional perspective at the ECB's action in the context of the ESM activity, it is first of all striking that, similar to monetary policy and unlike in the field of banking supervision, it is not bound by a strict normative framework that embeds its action and enables monitoring. Furthermore, the action is of a more analytical, advisory but not decision-making nature, which is particularly evident in the assessments under Art. 13(1) and Art. 18(2) TESM. It should be stressed that the complexity of the assessments to be taken, not least because of the great importance

---

[339] ECJ, Pringle, 27.11.2012, ECLI:EU:C:2012:756, para. 158 with further references; on the contrary, Advocate General Kokott emphasised in her opinion, that the ECB is under no obligation to perform the tasks allocated to it in the TESM, and referred to its independence established in Art. 130 TFEU, see Advocate General Kokott, Pringle, 26.10.2012, ECLI:EU:C:2012:675, para. 181.

[340] For a different view Mersch (2017) ("independence [. . .] is simply not relevant in this field, as the ECB does not adopt any decisions and does not have its own instruments for the implementation of decisions").

[341] Arts. 29, 30(2) TESM. Regarding the independence granted to the Managing Director by the ESM reform, see infra Sect. 5.3.3.

[342] See for a different view but without further explanation Karatzia and Markakis (2017), p. 249.

[343] ECJ, Pringle, 27.11.2012, ECLI:EU:C:2012:756, para. 121.

of forecasts, gives the Commission and the ECB a certain margin of discretion.[344] There is a similarly broad scope for the negotiation of the MoU being a political decision,[345] but also for its compliance monitoring under Art. 13(3), (7) TESM.

If one takes into account the extent to which legal positions worthy of protection, especially fundamental rights or competences of the Member States, are affected, a differentiated picture emerges.

First of all, it becomes clear that the actions of the ESM, including the conditions attached to macroeconomic adjustment programmes, can significantly limit the economic policy of the Member States.[346]

The institutions involved in ESM activities have a major macroeconomic impact on the economic governance of the concerned Member States and can thus impose measures that do not have to be supported by the will of the citizens.[347] This was seen in Greece where conditionality entailed economic reforms and measures like cutting public spending and therefore influencing labour and health policy, pension costs or judiciary systems.[348] This influence needs to be legitimated and controlled above all because, as we have seen, the Treaties in principle leave economic policy competence with the Member States. This capacity to shape policy can be constrained not only by action of the Union and its institutions but also by action of intergovernmental bodies.[349]

Moreover, restructuring measures imposed on Member States may also have a fundamental rights relevance, as the *Ledra Advertising decision* demonstrates.[350] There, the restructuring of the Cypriot banking system through national measures, but in accordance with a MoU negotiated with the Troika, resulted in significant losses for depositors concerned.[351] As the ECJ states, this constitutes an encroachment on the right of property granted under Art. 17(1) CFR.[352]

In that decision, the ECJ not only stated that the Commission, when performing tasks entrusted to it by the TESM, is obliged to ensure that the MoU is in conformity with Union law which may possibly result in liability under Art. 340 TFEU.[353]

---

[344] Cf. Bark and Gilles (2013), p. 370 with further references.

[345] Pennesi (2018), p. 527.

[346] Cf. Lettanie (2019), p. 327.

[347] Cf. Ritleng (2016), p. 12; see also Advocate General Cruz Villalón, Gauweiler, 14.1.2015, ECLI:EU:C:2015:7, para. 143.

[348] Cf. Pennesi (2018), p. 514.

[349] For complaints relating various "austerity measures" before the European Court of Human Rights (ECtHR) see Koskelo (2017), pp. 143–145.

[350] ECJ, Ledra Advertising, 20.9.2016, ECLI:EU:C:2016:701; see also Koskelo (2017), pp. 139–140.

[351] For details see Pennesi (2018), pp. 517–518.

[352] ECJ, Ledra Advertising, 20.9.2016, ECLI:EU:C:2016:701, para. 68; concerning justification see paras. 70–72.

[353] Cf. ECJ, Ledra Advertising, 20.9.2016, ECLI:EU:C:2016:701, paras. 58, 60, 67; preceding ECJ, Pringle, 27.11.2012, ECLI:EU:C:2012:756, para. 104; for details concerning the high requirements for non-contractual liability see Lettanie (2019), p. 329.

Moreover, the ECJ states that, while conducting ESM activities, the EU institutions are bound by fundamental rights enshrined in the CFR.[354] For if Art. 51(1) s. 1 CFR addresses the Member States only when implementing Union law, i.e. not within the framework of the ESM, this means, in reverse, that the EU institutions are bound by fundamental rights even when they act outside the EU legal framework.[355]

However, if this action is divided up into the respective contributions of the institutions involved, the picture is different. Thus, the ECJ has underlined that the ECB's duties within the ESM, like those of the Commission, are important but do not entail any power to make decisions of their own.[356] Rather, the activities of the Commission and the ECB can be seen as providing advice and assistance, which serves as a basis for the BoG to take decisions.[357] The technical support provided by the ECB is also specified in the General Terms and Conditions for ESM Financial Assistance Facility Agreements. According to 5.12.1. of these terms, the ECB transfers the Net Disbursement Amount on the disbursement date to the designated euro account of the beneficiary Member State as instructed by the ESM. This lack of decision-making power vis-à-vis third parties in principle lowers the requirements for legitimation.

If one further differentiates between the contributions of the Commission and the ECB, the role of the ECB seems to be even more supportive. The mode of cooperation mentioned in many passages of the TESM, namely the performance of tasks by the Commission "in liaison with the ECB",[358] indicates that the Commission has the right of final decision in the relationship between these institutions.[359] This is expressed particularly clearly in the German version of the text, which requires *"Benehmen"* (form of consultation) rather than *"Einvernehmen"* (approval).

This view is shared by the Advocate General, who, in her opinion on the *Pringle case*, emphasised the following with regard to the tasks entrusted to the ECB by the TESM:

> Those tasks are relatively minor in comparison with those of the Commission. Individual tasks of assessment are provided for only in the first sentence of the first subparagraph of Article 4(4) and Article 18(2) of the ESM Treaty. For the rest, the Commission is, under Article 13(1), (3) and (7) and Article 14(6) of the ESM Treaty at times to act 'in liaison' with the European Central Bank. In those cases therefore it is not so much that tasks are allocated to the European Central Bank but that it has a qualified right to be consulted.[360]

---

[354] ECJ, Ledra Advertising, 20.9.2016, ECLI:EU:C:2016:701, para. 67.

[355] Cf. ECJ, Ledra Advertising, 20.9.2016, ECLI:EU:C:2016:701, para. 67.

[356] ECJ, Pringle, 27.11.2012, ECLI:EU:C:2012:756, para. 161; later confirmed in ECJ, Ledra Advertising, 20.9.2016, ECLI:EU:C:2016:701, paras. 52–53; Mallis, 20.9.2016, ECLI:EU:C:2016:702, para. 53.

[357] Cf. Lettanie (2019), pp. 327 and 328 with reference to the ECB's opinion.

[358] See Arts. 5(6)(g), 13(1), (3), (7) TESM.

[359] Lettanie (2019), p. 327; see also Advocate General Cruz Villalón, Gauweiler, 14.1.2015, ECLI:EU:C:2015:7, para. 144.

[360] Advocate General Kokott, Pringle, 26.10.2012, ECLI:EU:C:2012:675, para. 179.

However, a higher level of legitimation and control is needed pertaining to the tasks which the ECB either carries out alone or where decisions are taken conclusively and on a par with the Commission. This applies to the mentioned analysis under Art. 18(2) TESM as well as the adoption of the urgency procedure under Art. 4 (4) sub-para. 1 TESM.

But even where the actions of the Commission and the ECB are not binding, the considerable influence on the BoG's decisions should not be underestimated. According to the Advocate General's opinion in the *Gauweiler case*, "[t]he rules of the ESM, but also the experience of financial assistance programmes which have been implemented or which are still ongoing, amply demonstrates that the ECB's role in the design, adoption and regular monitoring of those programmes is significant, not to say decisive".[361]

In this respect, it must not be disregarded that, on the basis of the analytical resources and available data, assessments of the ECB cannot similarly be made or reviewed by other institutions and thus may at least have a considerable factual binding effect.

3.3.3.5 Accountability

This influence of the ECB's actions on the assessment, granting and enforcement of financial assistance and the conditions attached to it must be contained by adequate accountability mechanisms.[362] In particular, the actions of the Troika, which is not institutionally anchored within the Treaties or the TESM, have been criticised for a lack of democratic legitimation, which has in some cases led the requesting Member States to seek to deal only with the Member States or the EU institutions representing them.[363]

Political and Administrative Accountability

With regard to the mechanisms that ensure political and administrative control, the BoG comes into focus as the central decision-making body. This body, which alone implements the intergovernmental principle, derives its legitimation directly from the governments of the Member States and is responsible for the mandating of the Managing Director, the Commission and the ECB. From the perspective of the delegation's approach, the Commission and the ECB (as well as the Managing Director) can be classified as delegates of the ESM's BoG and sub-delegates of the contracting Member States.[364]

[361] Advocate General Cruz Villalón, Gauweiler, 14.1.2015, ECLI:EU:C:2015:7, para. 143.

[362] Cf. Pennesi (2018), p. 514.

[363] Ritleng (2016), p. 3.

[364] Cf. Lettanie (2019), p. 327.

This is accompanied by the BoG's monitoring role vis-à-vis the Commission, the ECB and the Managing Director. Although the TESM provides for a compulsory mandate for these institutions, i.e. the BoG has no discretionary power and, in particular, cannot revoke the tasks and powers granted, it can nevertheless regularly override the decisions of the Commission and the ECB.[365] This is for example visible in Art. 13(2) TESM new version, which provides that the BoG shall take decisions "[o]n the basis of the request of the ESM Member and the assessments referred to in paragraph 1 [. . .]". Other control bodies are the contracting Member States, which may modify or terminate the TESM, in particular the involvement of the Union institutions.[366]

In contrast, control by the Union institutions, especially by the European Parliament, is much less pronounced.[367] Since the Commission and the ECB are merely integrated into a task falling to the Member States, they are not unconditionally subject to institutional checks and balances. In the past, this has led to the ECB in particular largely refusing to provide the European Parliament and the ECA with concrete information on its role in ESM activities and thus evading control.[368] The fact that, in addition, the Eurogroup is not subject to Union democratic control when it is involved in executive tasks beyond a mere political forum, can be deplored from a democratic perspective, as the European Parliament has done.[369]

Judicial Accountability

In addition to the Commission and the ECB, the ECJ is also involved in the performance of the ESM's tasks. According to Art. 37(3), (2) TESM disputes between the ESM and an ESM Member or between ESM Members concerning the interpretation and application of the TESM shall be submitted to the CJEU. This is an arbitration agreement permitted under Art. 273 TFEU because disputes in the context of the ESM relate to the subject matter of the Treaties.

As regards legal protection specifically against the ECB, it should be noted that, in the context of the ESM activity, the ECB does not adopt legal acts which may be challenged by way of an action for annulment under Art. 263 TFEU. Indeed, the ECJ assumes that the Union institutions are in principle also subject to non-contractual liability under Art. 340 TFEU when they act outside the Treaties. Nevertheless, in

[365] Lettanie (2019), p. 328. In respect of the Managing Director, see infra Sect. 5.3.3.

[366] See also Forsthoff and Lauer (2020), paras. 30.148, who underline the role of national parliaments.

[367] For details see Pennesi (2018), p. 515.

[368] For details see Lettanie (2019), pp. 329–330.

[369] European Parliament, Report on the enquiry on the role and operations of the Troika (ECB, Commission and IMF) with regard to the euro area programme countries, 28 February 2014, 2013/2277(INI), para. 50.

view of the high liability requirements, it must be assumed that such a claim will only be justified in exceptional cases.

As a result, judicial protection against the ECB in the context of the TESM is rather limited.[370] This also applies to measures of the ESM which do not qualify as Union acts and therefore cannot be challenged by the affected individuals before the CJEU.[371] Nor can measures taken by the Eurogroup, which does not have decision-making powers under the Treaties, be challenged before the ECJ by way of an action for annulment under Art. 263 TFEU, as the ECJ pointed out in its *Mallis decision*.[372] This gives rise not only to a deficit in democracy but also in the rule of law, which should be reduced in an ESM reform.[373]

3.3.4 Economic and Budgetary Surveillance of Member States in the Euro Area

Although the economic and fiscal policies remain within national competence, the Member States shall, according to Arts. 121 and 126 TFEU coordinate their economic policies within the Council and avoid excessive government deficits. Correspondingly, the Council and the Commission exercise power on the Members States through procedures provided by EU law. Pursuant to Art. 5(1) sub-para. 1 TFEU, the Council shall adopt measures, in particular broad guidelines for these coordinated policies.

In order to address the deficits that emerged in the course of the financial and sovereign debt crisis, in particular the high level of public debt, secondary legislation was adopted to strengthen economic and budgetary surveillance. The most relevant to the ECB's activities is the "Two Pack", consisting of two regulations applicable solely in the euro area Member States, which deal with the monitoring of national budgetary planning and tighter budgetary surveillance.[374]

---

[370] Lettanie (2019), p. 329.

[371] For details see Simone (2017), pp. 199–202; Pennesi (2018), p. 515.

[372] ECJ, Mallis, 20.9.2016, ECLI:EU:C:2016:702, paras. 59 and 61; preceding Advocate General Wathelet, Mallis, 21.4.2016, ECLI:EU:C:2016:294, paras. 59 and 64. Recently, the ECJ also answered in the negative the question of whether the Eurogroup is one of the institutions within the meaning of Art. 340(2) TFEU whose acts or conduct could form the subject matter of an action before the CJEU to establish non-contractual liability of the EU, see ECJ, Council/Chrysostomides, 16.12.2020, ECLI:EU:C:2020:1028, paras. 78–98.

[373] See infra Sect. 5.3.3.

[374] Regulation (EU) No 472/2013 of the European Parliament and of the Council of 21 May 2013 on the strengthening of economic and budgetary surveillance of Member States in the euro area experiencing or threatened with serious difficulties with respect to their financial stability, OJ 27.5.2013, L 140, p. 1; Regulation (EU) No 473/2013 of the European Parliament and of the Council of 21 May 2013 on common provisions for monitoring and assessing draft budgetary plans and ensuring the correction of excessive deficit of the Member States in the euro area, OJ 27.5.2013, L 140, p. 11; concerning ECB participation according to Six Pack see Beukers (2013), p. 1589, n. 51.

In this context, the ECB, in its supervisory capacity, is involved in the enhanced surveillance of Member States which are experiencing, or are threatened with, serious difficulties with regard to their financial stability or are receiving financial assistance, in particular from the ESM.[375] Under the supervision of the ECB, stress tests are carried out, particularly with a view to assessing resilience to macroeconomic and financial shocks, and peer reviews are conducted regarding the supervisory capacity over the financial sector.[376]

Similarly to its involvement in ESM tasks, the ECB participates under the Commission ("in liaison") in regular review missions on the progress made by Member States.[377] The ECB also has a supportive role in the case of granting financial assistance to the Member State concerning assessing debt sustainability, drafting a macroeconomic adjustment programme and monitoring its implementation.[378]

Unlike in the context of the ESM activity, the ECB does not act on the basis of an international treaty, but under Union law. In terms of competence, action cannot be based on the monetary policy mandate, at least not where the ECB is addressed in its supervisory function.[379] The supporting competence of Art. 127(1) s. 2 TFEU is most likely to be the relevant basis of competence,[380] although as with the granting of financial assistance[381] this raises certain doubts.

Concerning accountability, it has to be noted, that, during the course of the enhanced surveillance process, the competent committee of the European Parliament and the parliament of the Member State concerned may invite representatives of the Commission, the ECB and the IMF to participate in an economic dialogue.[382] This concept, which follows on from the monetary dialogue of Art. 284(2), (3) TFEU, can also be found in other regulations concerning the coordination of economic and fiscal policy.[383]

[375] See Art. 2(1) sub-para. 1, (3) Regulation (EU) No 472/2013.

[376] Art. 3(3) sub-para 1(b), (c), (4) sub-para. 1(b), (c) Regulation (EU) No 472/2013.

[377] Art. 3(5) sub-para. 1 Regulation (EU) No 472/2013.

[378] Arts. 6(1), 7(1) sub-para. 1, (4) sub-para. 1 Regulation (EU) No 472/2013.

[379] Similarly Beukers (2013), p. 1590.

[380] This is also the view of the ECB, see Opinion of 16 February 2011 on economic governance reform in the European Union, CON/2011/13, OJ 20.5.2011, C 150, p. 1; see also Beukers (2013), p. 1617.

[381] See supra Sect. 3.3.3.3.

[382] Art. 3(9) Regulation (EU) No 472/2013; for details see Repasi (2020), paras. 17.51-17-65.

[383] See Art. 2ab Council Regulation (EC) No 1466/97 of 7 July 1997 on the strengthening of the surveillance of budgetary positions and the surveillance and coordination of economic policies, OJ 2.8.1997, L 209, p. 1, amended by Regulation (EU) No 1175/2011 of the European Parliament and of the Council of 16 November 2011 amending Council Regulation (EC) No 1466/97 on the strengthening of the surveillance of budgetary positions and the surveillance and coordination of economic policies, OJ 23.11.2011, L 306, p. 12; Art. 15 Regulation (EU) No 473/2013; for details concerning economic dialogue see for instance Martucci (2017), pp. 42–44.

3.3.5 Recovery and Resolution of Credit Institutions Within the SRM

3.3.5.1 The ECB's Role Within the SRM

In order to achieve greater centralisation of crisis management, a further step towards a Banking Union was to create an SRM on the basis of Art. 114 TFEU. Although territorially linked to the SSM,[384] the SRM's institutional core is not the ECB, but the SRB, which is mainly[385] responsible for adopting resolution schemes in relation to entities and groups which are directly supervised by the ECB.[386] With regard to institutions not under direct ECB supervision, the national resolution authorities (NRAs) are in principle responsible for adopting decisions relating to resolution.[387] This system is completed by the Single Resolution Fund (SRF), established on 1 January 2016, which is financed by levies on institutions and aims to avoid burdens on public budgets.

Although the supervision and recovery/resolution of institutions on the territory of the Member States participating in the SSM are institutionally separate, these mechanisms are not isolated from each other. This is illustrated in particular by the fact that a representative of the ECB (as well as of the Commission) can participate (without vote) in the meetings of executive sessions and plenary sessions of the SRB as a permanent observer being entitled to participate in the debates and having access to all documents.[388]

As regards the institutions falling under the direct competence of the SRB, the ECB is involved in the procedure to determine whether the conditions for adopting a resolution scheme by the SRM are met.

The determination of the first condition, namely whether an entity is failing or is likely to fail, is solely within the competence of the ECB, which must prior to this consult the SRB.[389] The importance of this task should not be underestimated, as it is the ECB that takes the initiative and triggers potential resolutions by the SRB. The ECB is also involved, albeit to a lesser extent, in the assessment of the second condition, namely whether alternative private sector measures or supervisory action would prospectively prevent failure within a reasonable timeframe.[390]

Although this assessment is made by the SRB (or where applicable by the NRAs), Art. 18(1) sub-para. 4 s. 1 SRMR provides a close cooperation with the ECB. The

[384] Art. 4(1) SRMR.

[385] For a peculiar divergence between the SSM and SRM regarding their scope of application see Bassani (2019), p. 24, n. 82.

[386] Art. 18(6), 7(2), 6(4), (5)(b) SRMR.

[387] Art. 7(3) SRMR.

[388] Art. 43(3) SRMR.

[389] Art. 18(1) sub-para. 1(a), sub-paras. 2, 3 SRMR.

[390] Art. 18(1) sub-para. 1(b).

latter can even inform the SRB (resp. the NRAs) that it considers the condition laid down in that point to be met.[391]

In addition, the ECB is also involved in the decision to convert or write down capital instruments.[392] Indeed, the assessment of the viability of an institution may only be made by the SRB if the ECB does not make such an assessment within three calendar days of being informed.[393]

No less important, the ECB is consulted prior to the adoption of certain decisions, such as in the process of drawing up resolution plans,[394] *inter alia* the assessment of resolvability[395] and the determination of the minimum requirement for own funds and eligible liabilities.[396] However, the ECB does not have resolution powers, as Art. 4(1)(i) SSMR clarifies.

The involvement of the ECB in the resolution process has sometimes been criticised. In particular with regard to the determination of the conditions for resolution, there is criticism of the insufficient division of competences between the SRB and the ECB.[397] Precisely because the ECB's involvement is based on its expertise, it can in fact exert considerable influence.[398] This can further exacerbate the already existing trade-offs between monetary policy and banking supervision.[399]

3.3.5.2 Functional Characteristics Regarding Banking Resolution

As regards the independence of the performance of tasks, a risk of political influence is also virulent in the area of banking resolution, probably even more so than in the area of banking supervision. This is because political actors not only need capital, but also hold and manage public funds. They thus have an interest in ensuring that public budgets are not burdened, or at least as little as possible.[400] Even if the interest in reducing the burden in terms of government responsibility is reasonable,[401] it could be given disproportionate consideration in the event of political influence and thus displace other concerns that are crucial for an optimal decision from the outset. This argues in favour of the independence of the institutions responsible for resolution, in particular the ECB. On the other hand, it should not be overlooked that this

---

[391] Art. 18(1) sub-para. 4 s. 2 SRMR.

[392] Art. 21(1) SRMR.

[393] Art. 21(2) SRMR.

[394] Art. 8(2), (13) SRMR.

[395] Art. 10(1) SRMR.

[396] Art. 12(1) SRMR.

[397] Cf. Lamandini et al. (2015), pp. 19, 38–40.

[398] Cf. Manger-Nestler and Böttner (2019), p. 57.

[399] See infra Sect. 5.3.1.

[400] Bini Smaghi (2007), p. 49.

[401] Cf. Zilioli (2016), pp. 160–161.

potential influence on public funds requires strong mechanisms of democratic accountability.[402]

As regards the control capacity of other European and national actors and the fundamental rights dimension, there are clear parallels with SSM supervision. It can be noted that the action of the ECB, where it takes decisions, is guided by detailed normative requirements in Art. 18(4) SRM. In addition, the ECB's assessments, together with the final resolution decisions, have a significant impact on fundamental rights. Thus, resolution measures may encroach on the shareholders' right to property protected by Art. 17(1) CFR,[403] but may be justified for the purpose of ensuring the stability of the banking and financial system and preventing systemic risks.[404]

3.3.5.3 Accountability

Political and Administrative Accountability

As far as political accountability is concerned, such obligations only relate to the SRB, not to the ECB. Pursuant to Arts. 45, 46 SRMR, the SRB has reporting and accountability obligations to the EU institutions (European Parliament, Council, Commission and ECA) on the one hand, and to the national parliaments of the participating Member States on the other.[405] These obligations correspond to the guarantee of independence to the SRB, thus establishing a parallelism between the SSM and the SRM.

However, it is critical that these rules do not indicate whether this responsibility also extends to the ECB's contributions to action. Thus, an institutional separation between banking supervision and resolution, with different areas of responsibility, may lead to certain gaps in democratic control. Although, for instance, the adoption of resolution schemes falls within the competence of the SRB, it has no influence, in particular no rights vis-à-vis the ECB, e.g. on the assessment of whether an institution fails or is likely to fail.[406] This lack of control is reflected at the level of accountability.

However, not only the legal limits, but also the practical handling of parliamentary control can cause deficits. This applies in particular to the not always clear

---

[402]Cf. Mersch (2017).

[403]For the Banking Communication from the Commission, however, the ECJ denied an interference decisively based on the consideration that the shareholders "must fully bear the risk of their investments", see ECJ, Kotnik, 19.7.2016, ECLI:EU:C:2016:570, paras. 73 et seq.; for a critical view see Lamandini et al. (2017), pp. 221–222.

[404]Cf. ECJ, OC, 16.7.2020, ECLI:EU:C:2020:567, para. 92 regarding national regulation imposing an asset threshold on people's banks established as cooperative societies and allowing the right to redeem shares by the withdrawing shareholder to be limited; see also ECJ, Ledra Advertising, 20.9.2016, EU:C:2016:701, paras. 71, 74.

[405]For details see Manger-Nestler (2016), paras. 49–56; Ruccia (2017), pp. 330–331.

[406]For the ECJ's view see infra Sect. 3.3.5.3.2.

separation of functions and responsible authorities, not only in the relationship between monetary policy and banking supervision, but also in the relationship between these areas and banking resolution.[407]

Judicial Accountability

With regard to judicial review, it is questionable whether the ECB's actions under the SRM, in particular the assessment regarding the resolution trigger, can be subject to judicial review. As this is a separate decision from the adoption of a resolution scheme, it is argued that the institutions concerned can challenge both decisions before the CJEU.[408] However, the fact that the addressees are typically not yet legally affected by the ECB's assessment argues against this.[409] Moreover, at least a separate appeal against ECB measures could lack the interest in bringing proceedings, comparable to the rule on the valuation of assets and liabilities in Art. 20 (15) SRMR.[410] This opinion was recently shared by the EGC, which dismissed an action for annulment against an assessment by the ECB under Art. 18(1) SRMR as inadmissible. The court ruled, referring in particular to the *IBM case*, that "the contested acts must be considered to be preparatory measures in the procedure, which are designed to allow the SRB to take a decision regarding the resolution of the banks in question, and cannot, for that reason, form the subject of an action for annulment".[411]

The EGC, endorsing the view of the ECB, stressed that the ECB "has no decision-making power within the framework for the adoption of a resolution scheme"[412] and made explicit reference to Recital 26 SRMR, the second sentence of which provides that "[t]he Board, if it considers all the criteria relating to the triggering of resolutions to be met, should adopt the resolution scheme".[413] From this, the court deduced:

> [T]he SRB has the exclusive power to assess the conditions required for a resolution and to adopt a resolution scheme if it considers that all the conditions are met. In addition, it follows expressly from Article 18(1) of Regulation No 806/2014 that it is for the SRB to assess whether the three conditions set out in that provision are met. While the ECB does have the power to send an assessment with regard to the first condition, namely whether the entity is failing or is likely to fail, this nevertheless constitutes a mere assessment, which does not in any way bind the SRB.[414]

[407]Cf. Amtenbrink and Markakis (2019), pp. 18–22.

[408]Lamandini et al. (2015), p. 39; (2017), p. 30.

[409]Kämmerer (2016), p. 10.

[410]Ibid.

[411]EGC, Ernests Bernis, 6.5.2019, ECLI:EU:T:2019:295, paras. 32, 36; see also EGC, ABLV Bank, 6.5.2019, ECLI:EU:T:2019:296; approved by Advocate General Sánchez-Bordona, ABLV Bank, 14.1.2021, ECLI:EU:C:2021:16, paras. 47 et seq., 78 et seq..

[412]EGC, Ernests Bernis, 6.5.2019, ECLI:EU:T:2019:295, para. 34.

[413]Ibid.

[414]Ibid.

Pertaining to the ECJ's *Meroni doctrine*, which limits the delegation of tasks and powers especially to bodies established under secondary legislation,[415] this view is not without problems, as it does not assign decisive decision-making powers to the Union institutions, but to the SRB as an (independent) authority (agency).

It is therefore more convincing to assume that in the event that the ECB issues an assessment pursuant to Art. 18(1) sub-para. 1(a) SRMR, the SRB is bound by it because Art. 18(1) sub-para. 2 SRMR provides for ECB competence in this respect. This would have the consequence that the ECB's decision can and must be challenged separately. With regard to the assessment pursuant to Art. 18(1) sub-para. 1(b) SRMR, however, the assessment is made by the SRB, which only cooperates with the ECB pursuant to Art. 18(1) sub-para. 4 s. 1 SRMR. In this respect, an isolated challenge of the ECB's action would be inadmissible.

If one is willing to accept the reasoning of the court, the ECB's actions, comparable to the assessments within the ESM activity, are ultimately to be classified as advisory, in all respects non-binding activities. However, this does not change the fact that the influence on the (final) decision of the SRB is in fact nevertheless very high.

References

Almhofer M (2018) Die Haftung der Europäischen Zentralbank für rechtswidrige Bankenaufsicht. Mohr Siebeck, Tübingen

Amtenbrink F (2019) Independence and accountability in the new age of European central banking – revisiting Gormely and de Haan's 'The democratic deficit of the European Central Bank'. In: Amtenbrink F, Davies G, Kochenov D, Lindeboom J (eds) The internal market and the future of European integration – essays in honour of Laurence W. Gormley. Cambridge University Press, Cambridge, pp 305–321

Amtenbrink F, Markakis M (2019) Towards a meaningful prudential supervision dialogue in the euro area? – a study of the interaction between the European Parliament and the European Central Bank in the Single Supervisory Mechanism. Eur Law Rev 44:3–23

Armour J, Awrey D, Davies P, Enriques L, Gordon JN, Mayer C, Payne J (2016) Principles of financial regulation. Oxford University Press, Oxford

Athanassiou P (2020) Chapter 24 Payment systems. In: Amtenbrink F, Herrmann C (eds) The EU law of Economic and Monetary Union. Oxford University Press, Oxford, pp 711–735

Athanassiou P, Zagouras G (2015) Kommentierung zu Art. 142 AEUV. In: von der Groeben H, Schwarze J, Hatje A (eds) Europäisches Unionsrecht, 7th edn. Nomos, Baden-Baden

Bark F, Gilles A (2013) Der ESM in der Praxis – Rechtsgrundlagen und Funktionsweise. Europäische Zeitschrift für Wirtschaftsrecht, pp 367–371

Baroncelli S (2016) The Gauweiler Judgment in view of the case law of the European Court of Justice on European Central Bank independence: between substance and form. Maastricht J Eur Comp Law 23:79–98

Basel Committee on Banking Supervision (BCBS) Core Principles for Effective Banking Supervision, September 2012. https://www.bis.org/publ/bcbs230.pdf (26 February 2021)

[415]See infra Sect. 4.4.3.

Bassan F (2017) Criteria for determining the legality of the ECB's unconventional measures. In: Daniele L, Simone P, Cisotta R (eds) Democracy in the EMU in the aftermath of the crisis. Springer, Heidelberg, pp 235–248

Bassani G (2019) The legal framework applicable to the Single Supervisory Mechanism – tapestry or patchwork? Wolters Kluwer, Alphen aan den Rijn

Bauerschmidt J (2019) Finanzstabilität als Ziel der Bankenunion. Zeitschrift für das gesamte Handelsrecht und Wirtschaftsrecht 183:476–502

Beukers T (2013) The new ECB and its relationship with the Member States of the euro area – between central bank independence and central bank intervention. Common Mark Law Rev 50:1579–1620

Bini Smaghi L (2007) Independence and accountability in supervision – general principles and European setting. In: Masciandaro D, Quintyn M (eds) Designing financial supervision institutions – independence, accountability and governance. Elgar, Cheltenham/Northampton, pp 41–62

Bobić A, Dawson M (2020) Making sense of the "incomprehensible": the *PSPP* judgment of the German Federal Constitutional Court. Common Mark Law Rev 57:1953–1998

Borger V (2016) Outright Monetary Transactions and the stability mandate of the ECB: Gauweiler. Common Mark Law Rev 53:139–196

Brade A, Gentzsch M (2020) PSPP mit "PEPP" – Der währungspolitische Kontrollmaßstab des BVerfG als "Ultra-vires-Akt"?, VerfBlog, 2020/5/07. https://verfassungsblog.de/pspp-mit-pepp/ (26 February 2021)

Brito Bastos F (2019) Judicial review of composite administrative procedures in the Single Supervisory Mechanism: *Berlusconi*. Common Mark Law Rev 56:1355–1377

Cafaro S (2017) How the ECB reinterpreted its mandate during the euro-crisis (and why it was right in doing so). In: Daniele L, Simone P, Cisotta R (eds) Democracy in the EMU in the aftermath of the crisis. Springer, Heidelberg, pp 217–233

Calliess C (2016) Kommentierung zu Art. 5 EUV. In: Calliess C, Ruffert M (eds) EUV/AEUV, 5th edn. Beck, Munich

Craig P (2018) EU administrative law, 3rd edn. Oxford University Press, Oxford

Craig P, de Búrca G (2015) EU law – text, cases, and materials, 6th edn. Oxford University Press, Oxford

Cremer W (2016) Kommentierung zu Art. 263 AEUV. In: Calliess C, Ruffert M (eds) EUV/AEUV, 5th edn. Beck, Munich

Dawson M, Maricut-Akbik A, Bobić A (2019) Reconciling independence and accountability at the European Central Bank – the false promise of proceduralism. Eur Law J 25:75–93

Dawson M, Bobić A (2019) Quantitative easing at the Court of Justice – doing whatever it takes to save the euro – *Weiss and Others*. Common Mark Law Rev 56:1005–1040

De Boer N, van't Klooster J (2020) The ECB, the courts and the issue of democratic legitimacy after Weiss. Common Mark Law Rev 57:1689–1724

Dumitrescu-Pasecinic A (2019) International law in the European Banking Union – the case of non-euro periphery. Eur Law Rev 44:359–382

Eurogroup (2012) Euro Area Summit Statement of 29 June. https://www.bankingsupervision.europa.eu/about/milestones/shared/pdf/2012-06-29_euro_area_summit_statement_en.pdf (26 February 2021)

European Central Bank (1998) Press Release of 13 October. https://www.ecb.europa.eu/press/pr/date/1998/html/pr981013_1.en.html (26 February 2021)

European Central Bank (2000) Monetary policy transmission in the euro area, Monthly Bulletin, July. https://www.ecb.europa.eu/pub/pdf/other/mbjul2000_article07.pdf (26 February 2021)

European Central Bank (2012) Press Release of 6 September. https://www.ecb.europa.eu/press/pr/date/2012/html/pr120906_1.en.html (26 February 2021)

European Central Bank (2015) Press Release of 22 January. https://www.ecb.europa.eu/press/pr/date/2015/html/pr150122_1.en.html (26 February 2021)

European Central Bank (2016) Press Release of 4 May. https://www.ecb.europa.eu/press/pr/date/2016/html/pr160504.en.html (26 February 2021)

European Central Bank (2019) Press Release of 12 September. https://www.ecb.europa.eu/press/pr/date/2019/html/ecb.mp190912~08de50b4d2.en.html (26 February 2021)

European Central Bank (2020a) Key ECB interest rates. https://www.ecb.europa.eu/stats/policy_and_exchange_rates/key_ecb_interest_rates/html/index.en.html (26 February 2021)
European Central Bank (2020b) Press Release of 10 July. https://www.bankingsupervision.europa.eu/press/pr/date/2020/html/ssm.pr200710~ae2abe1f23.en.html (26 February 2021)
European Central Bank (2020c) Press Release of 10 July. https://www.bankingsupervision.europa.eu/press/pr/date/2020/html/ssm.pr200710_1~ead3942902.en.html (26 February 2021)
European Central Bank (2021) Press Release of 21 January. https://www.ecb.europa.eu/press/pr/date/2021/html/ecb.mp210121~eb9154682e.en.html (26 February 2021)
European Court of Auditors (2016) Single Supervisory Mechanism – good start but further improvements needed, Special Report No. 29. https://www.eca.europa.eu/Lists/ECADocuments/SR16_29/SR_SSM_EN.pdf (26 February 2021)
European Court of Auditors/European Central Bank (2019) Memorandum of Understanding regarding audits on the ECB's supervisory tasks, 9.10. https://www.eca.europa.eu/de/Pages/DocItem.aspx?did=51578 (26 February 2021)
Ferran E, Babis V (2013) The European Single Supervisory Mechanism, University of Cambridge Faculty of Law, Legal Studies Research Paper Series, Paper No. 10/2013. https://papers.ssrn.com/sol3/papers.cfm?abstract_id=2224538 (26 February 2021)
Forkel H-W (2011) Für eine unabhängige Bankenaufsicht. Zeitschrift für Rechtspolitik, pp 100–102
Forsthoff U, Lauer N (2020) Chapter 30 Policy conditionality attached to ESM financial assistance. In: Amtenbrink F, Herrmann C (eds) The EU law of Economic and Monetary Union. Oxford University Press, Oxford, pp 878–920
Freimuth C (2013) Kommentierung zu Art. 128 AEUV. In: Siekmann H (ed) EWU – Kommentar zur Europäischen Währungsunion. Mohr Siebeck, Tübingen
Garicano L, Lastra RM (2010) Towards a new architecture for financial stability – seven principles. J Int Econ Law 13:597–621
Gentzsch M (2019) Gerichtliche Kontrolle geldpolitischer Entscheidungen der EZB am Beispiel des Public Sector Purchase Programme. Europarecht, pp 279–301
Gentzsch M (2020) Die EZB ultra vires? – Die PSPP-Entscheidung und ihre Konsequenzen für das Recht der Währungsunion. Zeitschrift für Bank- und Kapitalmarktrecht, pp 576–585
Gentzsch M, Brade A (2019) Die Bankenunion vor dem Bundesverfassungsgericht – Neue Impulse für grundlegende Fragestellungen des Verfassungs- und Unionsrechts. Europarecht, pp 602–636
German Council of Economic Experts (2012/13) Annual report. https://www.sachverstaendigenrat-wirtschaft.de/fileadmin/dateiablage/gutachten/ga201213/ga12_ges.pdf (26 February 2021)
Goldmann M (2018) United in diversity? – the relationship between monetary policy and prudential supervision in the Banking Union. Eur Const Law Rev 14:283–310
Goldmann M (2020) Das BVerfG holt sich ein trojanisches Pferd ins Haus – Urteil zu EZB-Ankaufprogramm und EuGH, 6.5. https://www.lto.de/recht/hintergruende/h/bverfg 2bvr85915-ezb-anleihenkauf-eugh-europa-wirtschaft-geldpolitik-monetarismus-zentralbank-pspp-dialog-konfrontation/ (26 February 2021)
Gören E (2019) Der Einheitliche Aufsichtsmechanismus bei der Europäischen Zentralbank (Single Supervisory Mechanism). Nomos, Baden-Baden
Gurlit E (2013) Handlungsformen der Finanzmarktaufsicht. Zeitschrift für das gesamte Handelsrecht und Wirtschaftsrecht 177:862–901
Häde U (2016) Kommentierung zu Art. 130, 133 AEUV. In: Calliess C, Ruffert M (eds) EUV/AEUV, 5th edn. Beck, Munich
Hahn HJ, Häde U (2010) Währungsrecht, 2nd edn. Beck, Munich
Herdegen M (2012) Europäische Bankenunion – Wege zu einer einheitlichen Bankenaufsicht. Wertpapier-Mitteilungen (Zeitschrift für Wirtschafts- und Bankrecht), pp 1889–1898
Herrmann C, Dornacher C (2017) International and European monetary law – an introduction. Springer, Heidelberg
Herzog R (1999) Gesetzgebung und Einzelfallgerechtigkeit. Neue Juristische Wochenschrift, pp 25–28
High-Level Group on Financial Supervision in the EU (2009) Report of 25 February. https://ec.europa.eu/info/system/files/de_larosiere_report_en.pdf (26 February 2021)

Kämmerer JA (2016) Rechtsschutz in der Bankenunion (SSM, SRM). Wertpapier-Mitteilungen (Zeitschrift für Wirtschafts- und Bankrecht), pp 1–11
Kämmerer JA, Starski P (2013) Die Europäische Zentralbank in der Bankenunion oder: Vor Risiken und Nebenwirkungen wird gewarnt. Zeitschrift für Gesetzgebung, pp 318–338
Karagianni A, Scholten M (2018) Accountability gaps in the Single Supervisory Mechanism (SSM) framework. Utrecht J Int Eur Law 34:185–194
Karatzia A, Markakis M (2017) What role for the Commission and the ECB in the European Stability Mechanism? Cambridge Int Law J 6:232–252
Kaufhold A-K (2016) Systemaufsicht – Anforderungen an die Ausgestaltung einer Aufsicht zur Abwehr systemischer Risiken entwickelt am Beispiel der Finanzaufsicht. Mohr Siebeck, Tübingen
Kern A (2015) European Banking Union – a legal and institutional analysis of the Single Supervisory Mechanism and the Single Resolution Mechanism. Eur Law Rev 40:154–187
Koskelo P (2017) Relevance of fundamental rights for central bank policy and decision-making. In: ECB, Legal Conference 2017 – shaping a new legal order for Europe: a tale of crises and opportunities, Frankfurt a.M., pp 133–145. https://www.ecb.europa.eu/pub/pdf/other/ecblegalconferenceproceedings201712.en.pdf (26 February 2021)
Kröger M, Pilniok A (2016) Unabhängigkeit zählt – Amtliche Statistik zwischen Politik, Verwaltung und Wissenschaft. In: Kröger M, Pilniok A (eds) Unabhängiges Verwalten in der Europäischen Union. Mohr Siebeck, Tübingen, pp 131–157
Lamandini M, Ramos Muñoz D, Solana Álvarez J (2015) Depicting the limits to the SSM's supervisory powers – the role of constitutional mandates and of fundamental rights' protection. Quaderni di Ricerca Giuridica No. 79. https://ssrn.com/abstract=2733620 (26 February 2021)
Lamandini M, Ramos Muñoz D, Solana Álvarez J (2017) The European Central Bank (ECB) (powers) as a catalyst for change in EU law – the ECB's mandates (part 1), SSM, SRM and fundamental rights (part 2). Columbia J Eur Law 23:1–54 and 199–263
Lambrinoc S (2016) Die Unabhängigkeit der Europäischen Zentralbank als Aufsichtsbehörde für Kreditinstitute. In: Kröger M, Pilniok A (eds) Unabhängiges Verwalten in der Europäischen Union. Mohr Siebeck, Tübingen, pp 221–238
Lastra RM (2015) International financial and monetary law, 2nd edn. Oxford University Press, Oxford
Lehmann M (2017) Varying standards of judicial scrutiny over central bank actions. In: ECB, Legal Conference 2017 – shaping a new legal order for Europe: a tale of crises and opportunities, Frankfurt a.M., pp 112–132. https://www.ecb.europa.eu/pub/pdf/other/ecblegalconferenceproceedings201712.en.pdf (26 February 2021)
Lettanie U (2019) The ECB's performance under the ESM Treaty on a sliding scale of delegation. Eur Law J 25:317–332
Lo Schiavo G (2019) The ECB and its application of national law in the SSM. In: Lo Schiavo G (ed) The European Banking Union and the role of law. Elgar, Cheltenham/Northampton, pp 117–196
Maduro MP (2020) Some preliminary remarks on the PSPP decision of the German Constitutional Court, VerfBlog, 2020/5/06. https://verfassungsblog.de/some-preliminary-remarks-on-the-pspp-decision-of-the-german-constitutional-court/ (26 February 2021)
Majone G (1998) The regulatory state and its legitimacy problems, Institute for Advanced Studies Vienna, Political Science Series No. 56. https://nbn-resolving.org/urn:nbn:de:0168-ssoar-246700 (26 February 2021)
Manger-Nestler C (2016) B. II. Institutionell-organisatorische Aspekte des Einheitlichen Abwicklungsmechanismus. In: Jahn U, Schmitt C, Geier B (eds) Handbuch Bankensanierung und -abwicklung. Beck, Munich
Manger-Nestler C (2019) Die Außenwährungsbeziehungen der Europäischen Union an der Schnittstelle zwischen Europa- und Völkerrecht. In: Groh T, Knur F, Köster C, Maus S, Roeder T (eds) Verfassungsrecht, Völkerrecht, Menschenrechte – Vom Recht im Zentrum der Internationalen Beziehungen – Festschrift für Ulrich Fastenrath zum 70. Geburtstag. C.F. Müller, Heidelberg, pp 121–136
Manger-Nestler C, Böttner R (2019) Der Europäische Währungsfonds nach den Plänen der Kommission. Zeitschrift für ausländisches öffentliches Recht und Völkerrecht, pp 43–84

Manger-Nestler C, Gramlich L (2019) Nur Bares ist Wahres – Zur Reichweite des Rechts auf Barzahlung im Kontext währungsrechtlicher Regelungen. Wertpapier-Mitteilungen (Zeitschrift für Wirtschafts- und Bankrecht), pp 1949–1957, 1997–2004

Maricut-Akbik A (2020) Contesting the European Central Bank in banking supervision – accountability in practice at the European Parliament. J Common Mark Stud 58:1199–1214

Martini M, Weinzierl Q (2017) Nationales Verfassungsrecht als Prüfungsmaßstab des EuGH? – Der Vollzug nationalen Rechts durch die EZB und seine ungelösten Folgeprobleme. Neue Zeitschrift für Verwaltungsrecht, pp 177–183

Martucci F (2017) The democratic foundations of the EMU – the European Parliament and the national parliaments between cooperation and rivalry. In: Daniele L, Simone P, Cisotta R (eds) Democracy in the EMU in the aftermath of the crisis. Springer, Heidelberg, pp 27–50

Marzal T (2020) Is the BVerfG PSPP decision "simply not comprehensible"? – a critique of the judgment's reasoning on proportionality, VerfBlog, 2020/5/09. https://verfassungsblog.de/is-the-bverfg-pspp-decision-simply-not-comprehensible/ (26 February 2021)

Mayer FC, Kollmeyer D (2013) Sinnlose Gesetzgebung? – Die Europäische Bankenunion im Bundestag. Deutsches Verwaltungsblatt, pp 1158–1167

Mersch Y (2017) Central bank independence revisited, Keynote at the "Symposium on Building the Financial System of the 21st Century: An Agenda for Europe and the United States", Frankfurt a.M., 30 March 2017. https://www.ecb.europa.eu/press/key/date/2017/html/sp170330.en.html (26 February 2021)

Möllers TMJ (2020) Das PSPP-Urteil des BVerfG und die Europäische Rechtsunion – Drei Wege aus der Sackgasse. Europäische Zeitschrift für Wirtschaftsrecht, pp 503–505

Mooij AAM (2020) The legality of the ECB responses to COVID-19. Eur Law Rev 45:713–731

Muscheler-Lorange K (2013) Kommentierung zu Art. 5 ESZB/EZB-S. In: Siekmann H (ed) EWU – Kommentar zur Europäischen Währungsunion. Mohr Siebeck, Tübingen

Nettesheim M (2005) Demokratisierung der Europäischen Union und Europäisierung der Demokratietheorie. In: Bauer H, Huber PM, Sommermann K-P (eds) Demokratie in Europa. Mohr Siebeck, Tübingen, pp 143–189

Nettesheim M (2018) § 18 Wirtschaftsverfassung und Wirtschaftspolitik. In: Oppermann T, Classen CD, Nettesheim M (eds) Europarecht, 8th edn. Beck, Munich

Ohler C (2015) Bankenaufsicht und Geldpolitik in der Währungsunion. Beck, Munich

Omlor S (2015) Abschied vom Bargeld? – Überlegungen aus geldgeschichtlicher, währungs- und geldprivatrechtlicher Perspektive. Wertpapier-Mitteilungen (Zeitschrift für Wirtschafts- und Bankrecht), pp 2297–2303

Ossenbühl F (1980) Aktuelle Probleme der Gewaltenteilung. Die Öffentliche Verwaltung, pp 545–553

Pennesi F (2018) The accountability of the European Stability Mechanism and the European Monetary Fund – who should answer for conditionality measures? Eur Pap 3:511–545

Peuker E (2014) Die Anwendung nationaler Rechtsvorschriften durch Unionsorgane ein Konstruktionsfehler der europäischen Bankenaufsicht. Juristenzeitung, pp 764–771

Pilz S (2017) Ein Schatzamt für die Eurozone? – Überlegungen zu den Vorschlägen des Europäischen Parlaments und der Kommission zu einer Reform der Wirtschaftsunion. Europäische Zeitschrift für Wirtschaftsrecht, pp 637–645

Pliakos A, Anagnostaras G (2010) Adjudicating economics II: the quantitative easing programme declared valid. Eur Law Rev 45:128–146

Quintyn M, Taylor MW (2003) Regulatory and supervisory independence and financial stability. CESifo Econ Stud 49:259–294

Quintyn M, Taylor MW (2007) Robust regulators and their political masters – independence and accountability in theory. In: Masciandaro D, Quintyn M (eds) Designing financial supervision institutions – independence, accountability and governance. Elgar, Cheltenham/Northampton, pp 3–40

Repasi R (2020) Chapter 17 European Parliament and national parliaments. In: Amtenbrink F, Herrmann C (eds) The EU law of Economic and Monetary Union. Oxford University Press, Oxford, pp 456–506

Ritleng D (2016) Introduction. In: Ritleng D (ed) Independence and legitimacy in the institutional system of the European Union. Oxford University Press, Oxford, pp 1–14

Ruccia N (2017) The Single Resolution Mechanism and the Single Resolution Fund – substantive issues and the contradictory democratic deficit. In: Daniele L, Simone P, Cisotta R (eds) Democracy in the EMU in the aftermath of the crisis. Springer, Heidelberg, pp 319–331
Sandberger G (2019) Gefahr durch Target-Salden – Risikoreiche Kreditvergabe oder bedeutungslose Buchungsposten? Juristenzeitung, pp 599–608
Schneider SH (2014) Sanctioning by the ECB and national authorities within the Single Supervisory Mechanism. Europäische Zeitschrift für Wirtschaftsrecht Beilage, pp 18–23
Schuster G (2014) The banking supervisory competences and powers of the ECB. Europäische Zeitschrift für Wirtschaftsrecht Beilage, pp 3–9
Selmayr M (2015) Kommentierung zu Art. 127 AEUV. In: von der Groeben H, Schwarze J, Hatje A (eds) Europäisches Unionsrecht, 7th edn. Nomos, Baden-Baden
Siekmann H (2013) Kommentierung zu Art. 130 AEUV. In: Siekmann H (ed) EWU – Kommentar zur Europäischen Währungsunion. Mohr Siebeck, Tübingen
Simone P (2017) Respecting the democratic principle in ESM activities related to the context of the economic and financial crisis. In: Daniele L, Simone P, Cisotta R (eds) Democracy in the EMU in the aftermath of the crisis. Springer, Heidelberg, pp 195–214
Smits R (1997) The European Central Bank – institutional aspects. Kluwer Law International, The Hague
Steinbach A (2016) The lender of last resort in the Eurozone. Common Mark Law Rev 53:361–383
Steinbach A (2017) Das behördliche Unabhängigkeitsparadigma im Wirtschaftsverwaltungsrecht – Eine funktionell-rechtliche Betrachtung. Die Verwaltung 50:507–536
Streinz R (2018) Kommentierung zu Art. 5 EUV. In: Streinz R (ed) EUV/AEUV, 3rd edn. Beck, Munich
ter Kuile G, Wissink L, Bovenschen W (2015) Tailor-made accountability within the Single Supervisory Mechanism. Common Mark Law Rev 52:155–190
Thiele A (2014) Finanzaufsicht – Der Staat und die Finanzmärkte. Mohr Siebeck, Tübingen
Thiele A (2015) Krise der Europäischen Integration? – Die Bankenunion als Beleg für die Handlungsfähigkeit der EU. Gewerbearchiv, pp 111–116, 157–160
Tröger TH (2013) The Single Supervisory Mechanism – panacea or quack banking regulation?, SAFE Working Paper No. 27. https://papers.ssrn.com/sol3/papers.cfm?abstract_id=2311353 (26 February 2021)
van den Berg CCA (2004) The making of the Statute of the European System of Central Banks – an application of checks and balances. Rozenberg Publishers, Amsterdam
Viterbo A (2019) The European Union in the transnational financial regulatory arena – the case of the Basel Committee on Banking Supervision. J Int Econ Law 22:205–228
Waldhoff C (2013) Kommentierung zu Art. 127 AEUV. In: Siekmann H (ed) EWU – Kommentar zur Europäischen Währungsunion. Mohr Siebeck, Tübingen
Weinzierl J (2019) Der EuGH erklärt erstmalig nationales Recht für ungültig – Anmerkung zum Urteil des EuGH v. 26.2.2019, Rs. C-202/18 (Rimšēvičs). Europarecht, pp 434–458
Wolfers B, Voland T (2014) Level the playing field – the new supervision of credit institutions by the European Central Bank. Common Mark Law Rev 51:1463–1495
Wymeersch E (2014) The Single Supervisory Mechanism or "SSM" – part one of the Banking Union, National Bank of Belgium Working Paper No. 255. http://www.nationalebankvanbelgie.be/doc/ts/publications/wp/wp255en.pdf (26 February 2021)
Zilioli C (2016) The independence of the European Central Bank and its new banking supervisory competences. In: Ritleng D (ed) Independence and legitimacy in the institutional system of the European Union. Oxford University Press, Oxford, pp 125–179
Zilioli C (2017) Justiciability of central banks' decisions and the imperative to respect fundamental rights. In: ECB, Legal Conference 2017 – shaping a new legal order for Europe: a tale of crises and opportunities, Frankfurt a.M., pp 91–103. https://www.ecb.europa.eu/pub/pdf/other/ecblegalconferenceproceedings201712.en.pdf (26 February 2021)

Chapter 4
Independence as a Structural Characteristic of European Union Law

Although central bank independence deserves special attention, not least because of being fixed in the Treaties, it can perhaps be better understood if contrasted to other concepts of fulfilling EU tasks. In this respect, there are several provisions in primary, but above all in secondary law, which guarantee a certain degree of independence to institutions, bodies, offices and agencies/authorities. Such a system, composed of independent powers, has developed historically and is closely linked to the concept of the "Community method".[1] Nevertheless, increasing impulses for democratisation, which have been reflected in particular in the valorisation of the European Parliament, also affect the concept of independence. The latter must always be scrutinised because, as shown, it does not intrinsically represent a value, but has to be considered functionally, i.e. in the light of the tasks to be performed.

In the following, the independence of the CJEU, the European Commission, the ECA as well as the European Administration, esp. "regulatory" financial agencies like the EBA, will be examined more closely in the light of their respective roles.

[1]Cf. Ritleng (2016a), p. 3; for details Jacqué (2016), pp. 16–19.

C. Manger-Nestler, M. Gentzsch, *Democratic Legitimation of Central Bank Independence in the European Union*, https://doi.org/10.1007/978-3-030-75115-9_4

4.1 Court of Justice of the European Union

The ECB is sometimes considered to be judicially independent in view of the freedom of instruction and influence it has been granted.[2] Indeed, if one takes the CJEU in particular as a comparator institution, which is on an equal institutional footing with the ECB,[3] there are clear parallels in terms of autonomy provisions.[4]

This concerns in particular the personal independence of the Judges and Advocates General of the ECJ and the Judges of the EGC, who are to be appointed by common accord by the governments of the Member States and chosen from persons whose independence is beyond doubt.[5] This sets out personal requirements which are intended to prevent even the slightest appearance of external influence. Moreover, Judges and Advocates General may be deprived of their office only if they no longer fulfil the requisite conditions or no longer meet the obligations arising from their office.[6] However, this is attended by strict procedural safeguards requiring a unanimous opinion of the Judges and Advocates General of the ECJ. To increase independence, there are also immunity and incompatibility rules.[7] However, the personal independence of the Judges and Advocates General even falls a little short of that of the members of the ECB's decision-making bodies because their term of office is only 6 years and reappointment is permitted.[8,9] This should be viewed critically, because it provides at least abstract incentives for political considerations with a view to possible reappointment.[10] Political influence by the Member States on the judges they appoint is nevertheless prevented by procedural rules such as the secrecy of deliberations and the majority principle.[11]

As regards substantive independence, the Judges and Advocates General also enjoy a broad freedom of instruction and influence. Although this has not been provided for in any provisions comparable to Art. 130 TFEU or Art. 97(1) GG[12,13] it follows directly from the principle of the rule of law, which is one of the EU's constituent values according to Art. 2 s. 1 TEU.

---

[2]See for example Kirchhof, Interview with Focus Money, 3.10.2019, https://www.finanzen100.de/finanznachrichten/boerse/ex-verfassungsrichter-kirchhof-es-gibt-ein-grundrecht-auf-zinsen_H1534322580_11200605/ (26 February 2021).

[3]Art. 13(1) sub-para. 2 5th indent TEU.

[4]Cf. ECJ, OLAF, 10.7.2003, ECLI:EU:C:2003:395, para. 133; see also Heisenberg and Richmond (2002), p. 203.

[5]Art. 19(2) sub-para. 3 ss. 1, 2 TEU; see further Arts. 253(1), 254(2) s. 1 TFEU.

[6]Arts. 6(1) s. 1, 7 CJEU Statute.

[7]Arts. 3, 4, 7 CJEU Statute.

[8]Art. 19(2) sub-para. 3 ss. 2, 3 TEU.

[9]Similarly Selmayr (2015), para. 106.

[10]Ritleng (2016b), p. 98 with further references.

[11]Art. 32(1), (4) Rules of Procedure of the Court of Justice.

[12]It provides that judges are independent and subject only to the law.

[13]Cf. Zilioli (2016), p. 135.

The CJEU is also subject to important institutional arrangements to ensure its independence. For example, the number of Judges and Advocates General of the ECJ is laid down in the Treaties,[14] which prevents any increase in their number and thus political influence through so-called "court packing".[15] Moreover, the rules guaranteeing independence, which are laid down in Title 1 of the CJEU Statute, can only be changed by amending the Treaties.[16]

Looking at the function of the institutions, there are similarities, but also clear differences. Both institutions are shielded from influence that is perceived as inappropriate in order to ensure the credibility of the institutions. This applies in particular to influence by the Member States, for which incentives exist regarding the CJEU precisely when it is necessary to decide on the conformity of Member State measures with EU law or the imposition of sanctions on Member States.[17]

At the same time, both institutions are equipped with a specific technical expertise which is intended to reach the best possible decisions, while those decisions are deprived of direct influence and control by the citizens.[18]

However, there are some specific features of the judiciary which are not transposable to central bank action. The function of the CJEU is specifically marked by Art. 19(1) s. 2 TEU, according to which it shall ensure that in the interpretation and application of the Treaties the law is observed, which outlines a much broader mandate than that of the ECB.[19] Courts have the task of ensuring effective legal protection for individuals, thereby fulfilling the fundamental right to an effective remedy and a fair trial (judiciary as "third power").[20] Their independence serves above all the rule of law and above all the protection of minorities, which would be endangered if they were embedded in representative-democratic responsibility.[21]

However, the courts are subject to law and statute, the ECJ in particular to the provisions of the Treaties. Although the courts, in particular the ECJ, sometimes have considerable discretionary power in the interpretation of provisions,[22] the legal methodology prohibits the injection of political considerations of expediency. As *Lehmann* put it, judges typically do not have a political agenda, or if they have one, they cannot rely on it in legal arguments.[23] By contrast, the task of defining and

[14]Art. 19(2) sub-paras. 1 ss 1, 2 TEU. An increase in the number of Advocates General requires a request from the ECJ and a unanimous decision of the Council, Art. 252(1) s. 2 TFEU. The number of members of the Court, which should include at least one judge per Member State (Art. 19 (2) sub-para. 2 TEU), is laid down in Art. 48 CJEU Statute.

[15]Ritleng (2016b), p. 91.

[16]Art. 281(2) s. 1 TFEU.

[17]Dehousse (2016), p. 67.

[18]Cf. Zilioli (2017), p. 97.

[19]Heisenberg and Richmond (2002), pp. 205–206.

[20]Art. 47 CFR; see also Art. 6(1) ECHR.

[21]Cf. Ortino (2017), p. 304.

[22]For details see Ritleng (2016b), pp. 106 et seq.

[23]Lehmann (2017), p. 115.

implementing monetary policy which has been assigned to the ECB/Eurosystem makes it possible to formulate an entire policy area, which also leaves the necessary scope for the use of a broad range of instruments.

In addition, another aspect argues for greater institutional independence of the ECB in comparison with the CJEU, as pointed out by *Heisenberg* and *Richmond*.[24] The concept of the ESCB/Eurosystem as a European system is characterised by the fact that the ECB has a power of instruction vis-à-vis the NCBs, which finds no parallel in the multi-level jurisdictional system of the EU (*"Rechtsprechungsverbund"*), which consists of Union courts and national courts.[25] This strict subordination is strengthened by the Governing Council's right of action under Art. 271(d) TFEU vis-à-vis the NCBs to fulfil and enforce obligations under the Treaties and the ECB/ESCB Statute. As a result, the system as a whole is more strongly shielded from external, mainly Member State, influences, as became clearly visible in the aftermath of the *PSPP decision*. For if the German government (Bundesregierung) and the German Parliament (Deutscher Bundestag) had exerted undue influence on the German central bank (Deutsche Bundesbank) in order to exercise their responsibility with regard to European integration ("*Integrationsverantwortung*") and if the latter had withdrawn from the PSPP, this might have resulted in an action by the ECB under Art. 271(d) TFEU.[26] There is no comparable finding within the jurisdiction system of the EU. In the event of Member States acting in violation of Union law by interfering with the judiciary, only the infringement procedure under Art. 258 TFEU of the Commission[27] or the procedure under Art. 7 TEU, which is considered to be less effective due to the unanimity requirement, remains.

The different functions also illustrate the different approaches to democratic embedment. While the ECB is directly accountable to the representative bodies, which is mainly expressed through reporting and accountability obligations, such a linkage is not envisaged for the Judges and the Advocates General. In this respect, the legislator has only the possibility to change a particular case law in a forward-looking manner by enacting rules, in so far as he is competent to do so.

The fact that within the branch of judiciary there is further potential for, and possibly even a need for, democratic embedment without violating the independence of the judiciary becomes clear with regard to the public prosecution. For example, the European Public Prosecutor's Office (EPPO), which is responsible for investigating, prosecuting and bringing prosecutions in respect of offences affecting the

---

[24]Heisenberg and Richmond (2002), pp. 207–208.

[25]Ibid.

[26]For details see Gentzsch (2020), pp. 581–582.

[27]Recently ECJ, European Commission/Republic of Poland, 24.6.2019, ECLI:EU:C:2019:531; ECJ, European Commission/Republic of Poland, 5.11.2019, ECLI:EU:C:2019:924.

Union's financial interests,[28] is granted a high degree of independence, in particular freedom of instruction and influence.[29] At the same time, the EPPO is accountable to the European Parliament, the Council and the Commission for its general activities and issues annual reports.[30]

This liaison of the public prosecutor's office between judiciary and administration is particularly evident in the structure of the German public prosecutor's office. Public prosecutors are subject to instructions in accordance with §§ 146, 147 Gerichtsverfassungsgesetz (GVG), which extends to the Ministers of Justice and is ultimately intended to ensure democratic legitimation. The functional positioning of the public prosecutor's office ultimately determines the required degree of independence on the one hand and the nature and extent of democratic legitimation and control on the other. Nevertheless, the ECJ has rejected the German concept by not considering the German public prosecutor's office as an "issuing judicial authority"[31] for the European arrest warrant because of its obligation to follow instructions.[32] This makes it clear that although Union law allows for democratic embedment with regard to the tasks of the public prosecutor and itself provides for the EPPO, it does not include the instrument of binding instructions as a *conditio sine qua non*.

4.2 European Court of Auditors

The ECA carrying out the Union's audit consists of one national of each Member state.[33] Like other EU institutions, the ECA is endowed with independence.[34]

With regard to personal independence, the members of the ECA seem to have a similarly strong position as the members of the Governing Council of the ECB. According to Art. 285(2) s. 2 TFEU its members shall be completely independent in the performance of their duties, in the Union's general interest. Art. 286(1) s. 2 TFEU states that their independence must be beyond doubt. This provision has certain parallels with that concerning the judges of CJEU[35] and attaches

[28] Art. 4 s. 1 Council Regulation (EU) 2017/1939 of 12 October 2017 implementing enhanced cooperation on the establishment of the European Public Prosecutor's Office ('the EPPO'), OJ 31.10.2017, L 283, p. 1 (hereinafter: EPPOR).

[29] Art. 6(1) EPPOR.

[30] Arts. 6(2), 7 EPPOR.

[31] Art. 6(1) Council Framework Decision 2002/584/JHA of 13 June 2002 on the European arrest warrant and the surrender procedures between Member States, OJ 18.07.2002, L 190, p. 1.

[32] ECJ, OG/PI, 27.5.2019, ECLI:EU:C:2019:456.

[33] Art. 285(2) s. 1 TFEU.

[34] For an in-depth analysis see Vogiatzis (2019), pp. 667 et seq.

[35] Art. 253 TFEU.

independence precisely to the members as a necessary quality for the exercise of the mandate.

Similar to the members of the Commission,[36] the members of the ECA are subject to incompatibility rules during and after the termination of their mandate,[37] but also benefit from the privileges granted to judges.[38] Their term of office of 6 years, which is renewable, is also the same as that of the Judges and Advocates General of the CJEU. Here too, concerns about the possibility of reappointment are certainly warranted in terms of independence.[39]

Moreover, ECA members cannot be easily removed from office by the political institutions. Beyond the end of the term of office, death and resignation, the office only ends by removal from office by a ruling of the ECJ.[40] However, it should be noted that the deprivation of office presupposes that the regarding concerned no longer fulfils the requisite conditions or meets the obligations arising from their office.

Furthermore, Art. 286(3) TFEU constitutes substantive independence, as it stipulates that the members of the ECA in "the performance of these duties [...] shall neither seek nor take instructions from any government or from any other body" (s. 1) and "shall refrain from any action incompatible with their duties" (s. 2).

In contrast, Art 286(3) TFEU does not contain a prohibition imposed on the Union institutions and the Member States comparable to Art. 130 s. 2 TFEU. Instead, the ECA is assigned a support function vis-à-vis the European Parliament and the Council in exercising their powers of control over the implementation of the budget in Art. 287(4) TFEU. This gives them the opportunity to formulate their expectations regarding the audit, so that especially the Budgetary Control Committee of the European Parliament is prone to make certain recommendations.[41] However, the Member States are largely prohibited from influencing the members of the ECA in terms of freedom of instruction.

The independence of the ECA is reinforced and justified by its functions. These can in principle be divided into two categories, namely compliance and performance audit.[42,43] While the former comprises the examination of the legality and regularity of transactions, the latter concerns the value-for-money audit according to the principles of economy, efficiency and effectiveness.[44]

---

[36]See infra Sect. 4.3.

[37]Art. 286(4) TFEU.

[38]Art. 286(8) TFEU.

[39]Cf. Waldhoff (2016), para. 8.

[40]Art. 286(5) sub-para. 1 TFEU.

[41]Cf. Vogiatzis (2019), pp. 691–692.

[42]Art. 287(2) s. 1 TFEU.

[43]For details see Vogiatzis (2019), pp. 668 et seq.

[44]Art. 33 Regulation (EU, Euratom) 2018/1046 of the European Parliament and of the Council of 18 July 2018 on the financial rules applicable to the general budget of the Union, amending Regulations (EU) No 1296/2013, (EU) No 1301/2013, (EU) No 1303/2013, (EU) No 1304/2013,

The ECA's independence is probably not only justified by its legal status as an audit institution and the audit profession it represents, but rather by the fact that it acts on behalf of the Union interest.[45] If this view is shared, the ECA's independence is functionally similar to that of the Commission,[46] because the focus is less on the specific nature of the task and more on defending against Member State influence.

Looking at the ECA and its relationship with national audit bodies, there are also differences with the ESCB/Eurosystem. Union law addresses the national audit bodies in particular in so far as they cooperate with the ECA in a spirit of trust while maintaining their independence[47] and participate ("in liaison") in the audit in the Member States.[48] They may also be required by the ECA to forward the documents and information necessary for the performance of its tasks. Unlike the ESCB/ECB, this form of vertical cooperation is not marked by strict hierarchical subordination. Moreover, there are no independence rules in favour of the national audit bodies, so that the system as such is less shielded from external influences than the ESCB/Eurosystem.[49]

4.3 European Commission

As already pointed out, the European Commission also plays an important role in the institutional structure of the Economic and Monetary Union as well as in granting financial aids by the ESM.[50]

The functions of the Commission are various. As well as being the "guardian of the Treaties", it also has coordinating, executive and management functions, ensures the Union's external representation and, in principle, has a monopoly of initiative for the adoption of legislative acts.[51] However, the main focus is on the gubernatorial-administrative function, especially since the Commission, despite its monopoly on legislative initiative, cannot be regarded as a third branch of the EU legislature.[52]

Relevant for this investigation is that the Treaties also provide the Commission with independence. According to Art. 17(3) sub-para. 3 s. 1 TEU, the Commission shall be completely independent when carrying out its responsibilities. Without prejudice to Art. 18(2) TEU, according to which the High Representative for Foreign

(EU) No 1309/2013, (EU) No 1316/2013, (EU) No 223/2014, (EU) No 283/2014, and Decision No 541/2014/EU and repealing Regulation (EU, Euratom) No 966/2012, OJ 30.7.2018, L 193, p. 1.

[45]For details see Vogiatzis (2019), pp. 671–675.

[46]See infra Sect. 4.3.

[47]Art. 287(3) sub-para. 1 s. 3 TFEU.

[48]Art. 287(3) sub-para. 1 s. 2 TFEU.

[49]Cf. Vogiatzis (2019), p. 681.

[50]Cf. Ritleng (2016a), p. 4.

[51]Art. 17(1), (2) TEU.

[52]Cf. Jacqué (2016), p. 56; Ritleng (2016c), pp. 24–25.

Affairs and Security Policy is mandated by the Council, the members of the Commission shall neither seek nor take instructions from any Government or other institution, body, office or entity.[53] This freedom from instructions is rounded off by the fact that the members of the Commission shall refrain from any action incompatible with their duties or the performance of their tasks[54] and that they are chosen on the ground of their general competence and European commitment from persons whose independence is beyond doubt.[55] There are also incompatibility rules during the term of office and a requirement for restraint with regard to the acceptance of certain activities or benefits after the end of the term.[56]

Although there are similarities with the members of the ECB's Governing Council in this respect, which have been pointed out by the ECJ,[57] clear differences also occur. For example, the Commission's prohibition on seeking and taking instructions, which is compatible to Art. 130 s. 1 TFEU, is only partially covered by a prohibition of exerting influence on the Commission.[58] In this respect, Art. 245 (1) s. 2 TFEU provides that the Member States respect the independence of the members of the Commission and shall not seek to influence them in the performance of their tasks. In contrast, no comparable shielding is provided for the Union bodies.

With regard to personal independence, it should also be noted that the members of the Commission are obliged to resign from office if the President so requests.[59] This right of the President allows for a free political and therefore unconditional decision, in addition to removal from office in the event that the member concerned no longer fulfils the conditions required for the performance of their duties or has been guilty of serious misconduct.[60] At 5 years, the length of the term of office is significantly shorter than that of the members of the ECB's Executive Board.[61] Together with the possibility of reappointment, this contributes to making the members of the Commission more dependent.[62]

Moreover, a particularly striking difference is that under Art. 17(8) s. 1 TEU, the Commission is responsible to the European Parliament as a body, which is safeguarded by the parliamentary right to table a motion of censure, which, if carried, entails the Commission's resignation.[63] As a result of these sanction mechanisms,

---

[53] Art. 17(3) sub-para. 3 s. 2 TEU.

[54] Art. 17(3) sub-para. 3 s. 3 TEU; see further Art. 245(1) s. 1 TFEU.

[55] Art. 17(3) sub-para. 2 TEU.

[56] Art. 245(2) TFEU.

[57] ECJ, OLAF, 10.7.2003, ECLI:EU:C:2003:395, para. 133.

[58] Cf. Zilioli (2016), p. 135.

[59] Art. 17(6) sub-para. 2 s. 1 TEU.

[60] Art. 247 TFEU.

[61] Art. 17(3) sub-para. 1 TEU.

[62] Similarly Selmayr (2015), para. 106.

[63] Art. 17(8) ss. 2, 3 TEU.

the Commission's responsibility goes well beyond that of the ECB or its decision-making bodies.[64]

This concept of independence, particularly vis-à-vis the Member States, and of democratic accountability, becomes clearer when we look at the Commission's functions. The independence of the Commission is based primarily on the fact that it was created as a depoliticised, technocratic institution, which is to some extent comparable to the ECB. The Commission should not be bound by the interests of the Member States but by the interests of the Union, which is also reflected by its central position in Art. 17(1) s. 1 TEU. Recapturing it by national interests is particularly likely where Union law restricts the Member States' scope for action enforced by Union law procedures, in particular the infringement procedure under Arts. 258, 259 TFEU or the excessive deficit procedure under Art. 126 TFEU.[65] This aspect is also evident in the field of competition law, where the Commission has a central role, which serves in particular to break down the different approaches of the Member States.[66]

The right of legislative initiative is also based on this idea, in so far as the Council can only amend the Commission proposal unanimously in certain cases.[67] This strong position of the Commission in the legislative procedure, on the other hand, is becoming less and less convincing, especially since the European Parliament has been revalued. This applies in particular to the Commission's right, confirmed by the ECJ in the *Macro-Financial Assistance (MFA) decision*, to withdraw proposals under certain conditions "as long as the Council has not acted".[68] Interestingly, the Commission contested the argument that the respective decision affected the principle of democracy, by stating that, "like the other EU institutions, it has a democratic legitimacy of its own".[69]

Nevertheless, democratic legitimation and control must be particularly strong where measures encroach on the rights of individuals and also of the Member States. Against this background, it was important that the strengthened role of the Commission in the course of Six-Pack and Two-Pack legislation, the European Semester, the ESM Treaty and the Fiscal Compact Treaty (TSCG) was democratically accompanied, in particular by adequate accountability mechanisms, especially vis-à-vis parliaments.[70]

[64]Cf. Brentford (1998), p. 91; Selmayr (2015), para. 106.

[65]Cf. Jacqué (2016), pp. 52–54.

[66]Cf. Dehousse (2016), p. 68.

[67]Art. 293(1) TFEU; for details see Dehousse (2016), p. 68.

[68]ECJ, Macro-Financial Assistance, 14.4.2015, ECLI:EU:C:2015:217, para. 74; for details see Ritleng (2016c), pp. 15–19.

[69]ECJ, Macro-Financial Assistance, 14.4.2015, ECLI:EU:C:2015:217, para. 60.

[70]For details see Smits (2017), pp. 53–55.

4.4 European Administration, in Particular the European Banking Authority

4.4.1 Independent European Administration

In the context of European administration, Art. 298 TFEU contains another provision addressing the notion of independence. According to this provision, the institutions, bodies, offices and agencies of the Union shall, when carrying out their missions, have the support not only of an open and efficient European administration but also of an independent one.

However, the content of the independence referred to therein is far from clear. Commonly, the provision is understood as an imperative of impartial and fair administration, which follows from the rule of law and the principle of equal treatment.[71] Furthermore, the provision could also be understood as a concretisation of the principle of institutional balance or even as an expression of a constitutional division of functions under the rule of law with separation of legislative, executive and judicial powers.[72] It is also conceivable that Art. 298(1) TFEU could be interpreted to the effect that it standardises the concept of political independence as an organisational principle.[73]

The genesis of the provision reveals that the procedural principles contained in Art. 298(1) TFEU are closely related to the principle of "good administration" and give it concrete form.[74] Art. 41(1) CFR ("right to good administration") contains in particular the right of every person to have his or her affairs handled impartially by the Union institutions, bodies, offices and agencies. However, this impartiality differs from a concept of independence as a functional standard for the performance of duties, since its primary purpose is to examine all relevant aspects of the decision and to exclude any prejudiced officials.[75]

Thus, Art. 298(1) TFEU and Art. 41 CFR develop at most a small normative steering effect in the sense of a principle of the performance of tasks characterised by the division of functions and leave the corresponding formulations to Union legislation.

---

[71] Cf. Reithmann (2015), para. 13.

[72] Kotzur (2017), para. 3.

[73] Cf. Groß (2014), pp. 197–198; Michel (2015), pp. 54–55.

[74] Saurer (2017), para. 11.

[75] Cf. ECJ, Burban, 31.3.1992, ECLI:EU:C:1992:153, para. 7; EGC, max.mobil, 30.1.2002, ECLI:EU:T:2002:20, para. Rn. 49.

4.4.2 Agencies Within the European Administration

Notwithstanding the lack of primary legal foundations, a large number of secondary legal bodies have been set up and equipped with expertise to perform a wide range of tasks and relieve the Commission, particularly in highly complex and technical matters.[76]

The range of activities of these so-called agencies includes carrying out support and management tasks, collecting or exchanging information and data, making recommendations to the Commission, but also in the case of "regulatory" agencies setting standards or exercising decision-making powers.[77] This increasing "mushrooming"[78] meets with criticism from a political science and legal point of view and is seen in particular as an expression of a European lack of democracy.[79]

Above all, the lack of explicit primary law enabling the establishment of European administrative bodies is proving to be problematic, although at the time of the last major reform of the Lisbon Treaty, it was no longer possible to imagine the European administration without agencies. As a legal basis, the powers of harmonisation in Art. 114 TFEU or—in the absence of a specific provision—the dispositive powers of Art. 352 TFEU is regularly used.

The ECJ initially approved the establishment of bodies of the European Union on the basis of Art. 114(1) TFEU which are "responsible for contributing to the implementation of a process of harmonisation in situations where, in order to facilitate the uniform implementation and application of acts based on that provision, the adoption of non-binding supporting and framework measures seems appropriate".[80]

The court also states:

> It must be emphasised, however, that the tasks conferred on such a body must be closely linked to the subject-matter of the acts approximating the laws, regulations and administrative provisions of the Member States. Such is the case in particular where the Community body thus established provides services to national authorities and/or operators which affect the homogenous implementation of harmonising instruments and which are likely to facilitate their application.[81]

In the ESMA decision, the ECJ significantly extended the powers of harmonisation and has since then considered Art. 114(1) TFEU as a valid legal basis for the allocation of enforcement powers to EU institutions, bodies, offices and agencies with decision-making powers directly vis-à-vis natural and legal persons,[82] on the grounds of special circumstances and the limitation of intervention powers to

[76]Cf. Vos (2016), pp. 206, 211.

[77]For a detailed categorisation see Craig (2018), pp. 163–167.

[78]Busuioc (2009), p. 600.

[79]In general Majone (1998), p. 5.

[80]ECJ, ENISA, 2.5.2006, ECLI:EU:C:2006:279, para. 44.

[81]ECJ, ENISA, 2.5.2006, ECLI:EU:C:2006:279, para. 45.

[82]Cf. ECJ, ESMA, 22.1.2014, ECLI:EU:C:2014:18, paras. 106–107.

exceptional situations requiring rapid and temporary action, in particular in areas of high technical complexity.[83]

It is precisely this broad interpretation of the powers of harmonisation that has further intensified the criticism in the literature, which is mainly directed against the allocation of individual decision-making powers to individuals.[84] This is particularly true in so far as the establishment of agencies is accompanied by originally European administrative competences instead of harmonising national provisions.[85]

Also, the FCC, in its *Banking Union decision*, which indirectly concerned the compliance of the SRM with Union law, clearly criticised the establishment of bodies of the European Union on the basis of Art. 114(1) TFEU with regard to the principle of conferral, because neither the wording of Art. 114(1) TFEU nor its systematic position provides any support and, moreover, it cannot easily be justified by teleological reasons.[86] Therefore, with regard to the establishment of agencies vested with enforcement powers on the basis of Art. 114(1) TFEU, it urged in particular that such agencies be limited to narrowly defined exceptions and that they be set up only in order to avoid or remove differences in administrative practice that would otherwise be inevitable and that cannot be accepted because of the special nature of the matter in question.[87]

However, even Art. 352 TFEU, although limited by the unwritten element of the limit of the treaty amendment as well as the consensus principle, appears to be at best a second-best solution as a competence for Europeanised administrative competences which are not provided for in the Treaties.[88]

Not only the sustainability of the possible enabling clauses for the establishment of agencies, but also the normative design of organisation and procedures as well as the extent of assigning tasks and powers, raises legal questions. There are also numerous agencies in the various sectors of European administrative law, for instance environment (European Environment Agency, EEA), border management (FRONTEX) or financial supervision (EBA, ESMA, EIOPA), which are equipped with more or less extensive independence. It should be noted that supervision of the administration, e.g. by the Commission, comparable to the legal and technical supervision *("Rechts- und Fachaufsicht")* in the German ministerial administration is hardly ever found and thus does not constitute a structural feature of the European administration.[89]

[83]Cf. ECJ, ESMA, 22.1.2014, ECLI:EU:C:2014:18, para. 105.

[84]For details see Manger-Nestler (2015), pp. 324–328 with further references.

[85]See for example the criticism of Advocate General Kokott, ENISA, 22.9.2005, ECLI:EU:C:2005:574, para. 22; Advocate General Jääskinen, ESMA, 12.9.2013, ECLI:EU:C:2013:562, para. 52; see on the envisaged EDIS Herdegen (2016), pp. 1858 et seq.

[86]FCC, Banking Union, 30.7.2019, 2 BvR 1685/14 et al., paras. 240–245.

[87]FCC, Banking Union, 30.7.2019, 2 BvR 1685/14 et al., para. 246.

[88]Cf. Manger-Nestler (2015), p. 328.

[89]Ruffert (2011), pp. 404–405.

From a functional point of view, this independence is based on the assumption that the politically uninfluenced performance of tasks ensures a high quality of results, especially when developing technical and complex decisions.[90] In addition, to varying degrees, the need to fend off private interests, especially those of market participants, can also play a role.

However, it is difficult to determine its content in abstract terms, not least because, in the absence of central codification, they derive their legal origin from various secondary acts. Although the legal classifications are diverse, it is useful to measure the concretely established autonomy in the dimensions of institutional, personnel, financial and functional independence.[91] *Prima facie*, this creates parallels to central bank independence. However, these rules differ categorically, which is particularly evident from the criteria developed by the ECJ for the legal restriction of agency action.

4.4.3 Meroni Doctrine Limiting and Controlling the Delegation of Tasks and Powers

The questions of the extent to which tasks and powers can be delegated to agencies and the requirements for their organisation and procedures overlap to some extent, but are crucial in terms of compliance with Union democratic principles. Primary law is silent on the extent to which such delegation of decision-making powers is permissible. Whether Arts. 290, 291 TFEU, which concern the adoption of delegated acts and implementing acts, sets certain limits here, is a matter of controversy.[92]

In this context, the *Meroni doctrine* developed early on by the ECJ should be taken into account,[93] which the ECJ continued in its *Romano decision*[94] and adhered to in principle in its *ESMA decision*[95] despite some modifications. This underpins the delegation of powers to institutions established under secondary legislation with conditions and limits to the effect that only "clearly defined executive powers the exercise of which can, therefore, be subject to strict review in the light of objective criteria determined by the delegating authority"[96] can be delegated, but not "a discretionary power, implying a broad margin of discretion which may, according to the use which is made of it, make possible the execution of actual economic

[90]See Communication from the Commission of 11 December 2002, The operating framework for the European Regulatory Agencies, COM(2002), 718 final, p. 5.

[91]See for example Vos (2016), pp. 216–226; see also typology by Orator (2017), pp. 53–59.

[92]Stelkens (2012), p. 536 with further references.

[93]ECJ, Meroni I, 13.6.1958, ECLI:EU:C:1958:7; Meroni II, 13.6.1958, ECLI:EU:C:1958:8; for details see Craig (2018), pp. 168–169.

[94]ECJ, Romano, 14.5.1981, ECLI:EU:C:1981:104; for details see Craig (2018), pp. 169–170.

[95]ECJ, ESMA, 22.1.2014, ECLI:EU:C:2014:18; for details see Craig (2018), pp. 170–172.

[96]ECJ, Meroni I, 13.6.1958, ECLI:EU:C:1958:7, p. 152.

policy”,[97] because the latter “since it replaces the choices of the delegator by the choices of the delegate, brings about an actual transfer of responsibility”.[98] In that regard, the ECJ considered that there is a risk that the “balance of powers which is characteristic of the institutional structure of the community”[99] may be affected.

Developed at the time of the Treaty establishing the European Coal and Steel Community (TECSC), which did not provide the same level of legal protection as now exists in Arts. 263, 267 TFEU, and in terms of the delegation of powers to private-law bodies, these criteria seem at first sight hardly transferable to European agencies.[100] In view of the increasing regulatory and supervisory activity of modern agencies, which goes hand in hand with the harmonisation of highly complex areas, these criteria appear to be impossible to meet. The ECJ maintained this in the *Romano case*, ruling that the power “to adopt acts having the force of law”[101] cannot be delegated.

Nevertheless, in its *ESMA decision*, the ECJ explicitly referred to these *Meroni criteria*, but at the same time developed them further and gave them a new shape.

According to the ECJ, the delegation of powers to agencies under secondary legislation depends on “whether it involves clearly defined executive powers the exercise of which can, therefore, be subject to strict review in the light of objective criteria determined by the delegating authority, or whether it involves a ‘discretionary power implying a wide margin of discretion which may, according to the use which is made of it, make possible the execution of actual economic policy’”.[102] This excludes powers which are discretionary and require a wide margin of discretion, since this entails an “actual transfer of responsibility”.[103] In this respect, the secondary legislation must contain criteria and conditions which limit the agency’s discretion.[104] With regard to the powers of ESMA under Art. 28 of the Short Selling Regulation,[105] the exercise of which was the subject of the dispute, the ECJ underlined the subsidiarity of the powers of intervention[106] and the provisional nature of the measures,[107] but also the obligation “to consult ESRB and, if necessary, other relevant bodies and [. . .] [to] notify the competent national authorities concerned of the measure it proposes to take, including the details of the proposed

[97]Ibid.

[98]Ibid.

[99]Ibid.

[100]Manger-Nestler (2015), p. 330.

[101]ECJ, Romano, 14.5.1981, ECLI:EU:C:1981:104, para. 20.

[102]ECJ, ESMA, 22.1.2014, ECLI:EU:C:2014:18, para. 41.

[103]ECJ, ESMA, 22.1.2014, ECLI:EU:C:2014:18, para. 42.

[104]ECJ, ESMA, 22.1.2014, ECLI:EU:C:2014:18, paras. 45, 53.

[105]Regulation (EU) No 236/2012 of the European Parliament and of the Council of 14 March 2012 on short selling and certain aspects of credit default swaps, OJ 24.3.2012, L 86, p. 1.

[106]ECJ, ESMA, 22.1.2014, ECLI:EU:C:2014:18, para. 46.

[107]ECJ, ESMA, 22.1.2014, ECLI:EU:C:2014:18, para. 50.

measure and the evidence supporting the reasons why it must be adopted".[108] The ECJ also points out the "emphasis on the technical factual assessment that must be carried out by ESMA".[109]

Not least because of the finding that the *ESMA decision* on short selling restrictions was based on a specific case constellation, the scope of permissible delegation of tasks and powers to decision-making authorities is not yet clarified in a generally applicable manner. From a dogmatic point of view, the *Meroni criteria*, together with Arts. 290, 291 TFEU may well be considered as a kind of European doctrine of essentiality ("*Wesentlichkeitslehre*"),[110] but they also take up elements of the rule of law. *Weiß*, in particular, has emphasised that *Meroni jurisprudence* not only enshrines the principle of separation of powers and institutional aspects concerning institutional competences ("*Organzuständigkeiten*"), but also implicitly reflects democratic requirements.[111]

Since the core issue is the *ex ante* and *ex post* control of the exercise of tasks and powers by various mechanisms, numerous approaches can be found in the literature that refer to principal agent theory established in the political sciences.[112] Since modern representative democracies can also be described as principal-agent relationships, in which primarily administrative units act in the interests of the representative bodies or the citizens,[113] approaches which seek to measure the delegation of tasks and powers to decision-making bodies under secondary law in accordance with a democratic principle of Union law appear to be desirable.[114]

This relationship between the *Meroni doctrine* on the one hand and requirements of Union law, arising from Art. 2 and Arts. 10 to 12 TEU, regarding the democratic legitimation and control of independent authorities on the other hand was also remarkably emphasised by the FCC in its *Banking Union decision*.[115] In this respect, the court underlined that "as regards EU bodies, offices and agencies, it follows from the CJEU's so-called *Meroni doctrine* that solely clearly defined executive powers may be delegated to 'third parties' (not subject to parliamentary oversight) that must then adhere to objective criteria".[116] It also points out, with reference to the *ESMA*

[108]ECJ, ESMA, 22.1.2014, ECLI:EU:C:2014:18, para. 50.

[109]ECJ, ESMA, 22.1.2014, ECLI:EU:C:2014:18, para. 52.

[110]See also Ohler (2014), pp. 250–251; in regard of Art. 290 TFEU Gärditz (2010), p. 456.

[111]Weiß (2016), p. 658.

[112]Cf. Müller et al. (2006), pp. 23–26; Lupia (2006), pp. 33 et seq.; Strøm (2006), pp. 59–61.

[113]Cf. Müller et al. (2006), pp. 20–21, Bovens (2007), p. 463.

[114]Manger-Nestler (2015), p. 331; Ritleng (2016c), pp. 30 et seq., who criticises that the ECJ does "not seem to consider the principle of democracy as an impediment to the granting of increasing powers to independent bodies".

[115]FCC, Banking Union, 30.7.2019, 2 BvR 1685/14 et al., paras. 135 et seq. With regard to independent regulatory authorities in the electricity and natural gas sectors, the Advocate General, while leaving open whether the *Meroni doctrine* applies to national authorities, located its requirements in the principle of democracy, see Advocate General Pitruzzella, Internal markets for electricity and natural gas, 14.1.2021, ECLI:EU:C:2021:20, paras. 134, 141.

[116]FCC, Banking Union, 30.7.2019, 2 BvR 1685/14 et al., para. 137.

decision, that "[t]he delegation of powers must be based on the Treaties and may not provide for free choices or a wide margin of discretion given that this would lead to an impermissible 'actual transfer of responsibility'".[117]

In doing so, the FCC emphasises the democratic elements of the *Meroni doctrine*, which are reflected above all in the requirement of responsibility. A further limitation of powers—here too, the court refers to the *ESMA decision*—is to be achieved by procedural safeguards such as consultation, notification and review requirements, whereby considerable importance is attached in particular to judicial review by the CJEU.[118] In this respect too, a reference to democratic requirements is persuasive. The legislator's procedural steering options provide a representative democratic basis and enable forms of *ex-post* control. In addition, judicial control mentioned above forms a component of the accountability concept.

In principle, this could also allow the delegation of tasks and powers with a wider range of discretion, as called for in the literature,[119] provided that adequate mechanisms of democratic embedment are provided for.[120] With regard to the control of agency action, *Craig* emphasised *inter alia* the importance of judicial control, procedural law, specification of the scope of tasks, appointment and reporting obligations and parliamentary influence.[121] This paves the way for European administrative bodies which are at least partially independent, but which are bound by accountability mechanisms and other forms of control back to the objectives set out in their legal basis.

4.4.4 European Banking Authority

The EBA, which competes with the ECB in the area of banking regulation, is proving to be a reference model for independent bodies established by secondary legislation. Established on the basis of Art. 114(1) TFEU, the EBA is intended in particular to contribute to the harmonisation of supervisory rules by "assisting competent national supervisory authorities in the consistent interpretation and application of Union rules and contributing to financial stability necessary for financial integration".[122] The main tasks of EBA[123] are therefore two main groups, on the one hand, to contribute to the establishment of high-quality common regulatory and

---

[117]Ibid.

[118]Ibid.

[119]Also in this direction Priebe (1979), pp. 113–114; Berger (1999), pp. 89–91; Groß (2005), p. 66; Kohtamäki (2014), p. 332; Manger-Nestler and Böttner (2019), p. 75.

[120]Cf. Vos (2016), p. 227.

[121]Craig (2018), pp. 194–197.

[122]Recital 17 s. 3 EBAR.

[123]Art. 8(1)(a)-(l) EBAR.

supervisory standards[124] and the development of a Union supervisory handbook (single rule book) on the supervision of financial institutions,[125] and, on the other hand, to contribute to the consistent application of legally binding Union acts, in particular by building a common supervisory culture, ensuring consistent, efficient and effective application of the legislative acts, preventing regulatory arbitrage, fostering and monitoring supervisory independence, mediating and settling disagreements between competent authorities, ensuring effective and consistent supervision of financial institutions, ensuring a coherent functioning of colleges of supervisors and taking actions, *inter alia*, in emergency situations.[126]

In order to carry out its tasks, the EBA has been given specific powers. In particular, it drafts regulatory technical standards[127] and implementing standards,[128] issues guidelines and recommendations,[129] but also takes (individual) decisions vis-à-vis national supervisory authorities[130] and financial institutions.[131] In the course of the last ESA reform (2019), the issue of questions and answers (Q&A) has also been included in the EBA's toolbox.[132]

With regard to independence, it should first of all be stressed that the EBA, as an agency, has its own legal personality[133] and is thus institutionally separate, especially from the Commission.

In addition, the EBA and their bodies are granted a high degree of personal and substantive independence.[134] This applies in particular to the main decision-making body of the EBA, the Board of Supervisors,[135] which consists of the Chairperson of the EBA, the heads of the national banking supervisory authorities, one representative of each of the Commission, the ESRB and the two other EU supervisory authorities (ESMA, EIOPA), and a representative appointed by the ECB's Supervisory Board, but with voting rights only for the heads of the national supervisory authorities and, since the ESA reform (2019), for the Chairperson of the EBA.[136]

This independence of the members of the Board of Supervisors is established in several ways, albeit not constitutionally and thus not as strong as ECB independence. Firstly, they "shall act independently and objectively in the sole interest of the Union as a whole and shall neither seek nor take instructions from Union institutions

---

[124] Art. 8(1)(a) EBAR.

[125] Art. 8(1)(aa) EBAR.

[126] Art. 8(1)(b) EBAR.

[127] Arts. 8(2)(a), 10 EBAR.

[128] Arts. 8(2)(b), 15 EBAR.

[129] Arts. 8(2)(c)(d), 16, 17(3) EBAR.

[130] Arts. 8(2)(e), 18(3), 19(3) EBAR.

[131] Arts. 8(2)(f), 17(6), 18(4), 19(4) EBAR.

[132] Arts. 8(2)(ga), 16b EBAR.

[133] Art. 5(1) EBAR.

[134] See Art. 1(5) sub-para. 4 s. 1 EBAR.

[135] Art. 6 No. 1 EBAR in conjunction with Art. 43 EBAR; for the other bodies, see Nos. 2-5.

[136] Art. 40(1) EBAR.

or bodies, from any government or from any other public or private body".[137] In addition, "Member States, Union institutions or bodies, and any other public or private body, shall not seek to influence the members of the Board of Supervisors in the performance of their tasks".[138,139] These regulations were obviously modelled after Art. 130 TFEU and are intended to eliminate influence by political and economic players for each individual body of EBA.[140]

Despite this extensive substantive independence of the members of the Board of Supervisors, personal independence is not particularly pronounced. For the voting members, there are only protective provisions for the Chairperson, in particular the 5-year term of office which may be extended once[141] as well as integrity rules.[142] Furthermore, the Chairperson can be removed from office only for serious reasons, which is procedurally hedged by the competence of the European Parliament for such a removal, following a decision of the Council, adopted after consulting the Board of Supervisors.[143] There are no comparable protective provisions for the heads of national banking supervisory authorities. However, the requirement for the Member States to refrain from exercising any influence is likely to preclude dismissal decisions based on the performance of tasks under the EBA.

Although the EBA is to be classified as an institution between Union and Member State administration due to the dominance of Member State representatives in the decision-making body,[144] there should nevertheless be no channels of influence for Member State interest groups, but European financial supervision should be strengthened through the institutionalised integration of national expertise. For EBA this has been achieved in that, unlike other European agencies and thus comparable to the ECB, the CJEU and the Commission, it consists of personally independent members rather than mere representatives.[145]

However, EBA is criticised for the fact that governance is dominated by national authorities and thus national interests and perspectives find their way into the process of regulation and supervision, with the result that decision-making tends to be guided by the common interest of the majority rather than the Union interest.[146] This logic has not been fundamentally altered by the double majority requirement introduced with the establishment of the ECB supervision in order to avoid dominance of the authorities participating in the SSM.[147]

---

[137] Art. 42(1) EBAR.

[138] Art. 42(2) EBAR.

[139] Regarding the other bodies, see Arts. 46, 49(1), (2), 52(1), (2), 59(1) EBAR.

[140] Zilioli (2016), p. 156, n. 144, who considers this multiple coverage not necessary.

[141] Art. 48(3) EBAR.

[142] Art. 49(3) EBAR.

[143] Art. 48(5) EBAR.

[144] In general Dehousse (2016), pp. 70–72; Vos (2016), pp. 212 et seq.

[145] See Vos (2016), pp, 218 et seq.; Ritleng (2016a), pp. 9 et seq.

[146] Cf. Ortino (2017), pp. 310 et seq.

[147] See Art. 44 EBAR; for details Gurlit (2014), p. 16.

Since the ESA reform (2019), EBA's independence vis-à-vis third parties, both public and private, is further ensured by the fact that the members of the Board of Supervisors, the Chairperson as well as non-voting representatives and observers participating in the meetings of the Board of Supervisors shall, before such meetings, accurately and completely declare the absence or existence of any interest which might be considered prejudicial to their independence in relation to any items on the agenda, and shall abstain from participating in the discussion of, and voting upon, such points.[148] In addition, the Chairperson shall make public all meetings held with external stakeholders within a period of two weeks following the meeting and any hospitality received.[149]

Complementary to this far-reaching independence, however, is the need for democratic embedment. This is particularly true in view of the fact that the EBA not only sets abstract and general standards, but can also intervene (as ultima ratio) in the rights of the Member States or their authorities and of market participants entitled to fundamental rights. There are therefore crucial limits to the independence of the EBA.

Although the EBA has a wide range of powers in the field of banking regulation, some of these are linked back to the Commission. Although the EBA is not subject to supervision *("Rechts- und Fachaufsicht")* in the narrower sense,[150] the technical regulatory and implementing standards are adopted by the Commission in accordance with Arts. 290, 291 TFEU. Furthermore, the EU institutions, above all the Commission, are involved in the procedure for adopting intervention measures under Art. 17 and Art. 18 EBAR and thus enable control.[151] In this context it should also be mentioned that decisions of the EBA are subject to appeal under Art. 60 EBAR, which is decided on by the Board of Appeal, which is also endowed with independence and even impartiality.[152] Moreover, there is legal protection in so far as decisions of the EBA, more precisely of the Board of Appeal or, in the absence of a right of appeal, of the authority, are subject to control by the CJEU.[153]

The accountability of the EBA is also of great importance, which was noticeably expanded in the course of the ESA reform (2019) and has obviously borrowed from the accountability framework of the ECB's Supervisory Board.[154,155] Although EBA is accountable to the European Parliament and the Council,[156] those bodies

[148] Art. 42(3) EBAR; see also Art. 42(4) EBAR.

[149] Art. 49a s. 1 EBAR.

[150] Cf. Häde (2011), pp. 663–664.

[151] Cf. Ortino (2017), p. 312, who considers this to be above all a Union counterbalance to a Member State dominated decision-making.

[152] Art. 59 EBAR. See Zilioli (2016), p. 156, n. 144, who explains the additional guarantee of impartiality with the quasi-judicial function of the Board of Appeal.

[153] Art. 61 EBAR.

[154] Art. 3 EBAR.

[155] Cf. Repasi (2020), para. 17.74.

[156] Arts. 3(1) s. 1, 2(2)(b) EBAR.

regularly lack hard sanctioning and overriding instruments in line with the concept of democratic accountability. Only with regard to the EBA's rule-making capacity, the representative bodies have certain powers, as the European Parliament or the Council can object to regulatory technical standards according to Art. 13(1) EBAR and revoke the delegation of power according to Art. 12(1) EBAR. Control, which at the same time limits the financial independence of the EBA, is also provided by the rights of the European Parliament and the Council in the establishment of the budget.[157]

4.5 Consequences for Central Bank Action

Not only the ECB, but also other European institutions, bodies, offices and agencies of the Union are endowed with independence. In addition to institutional arrangements and the prohibition of material influence, in particular through instructions, personnel provisions play an important role here, which are intended to protect against improper influence through the implementation of longer terms of office and dismissal under exceptional conditions.

Despite common features in the independence norms, the specific function of the respective institutions must be taken into account. This provides indications of their performance potential, but also of their vulnerability to external influence.

In comparison with the CJEU, it is particularly striking that its independence is primarily determined by the commitment of the courts to the rule of law. This implies that the actions of the courts can be guided more strongly by legal provisions than those of the ECB, which enjoys considerable material scope for action, at least in the area of the stability objective. At the same time, reporting and accountability requirements do not prove to be the optimal instrument to constrain the action of the courts.

In contrast, there are functional parallels to the Commission, at least in so far as the ECB, at least in its supervisory function, is also more likely to be regarded as an administrative authority in the sense of an actor who enforces rules. The independence of the Commission, which also enjoys considerable power to shape policy in some cases, is nevertheless significantly weaker, which is mainly due to direct and sanctionable parliamentary responsibility.

There are also parallels in the relationship between the ECA and the ECB. From a functional point of view, however, it is important to bear in mind that the activities of the ECA mainly relate to opinions and recommendations and therefore do not directly affect certain legal interests.

The independence of the ECB must therefore be regarded as extremely widespread in relation to the other institutions. This is due to the fact that, on the one hand, the ECB has a wide scope for policy-making and powers to intervene in

[157] Arts. 63, 64 EBAR; for details see Repasi (2020), para. 17.91.

individual legal interests and, on the other hand, there is no direct parliamentary accountability characterised by harsh sanctions. In addition, its tasks are performed within a European system, which is characterised by guarantees of independence under European law in favour of the NCBs/NCAs as national institutions and by the ECB's power of leadership in the system. This shields the entire system even more strongly from external, above all Member State, influences.

In the relationship of the ECB to secondary law bodies, it is striking that these may also be characterised by independence-related provisions. However, it should be noted that the *Meroni doctrine*, as currently formulated by the ECJ, sets certain limits, which in particular prevent the establishment of largely independent institutions. This requires a stronger link to the Union's institutions, which can be established, for example, through rights of final decision as well as rights of consent and approval.

Nevertheless, it should be criticised that the discussion is only about the legal embedding of bodies established under secondary legislation and therefore ends with the allocation of decision-making powers to the European institutions. The fact that the actions of the European institutions, especially independent ones, also require democratic authorisation was rightly emphasised in the FCC's *Banking Union decision*, thus placing the *Meroni debate* in the context of a European principle of democracy. The decision states:

> Thus, there are no fundamental objections to the establishment of independent agencies; however, such practice remains precarious in light of the principle of democracy. At least where institutions, bodies, offices and agencies of the European Union drift towards a complete disconnect from democratic oversight, they come up against the limits of the EU's principle of democracy. This also applies to the ECB.[158]

However, this prohibits an all too formal approach that places too much emphasis on the European hierarchy of norms. Rather, an examination of other European standards of independence supports the finding that the reasons for guaranteeing independence must always be considered and that the nature and scope of control mechanisms are also decisive. Therefore, the concrete action in question must always be subjected to a functional consideration which identifies the level of independence and legitimation required in the individual case and therefore determines the design of decision-making bodies, depending on the task to be performed and the powers available for this purpose.[159]

This can mean that the mechanisms of legal embedment modernised within the context of the *ESMA decision* can also become important for the ECB's actions precisely in so far as the independence of the ECB is not justified by the mandate for price stability laid down in primary law. Taking into account the independence of European central banks, procedural requirements such as reporting, consultation and

[158]FCC, Banking Union, 30.7.2019, 2 BvR 1685/14 et al., paras. 138–139.

[159]See also Masing (2010), pp. 189–211, 218; Ruffert (2011), pp. 411–412; Manger-Nestler (2015), pp. 336–338; Orator (2017), pp. 372–373; Steinbach (2017), pp. 507 et seq.; in regard of central bank action see also Mersch (2017).

review obligations would therefore have to be thought through in a function-related way and examined with regard to their feasibility. The functional criteria already discussed can serve as criteria for the need for legitimation, i.e. the performance of the acting and monitoring bodies with regard to compliance with the specified objectives, the weight of the reasons for demanding independence, the fact that fundamental rights are affected and the existence of multi-target mandates and balancing decisions.

This should be supplemented by other mechanisms of democratic legitimation, accountability and control, which are reflected in European primary law and which are dealt with in the following chapter.

References

Berger M (1999) Vertraglich nicht vorgesehene Einrichtungen des Gemeinschaftsrechts mit eigener Rechtspersönlichkeit – Ihre Gründung und die Folgen für Rechtsschutz und Haftung. Nomos, Baden-Baden

Bovens M (2007) Analysing and assessing accountability – a conceptual framework. Eur Law J 13:447–468

Brentford P (1998) Constitutional aspects of the independence of the European Central Bank. Int Comp Law Quart 47:75–116

Busuioc M (2009) Accountability, control and independence – the case of European agencies. Eur Law J 15:599–615

Craig P (2018) EU administrative law, 3rd edn. Oxford University Press, Oxford

Dehousse R (2016) The politics of delegation in the European Union. In: Ritleng D (ed) Independence and legitimacy in the institutional system of the European Union. Oxford University Press, Oxford, pp 57–82

Gärditz KF (2010) Die Verwaltungsdimension des Lissabon-Vertrages. Die Öffentliche Verwaltung, pp 453–465

Gentzsch M (2020) Die EZB ultra vires? – Die PSPP-Entscheidung und ihre Konsequenzen für das Recht der Währungsunion. Zeitschrift für Bank- und Kapitalmarktrecht, pp 576–585

Groß T (2005) Die Kooperation zwischen europäischen Agenturen und nationalen Behörden. Europarecht, pp 54–68

Groß T (2014) Ist die Wirtschaftskrise ein Katalysator für das Entstehen unabhängiger Behörden? – Reformen der Bankaufsicht im Vergleich. Die Verwaltung 47:197–219

Gurlit E (2014) The ECB's relationship to the EBA, Europäische Zeitschrift für Wirtschaftsrecht Beilage, pp 14–18

Häde U (2011) Jenseits der Effizienz – Wer kontrolliert die Kontrolleure? – Demokratische Verantwortlichkeit und rechtsstaatliche Kontrolle der europäischen Finanzaufsichtsbehörden. Europäische Zeitschrift für Wirtschaftsrecht, pp 662–665

Heisenberg D, Richmond AL (2002) Supranational institution-building in the European Union – a comparison of the European Court of Justice and the European Central Bank. J Eur Public Policy 9:201–218

Herdegen M (2016) Der Verordnungsvorschlag der EU-Kommission zur Schaffung eines Europäischen Einlagenversicherungssystems – Würdigung aus europa- und staatsrechtlicher Sicht. Wertpapier-Mitteilungen (Zeitschrift für Wirtschafts- und Bankrecht), pp 1857–1865, 1905–1911

Jacqué JP (2016) Lost in transition – the European Commission between intergovernmentalism and integration. In: Ritleng D (ed) Independence and legitimacy in the institutional system of the European Union. Oxford University Press, Oxford, pp 15–56

Kohtamäki N (2014) Die ESMA darf Leerverkäufe regeln – Anmerkung zum Urteil des EuGH vom 22. Januar 2014. Europarecht, pp 321–332

Kotzur M (2017) Kommentierung zu Art. 298 AEUV. In: Geiger R, Khan D-E, Kotzur M (eds) EUV/AEUV – Kommentar, 6th edn. Beck, Munich

Lehmann M (2017) Varying standards of judicial scrutiny over central bank actions. In: ECB, Legal Conference 2017 – shaping a new legal order for Europe: a tale of crises and opportunities, Frankfurt a.M., pp 112–132. https://www.ecb.europa.eu/pub/pdf/other/ecblegalconferenceproceedings201712.en.pdf (26 February 2021)

Lupia A (2006) Delegation and its perils. In: Strøm K, Müller WC, Bergman T (eds) Delegation and accountability in parliamentary democracies, 2nd edn. Oxford University Press, Oxford, pp 33–54

Majone G (1998) Europe's 'democratic deficit' – the question of standards. Eur Law J 4:5–28

Manger-Nestler C (2015) EU-Agenturen als Ausdruck des europäischen Demokratiemangels? Zeitschrift für Europäische Studien, pp 315–346

Manger-Nestler C, Böttner R (2019) Der Europäische Währungsfonds nach den Plänen der Kommission. Zeitschrift für ausländisches öffentliches Recht und Völkerrecht, pp 43–84

Masing J (2010) Unabhängige Behörden und ihr Aufgabenprofil. In: Masing J, Marcou G (eds) Unabhängige Regulierungsbehörden – Organisationsrechtliche Herausforderungen in Frankreich und Deutschland. Mohr Siebeck, Tübingen, pp 181–219

Mersch Y (2017) Central bank independence revisited, Keynote at the "Symposium on Building the Financial System of the 21st Century: An Agenda for Europe and the United States", Frankfurt a.M., 30 March 2017. https://www.ecb.europa.eu/press/key/date/2017/html/sp170330.en.html (26 February 2021)

Michel K (2015) Institutionelles Gleichgewicht und EU-Agenturen – Eine Analyse unter besonderer Berücksichtigung der European Banking Authority. Duncker & Humblot, Berlin

Müller WC, Bergman T, Strøm K (2006) Parliamentary democracy – promise and problems. In: Strøm K, Müller WC, Bergman T (eds) Delegation and accountability in parliamentary democracies, 2nd edn. Oxford University Press, Oxford, pp 3–32

Ohler C (2014) Anmerkung zum Urteil des EuGH v. 22.1.2014, Rs. C-270/12 (ESMA). Juristenzeitung, pp 249–252

Orator A (2017) Möglichkeiten und Grenzen der Einrichtung von Unionsagenturen. Mohr Siebeck, Tübingen

Ortino M (2017) Negative democratic externalities in the European banking system. In: Daniele L, Simone P, Cisotta R (eds) Democracy in the EMU in the aftermath of the crisis. Springer, Heidelberg, pp 299–317

Priebe R (1979) Entscheidungsbefugnisse vertragsfremder Einrichtungen im Europäischen Gemeinschaftsrecht. Nomos, Baden-Baden

Reithmann U (2015) Kommentierung zu Art. 298 AEUV. In: von der Groeben H, Schwarze J, Hatje A (eds) Europäisches Unionsrecht, 7th edn. Nomos, Baden-Baden

Repasi R (2020) Chapter 17 European Parliament and national parliaments. In: Amtenbrink F, Herrmann C (eds) The EU law of Economic and Monetary Union. Oxford University Press, Oxford, pp 456–506

Ritleng D (2016a) Introduction. In: Ritleng D (ed) Independence and legitimacy in the institutional system of the European Union. Oxford University Press, Oxford, pp 1–14

Ritleng D (2016b) The independence and legitimacy of the European Court of Justice. In: Ritleng D (ed) Independence and legitimacy in the institutional system of the European Union. Oxford University Press, Oxford, pp 83–124

Ritleng D (2016c) Does the European Court of Justice take democracy seriously? – some thoughts about the Macro-Financial Assistance case. Common Mark Law Rev 53:11–33

Ruffert M (2011) Die neue Unabhängigkeit – Zur demokratischen Legitimation von Agenturen im europäischen Verwaltungsrecht. In: Müller-Graff P-C, Schmahl S, Skouris V (eds) Europäisches Recht zwischen Bewährung und Wandel – Festschrift für Dieter H. Scheuing. Nomos, Baden-Baden, pp 399–414

Saurer J (2017) Kommentierung zu Art. 298 AEUV. In: Pechstein M, Nowak C, Häde U (eds) Frankfurter Kommentar zu EUV, GRC und AEUV. Mohr Siebeck, Tübingen

Selmayr M (2015) Kommentierung zu Art. 282 AEUV. In: von der Groeben H, Schwarze J, Hatje A (eds) Europäisches Unionsrecht, 7th edn. Nomos, Baden-Baden

Smits R (2017) From subordinated to prominent – the role of the European Commission in EMU – reflections on euro area democracy. In: Daniele L, Simone P, Cisotta R (eds) Democracy in the EMU in the aftermath of the crisis. Springer, Heidelberg, pp 51–71

Steinbach A (2017) Das behördliche Unabhängigkeitsparadigma im Wirtschaftsverwaltungsrecht – Eine funktionell-rechtliche Betrachtung. Die Verwaltung 50:507–536

Stelkens U (2012) Art. 291 AEUV, das Unionsverwaltungsrecht und die Verwaltungsautonomie der Mitgliedstaaten – zugleich zur Abgrenzung der Anwendungsbereiche von Art. 290 und Art. 291 AEUV. Europarecht, pp 511–545

Strøm K (2006) Parliamentary democracy and delegation. In: Strøm K, Müller WC, Bergman T (eds) Delegation and accountability in parliamentary democracies, 2nd edn. Oxford University Press, Oxford, pp 55–106

Vogiatzis N (2019) The independence of the European Court of Auditors. Common Mark Law Rev 56:667–701

Vos E (2016) EU agencies and independence. In: Ritleng D (ed) Independence and legitimacy in the institutional system of the European Union. Oxford University Press, Oxford, pp 206–227

Waldhoff C (2016) Kommentierung zu Art. 286 AEUV. In: Calliess C, Ruffert M (eds) EUV/AEUV, 5th edn. Beck, Munich

Weiß W (2016) Dezentrale Agenturen in der EU-Rechtsetzung. Europarecht, pp 631–665

Zilioli C (2016) The independence of the European Central Bank and its new banking supervisory competences. In: Ritleng D (ed) Independence and legitimacy in the institutional system of the European Union. Oxford University Press, Oxford

Zilioli C (2017) Justiciability of central banks' decisions and the imperative to respect fundamental rights, in: ECB, Legal Conference 2017 – shaping a new legal order for Europe: a tale of crises and opportunities, Frankfurt a.M., pp 91–103. https://www.ecb.europa.eu/pub/pdf/other/ecblegalconferenceproceedings201712.en.pdf (26 February 2021)

Chapter 5
Democratic Legitimation and Control of Central Bank Action

After describing various dimensions of central bank independence in functional terms and comparing them with other implementations of independence in Union law, further mechanisms shall be found to ensure democratic legitimation and control. Although accountability is an important counterbalance, it should not be narrowed down. Rather, the principles of democracy as reflected in the Treaties should be examined for their potential to constrain the administration in general and the ECB action in particular. The principle of democracy enshrined in the national constitutional provision of Art. 20(1), (2) GG and the requirements derived from it by the FCC should also be considered in order to determine their potential for democratising the European administration.

In addition, consideration should be given to the extent to which greater democratic legitimation and control of central bank actions can also be established *de lege ferenda*. This does not necessarily have to be accompanied by a curtailment of independence, but can even strengthen it, depending on the type and extent of the instruments.

The debate itself is not a new one. The establishment of independent administrative authorities is being discussed for numerous legal systems and gains particular importance in the supranational, multi-level governance system of the EU.[1]

The common goal of the various approaches can be seen as being to tie the actions of independent institutions back to the objectives intended with their establishment through adequate regulations and arrangements. Access via principal-agent theory shows the need for *ex ante* and *ex post* control mechanisms to reduce agency loss, in particular regarding moral hazard and adverse selection.[2] Moreover, there are accountability concepts in the literature which attempt to contain central bank actions by means of numerous mechanisms. In this respect, *Amtenbrink* is influential

[1] See for example the articles in Caranta et al. (2004).

[2] Cf. Majone (1998), pp. 13–16; Lupia (2006), pp. 44–51; Strøm (2006), pp. 67–73; Lettanie (2019), pp. 322–323.

C. Manger-Nestler, M. Gentzsch, *Democratic Legitimation of Central Bank Independence in the European Union*, https://doi.org/10.1007/978-3-030-75115-9_5

in that he has identified eight criteria which, taken together, make it possible to assess democratic accountability.[3] The following study builds on this, but aims to establish even stronger links to the principles of democracy.

5.1 Democracy-Related Provisions in the Treaties Embedding Central Bank Independence

5.1.1 Representation

As already demonstrated the EU is based on the principle of representative democracy (Art. 10(1) TEU), which is further detailed in a dual legitimation concept (Art. 10(2) TEU). This, together with the principle of institutional balance enshrined in Art. 13(1), (2) TEU, forms the normative basis for a concept of political, administrative and judicial accountability, in which democratic responsibility is established not by mere formal relations but by the existence and effective functioning of institutional control mechanisms.

This is complemented by the ECJ's statements of democratic principles on the containment of independent bodies.[4] Indeed, the context of the *Data Protection Authorities decision*, which was concerned with the national, German administrative organisation, must be taken into account.

Nevertheless, the ECJ gave its opinion on the democratic principle of the Union, so that in the following it will be determined to what extent further conclusions can be drawn from this for the democratic embedding of central bank action.

Literature has sometimes pointed out that the transfer of monetary policy to the ECB is a transfer of powers rather than a delegation.[5] However, this does not alter the fact that the democratic provisions of the Treaties are, by law, on a par with central bank independence and can therefore set limits on it.

5.1.1.1 Legal Basis and Binding Effect of Law

According to the ECJ, it is important that the existence and conditions of operation of independent authorities are regulated by the law or by the Constitution and that those authorities are required to comply with the law.[6] In view of the possible parliamentary influence, the ECJ emphasises the legislator's competence to define

[3] Amtenbrink (1999), pp. 41–59 with reference to Eijffinger and de Haan (1996), p. 15; Gormley and de Haan (1996), pp. 97 et seq; following on this Lastra (2015), para. 2.178; Zilioli (2016a), p. 131, n. 23.

[4] See supra Sect. 2.3.4.

[5] Zilioli and Selmayr (2001), pp. 13 et seq; Zilioli (2016a), p. 130, n. 16.

[6] ECJ, Data Protection Authorities, 9.3.2010, ECLI:EU:C:2010:125, para. 42.

the powers of these authorities.[7] This particular role of the legal basis for democratic control of central bank actions was also highlighted by *Amtenbrink*, who referred to both *exante* control (through parliamentary rules) and *expost* control (through changes resulting from certain behaviour).[8]

The first characteristic pointed out by the ECJ can be understood as an institutional reservation of the law ("*institutioneller Gesetzesvorbehalt*"), according to which the establishment and organisation of independent authorities must be decided by the legislator. The second characteristic ensures that the actions of the authorities are linked to the legal basis and thus to the representative institutions. The third characteristic underlines the possibilities for representative bodies to exert *ex ante* influence on decisions to be taken by the authorities by defining the framework for action.

This concept seems suitable at least for the establishment of "secondary bodies" of Union law, but is subject to certain restrictions with regard to the Union's institutions. For here it must be noted that the institutions have already been established under primary law and have been given guarantees of independence, and that in the functionally structured Union legal order all institutions are endowed with certain competences. The representative institutions, the European Parliament and the Council, but also the ECB, must therefore comply with the powers conferred on them by the Treaties, without, in principle, any one institution having priority.

Nevertheless, the ECB offers scope for differentiation in view of the range of its tasks. In this respect, it should be noted that the ECB and the Eurosystem have been granted exclusive competence only in the field of monetary policy. Therefore, a revision of the Treaties would be necessary in order to realise the demand put forward in the literature that the political institutions should determine the objectives of monetary policy.[9]

Nevertheless, the representative institutions do have certain competences in the field of monetary law, in particular the basis for authorisation in Art. 133(1) TFEU, according to which the European Parliament and the Council, acting in accordance with the ordinary legislative procedure, shall adopt the measures necessary for the use of the euro as the single currency.

In other areas, in particular in the field of banking supervision based on shared competence (*arg. ex* Art. 127(5), (6) TFEU), the European Parliament and the Council have more room for regulatory manoeuvre in terms of both procedural and substantive law. This applies in particular to the SSM which has been established on the basis of Art. 127(6) TFEU, which can be amended or abolished

---

[7]ECJ, Data Protection Authorities, 9.3.2010, ECLI:EU:C:2010:125, para. 44. However, this raises the question to which extent the necessary guarantees of independence under Union law preclude normative regulation *(„normative Regulierung")* by the Member States, in particular by governments, but also by parliaments. With respect to the electricity and natural gas sectors, the Advocate General recently argued in favor of far-reaching independence of national regulatory authorities from any advance structuring by the national legislature *(„Vorstrukturierung")*, Advocate General Pitruzzella, Internal markets for electricity and natural gas, 14.1.2021, ECLI:EU:C:2021:20, paras. 85 et seq.

[8]Amtenbrink (1999), p. 42.

[9]Amtenbrink (1999), pp. 364–365; recently De Boer and van't Klooster (2020), pp. 1721–1722.

by the Council at any time. The Capital Requirements Regulation (CRR)[10] and the Capital Requirements Directive (CRD IV),[11] which are legal acts by the representative bodies, also determine the substantive law governing the ECB's supervisory activities.

5.1.1.2 Influence on Appointment Decisions

With regard to the relationship between the representative bodies and the members of the ECB's decision-making bodies called upon to take decisions, the influence on the selection of public officials plays a not inconsiderable role, also and precisely because *expost* sanctioning measures are eliminated regularly.

From the point of view of parliamentary influence, the ECJ has also stressed that the management of the supervisory authorities may be appointed by the parliament or the government.[12] *Amtenbrink* also attributes the appointment of central bank officials to democratic legitimation, whereby he also considers the allocation of appointment decisions to parliaments or governments to be relevant.[13]

With regard to the ECB and the members of its decision-making bodies, but also with regard to the members of the SSM Supervisory Board, it can be noted that both the Union and the Member State pillar of legitimation has been realised with regard to the appointment. The members of the Executive Board (President, Vice-President and four other members) are appointed by the European Council on a recommendation from the Council, after consulting the European Parliament and the Governing Council of the ECB, in accordance with Art. 11.2. sub-para. 1 ESCB/ECB Statute. With regard to the appointment of the Chair and the Vice-Chair of the SSM Supervisory Board, the role of the European Parliament is significantly enhanced. Its approval is required before the Council adopts an implementing decision on the appointment.[14] However, this is somewhat relativised by the fact that the supervisory body also includes four representatives of the ECB, who are appointed by the ECB itself,[15] without any further involvement of the representative bodies of the Council and the Parliament.

Nevertheless, the personal legitimation of the Supervisory Board can serve as a model for a possible reform of the Governing Council. In view of the significant strengthening of the European Parliament under the Treaty of Lisbon, some voices in

[10]Regulation (EU) No 575/2013 of the European Parliament and of the Council of 26 June 2013 on prudential requirements for credit institutions and investment firms and amending Regulation (EU) No 648/2012, OJ 27.6.2013, L 176, p. 1.

[11]Directive 2013/36/EU of the European Parliament and of the Council of 26 June 2013 on access to the activity of credit institutions and the prudential supervision of credit institutions and investment firms, amending Directive 2002/87/EC and repealing Directives 2006/48/EC and 2006/49/EC, OJ 27.6.2013, L 176, p. 338.

[12]ECJ, Data Protection Authorities, 9.3.2010, ECLI:EU:C:2010:125, para. 44.

[13]Amtenbrink (1999), p. 49.

[14]Art. 26(3) ss. 1, 2 SSMR.

[15]Art. 26(5) s. 1 SSMR.

literature have also called for this requirement of approval to be applied to the appointment of the members of the ECB's Executive Board.[16]

As regards the other members of the Governing Council (the Governors of the NCBs) and the Supervisory Body (representatives of the NCAs), the Member State pillar of legitimation is realised. As there are no provisions on this matter in the Treaties, the ESCB/ECB Statute or the SSMR, it is up to the Member States to decide to what extent they ensure direct or indirect parliamentary involvement in the appointment process.

5.1.1.3 Improving Political Accountability

An important element of the principle of representative democracy is the substantive influence and control of the representative bodies, in particular parliaments. In this context, die ECJ underlined the relevance of the legislator imposing obligation to authorities to report their activities to the parliament,[17] which provides the basis for democratic accountability in the strictest sense.[18] Whether these mechanisms, which have already been presented, are actually effective depends on a variety of aspects.

Inter alia, the importance of inter-institutional agreements between the ECB and the European Parliament can be stressed, which involve regular exchanges between the members of the ECB's Executive Board and the members of the ECON committee.[19] This monetary dialogue, provides a platform for MEPs from various political groups and the President of the ECB not only to exchange views but also to defend their positions publicly.[20] In the case of the SSM, these mechanisms have been made even more normative (Art. 20, 21 SSMR), while the role of the national parliaments has also been strengthened. In this respect, it should also be considered to what extent the legal framework of the banking dialogue can serve as a model for a newly conceived monetary dialogue.[21]

However, political accountability also faces certain limitations. This applies in particular to the ability of parliaments to grasp and assess complex economic issues. Moreover, the confidentiality of information, which must be maintained not only to protect financial stability but also the fundamental rights of market participants, may conflict with far-reaching information requirements.[22] Moreover, the large number of actors in the field of monetary and fiscal policy as well as financial supervision (and banking resolution) may lead to a risk of diffusion of spheres of responsibility. For accountability to be effective, it is important that the representative bodies assign

[16]Cf. Peroni (2017), p. 260; Amtenbrink and Markakis (2019), pp. 14, 22.

[17]ECJ, Data Protection Authorities, 9.3.2010, ECLI:EU:C:2010:125, para. 45.

[18]See also Amtenbrink (1999), pp. 54–55.

[19]Amtenbrink (2019), p. 318.

[20]Ibid.

[21]See for example Fromage and Ibrido (2018), pp. 295 et seq.

[22]Cf. Maricut-Akbik (2020), p. 1211; see also Curtin (2017), pp. 37–38.

the respective areas of responsibility horizontally to the ECB in its monetary policy and supervisory function, the Commission, the ESM and the SRB, and vertically within the respective systems. Here, qualitative assessments, especially by *Amtenbrink* and *Markakis*,[23] have revealed some deficits.

Improvements in political accountability of the SSM were also recently identified by *Lamandini* and *Ramos Muñoz*. They not only demand proactivity in political accountability, also with a more intrusive and regular political control by the Chair and Vice-Chair of the European Parliament's ECON committee (at a selected subgroup of the Banking Union Working Group [BUWG]) under appropriate confidentiality, but also more coordination in the "multi-polar" administrative accountability, with enhanced recourse from the BUWG to technical opinions of the EBA as a source of expert judgment instrumental to political control.[24] This is supplemented by a better coordination with judicial, quasi-judicial and administrative review, to regularly channel and incorporate into the political and administrative accountability framework also the most controversial issues, which give rise to litigation, and the responses offered to them by courts or administrative review bodies.[25]

In principle, it is convincing that, in view of the principle of democracy, other control mechanisms are also taken into account, which ultimately ensure that the actions of the central bank are geared to the objectives described. Nevertheless, the respective functions of administrative, judicial and parliamentary control and the resources made available for this purpose must not be neglected.

For example, the increased involvement of the EBA and the ECA and the specific expertise assigned to them in the parliamentary control of the SSM may well be useful, particularly as it allows external experts to assess confidential information on a confidential basis.[26] At the same time, however, the requirements of the institutional balance in terms of allocation of competences must be respected and, moreover, the control functions thus assigned must be covered by an adequate accountability framework and brought into line with the other tasks of these bodies. This also applies to any dialogue between parliaments and courts,[27] which has to preserve judicial independence and impartiality and in no case give the appearance of politically influenced jurisdiction.

5.1.1.4 Involvement of National Parliaments

In addition, the establishment of the SSM has provided further forms of political accountability by also involving national parliaments in the monitoring of the ECB

[23] Amtenbrink and Markakis (2019), pp. 3 et seq.

[24] Lamandini and Ramos Muñoz (2020), p. 10.

[25] Ibid.

[26] Lamandini and Ramos Muñoz (2020), pp. 41–42, 43–44.

[27] Lamandini and Ramos Muñoz (2020), p. 46.

pursuant to Art. 21 SSMR.[28] The fact that a Union institution is controlled by the national parliaments is a novelty, but it increases and improves the contribution of the national parliaments to the good functioning of the Union, as already provided for in Art. 12 TEU. The fact that the national parliaments lack the necessary instruments to monitor the actions of the Union bodies, in particular compliance with the principle of conferral under Art. 5(1) s. 1 TEU, has become obvious in the course of the *PSPP judgments*. Thus, the constitutional institutions/organs, like the Bundesregierung and the Bundestag, exercising their responsibility with regard to European integration *("Integrationsverantwortung")* could effectively only ensure ECB's compliance with its mandate by the participation of the Deutsche Bundesbank. Due to the FCC's *PSPP judgment*, the German central bank provided the necessary information to the Bundesregierung and, through the latter, also to the Bundestag in accordance with § 13(1) BBankG.[29] A direct accountability of the ECB towards national parliaments would be a *petitum* that would provide a legally sound basis for such a practice, which is not without risks with regard to the independence of the ECB and NCBs. However, this would require an amendment of the Treaties.

The control of the ECB in its supervisory function by the national parliaments was also underlined by the FCC in its *Banking Union decision*. In this context, Art. 21 SSMR is mentioned especially in the context of the democratic legitimation of the national authorities (Bundesanstalt für Finanzdienstleistungsaufsicht [BaFin] and Deutsche Bundesbank), namely as special rights to receive information, "ensuring that the Bundestag remains accountable to citizens regarding the activities of German supervisory authorities".[30] This is of decisive importance for democratic control in the multi-level governance system of the EU *("Verwaltungsverbund")*. In so far as the action of the national authorities is to some extent removed from the responsibility of the national governments by establishing independence from instructions and at the same time integrated into a system characterised by hierarchical elements,[31] the control of the European body by the national parliaments can also contribute to the control of the national authorities. This applies at least to the extent that the European body, like the ECB in the SSM, has responsibility for the effective and consistent functioning of the system,[32] while at the same time having rights of access and control, in particular rights of instruction and information.[33] If, in addition, this is supplemented by national accountability of national authorities, which is explicitly permitted under Art. 21(4) SSMR, parliamentary control would be established which, on the one hand, respects the independence of central banks

[28]See supra Sect. 3.3.1.4.1.

[29]See Gentzsch (2020), pp. 581–582.

[30]FCC, Banking Union, 30.7.2019, 2 BvR 1685/14 et al., para. 224, see also para. 230.

[31]See supra Sect. 4.5.

[32]Art. 6(1) s. 2 SSMR.

[33]Art. 6(2), (3), (5)(a) SSMR.

and, on the other hand, takes into account the specificities of European administration.

5.1.2 *Participation*

Apart from the principle of representative democracy, the Treaties contain other important democratic principles in Title II TEU. These include in particular the participation of the citizens of the Union as well as openness and transparency. According to Art. 11(1) TEU, the institutions shall, by appropriate means, give citizens and representative associations the opportunity to make known and publicly exchange their views in all areas of Union action. Pursuant to Art. 11(2) TEU, the institutions shall maintain an open, transparent and regular dialogue with representative associations and civil society. Moreover, Art. 11(3) TEU provides, that the Commission shall carry out broad consultations with parties concerned in order to ensure that the Union's actions are coherent and transparent. Not to be left unmentioned is the institute of the European Citizens' Initiative, which is laid down in Art. 11(4) TEU.

The EU's understanding of democracy expressed in these rules finds its vanishing point in the individual citizens of the Union, who are also the subject of legitimation, at least for the Union's pillar of legitimation. Its strong position is not only systematically expressed by the fact that Art. 9 TEU stands at the beginning of democratic principles. Rather, the non-existence of any kind of Union people leads to the fact that self-determination as a basic democratic value loses its collective character and instead refers to the individual's possibilities of influence.[34] The participation of Union citizens thus becomes a cornerstone of a pluralistic Union-democratic concept of legitimation.

In this way, participatory theories of democracy are given normative expression, which are represented in numerous facets in political science.[35] Particularly worthy of mention here are participatory democracy, which presupposes a high and, if possible, increasing number of participants and matters to be decided democratically and aims to exert an effective influence on political decisions, and deliberative democracy, which requires elaborate procedures of deliberation and decision-making and places reasoned political debate at the centre of participation.[36] In general, participatory and deliberative models of democracy must ensure that the central democratic ideas of self-determination and equality are implemented and

[34]See for example Zuleeg (1993), pp. 1071–1072; Peters (2001), pp. 657–660; Huber (2005), pp. 498–499, 503, 511.

[35]Cf. M. G. Schmidt (2019), pp. 228 et seq.; Petersen (2010), pp. 165–168; for a critical view see Peuker (2011), pp. 183–185, pp. 188–191.

[36]In summary M. G. Schmidt (2019), pp. 229, 233.

that, in the end, not a few people take over the authority's action for their particular interests.[37]

This has shown in particular public consultation on EU summer-time arrangements, in which the *Juncker* Commission gave European citizens, stakeholders and Member States the opportunity to comment on the existing summer-time arrangements and potential changes during July/August 2018.[38] As part of the methodological considerations for interpreting the results, the Commission pointed out that, unlike surveys, public consultations are not statistically representative and, as web-based ones, also have a self-selection bias of the respondents towards the views of those who choose to respond to the consultation against those who do not.

Although the number of respondents, at 4.6 million, including 99% of citizens, generated the largest amount of responses ever received in any Commission consultation, it should be noted that 70% of the replies came from Germany. Although a majority of 84% was in favour of abolishing the biannual daylight savings, this can hardly be characterised as a legitimating element for decisions based on it. The same applies to the public consultation launched by the Commission in September 2020 on whether one and two cent coins are useful or should be abolished.[39]

In addition, it must also be borne in mind that complex matters in particular can overwhelm the citizens, who will then focus solely on their own advantage.[40] Moreover, citizens have different levels of socio-economic resources, so that a high expenditure of time and resources in particular promotes political inequality.[41]

In January 2020, as part of the strategy review, the ECB also launched the project "ECB listens", which invites "euro area citizens and organisations to contribute ideas and comments on the way the central bank conducts its monetary policy within the framework set out by the Treaty on the Functioning of the European Union".[42] In addition to the planned series of events, which met organisational changes due to the COVID-19 pandemic and were mostly digital,[43] an online form was also provided for submitting proposals and comments.

Although such formats, if properly designed, can develop a great potential for gathering information, their function for democratic legitimation is rather limited.

This is especially due to the fact that, because of the particular importance of online formats, not all citizens of the Union have open access to them and therefore the democratic element of equality is not fully developed. Moreover, brainstorming

[37]Cf. von Bogdandy (2000), p. 33; Peuker (2011), p. 184.

[38]Commission Staff Working Document, Public Consultation on EU Summertime Arrangements of 12 September 2018, SWD(2018) 406 final.

[39]See https://ec.europa.eu/info/law/better-regulation/have-your-say/initiatives/12566-Uniform-rounding-rules-for-cash-payments (26 February 2021).

[40]Peuker (2011), p. 183.

[41]Cf. Peuker (2011), p. 184.

[42]ECB, Press Release of 24 February 2020a.

[43]See for example the event "Ihre Bundesbank hört zu" in November 2020, https://www.bundesbank.de/de/aufgaben/themen/bundesbank-hoert-zivilgesellschaftlichen-organisationen-zu-849296 (26 February 2021).

forums and forms do not appear to be suitable for exploring monetary policy in its various facets, such as economics, law, political science and social sciences. Moreover, central bank independence sets a limit to the extent that the participation of citizens and associations goes beyond mere discourse and creates real influence.

5.1.3 Transparency

The aspect of transparency is closely linked to the aspect of participation just described. For central banks, whose performance of tasks is determined to a considerable extent by the expectations of market participants, transparency takes on particular importance.[44] *Mersch*, for example, has formulated that "[t]ransparency is aimed at increasing the effectiveness of a central bank's policies by communicating them in real time, or even in advance, thus facilitating the public's understanding of the central bank's objectives, behaviour and decisions".[45]

According to Art. 11(2) TEU, the institutions shall maintain an open, transparent and regular dialogue with representative associations and civil society. This provision, which systematically adheres to democratic principles,[46] is reinforced by the fact that Art. 1(2) TEU already contains a commitment to transparency. According to that provision, the TEU marks a new stage in the process of creating an ever closer union among the peoples of Europe, in which decisions are taken as openly as possible and as closely as possible to the citizen. This is supplemented by Art. 15 TFEU. According to Art. 15(1) TFEU, the Union's institutions, bodies, offices and agencies shall conduct their work as openly as possible, in order to promote good governance and ensure the participation of civil society.

This is complemented by the right of citizens and residents of the EU to have access to documents of the Union's institutions, bodies, offices and agencies, subject to limits imposed by public or private interests.[47] Therefore, all of them shall ensure that their proceedings are transparent and shall elaborate in their Rules of Procedure specific provisions regarding access to their documents.[48]

In this context, it has to be mentioned that according to Art. 296(2) TFEU legal acts shall state the reasons on which they are based and shall refer to any proposals, initiatives, recommendations, requests or opinions required by the Treaties. Only when the reasons which led to the adoption of a measure are explained, parties concerned, in particular citizens and Member States, are in a position to control the

[44]In general Lastra (2015), paras. 2.183–2.186.

[45]Mersch (2017) with further references.

[46]Cf. Lenaerts (2013), pp. 300 et seq.

[47]Art. 15(3) sub-paras. 1, 2 TFEU.

[48]Art. 15(3) sub-para. 3 TFEU.

Union's institutions in the performance of their tasks.[49] The duty to state reasons thus fulfils an informative and thus transparent function.[50]

All in all, the disclosure of decision-making procedures and the subjects of decisions becomes an important component of the democratic legitimation of Union action, because it creates public control by the citizens of the Union, but also by other actors such as associations or the media.[51] It also enables citizens to make informed choices. The right of access to documents, but also the obligation to state reasons, are important requirements for central bank action, so that transparency can in principle have a legitimating effect.

5.1.3.1 Right of Access to Documents

With regard to the right of access to documents, Art. 15(3) sub-para. 4 TFEU has to be observed, according to which the ECB as well as the CJEU and the European Investment Bank (EIB) shall be subject to this paragraph only when exercising their administrative tasks. The purpose of this provision is to protect the confidentiality of the judicial or monetary or financial activities of these institutions and bodies.[52] However, the interpretation is based on the premise that exceptions must in principle be interpreted narrowly, which in this case means a broad interpretation of the notion of "administrative activity".[53] In so far as the scope of application of Art. 15(3) TFEU extends, the right of access to documents is also protected by Art. 42 CFR. The fact that Art. 42 CFR does not grant any further-reaching rights within its scope of application is derived from Art. 52(2) CFR.

Notwithstanding the above, it should be noted that the principles and conditions for such access to documents need to be further defined, whereas Art. 15 (3) sub-para. 2 TFEU also recognises limits on grounds of public or private interest. While public access to European Parliament, Council and Commission documents is further specified in Regulation (EC) No. 1049/2001,[54] the ECB further elaborated public access to ECB documents in a decision of 4 March 2004 and amended it by decision of 21 January 2015 on the occasion of the establishment of the SSM.[55] In this decision, the ECB acknowledged that openness enhances the administration's

[49]Cf. ECJ, Commission/Council, 19.11.2013, ECLI:EU:C:2013:752, para. 98 with further references.

[50]Calliess (2016), para. 11.

[51]Cf. Curtin (2017), p. 39.

[52]Heselhaus (2017), Art. 15 TFEU para. 76.

[53]Ibid.

[54]Regulation (EC) No 1049/2001 of the European Parliament and of the Council of 30 May 2001 regarding public access to European Parliament, Council and Commission documents, OJ 31.5.2001, L 145, p. 43.

[55]Decision 2004/258/EC of the European Central Bank of 4 March 2004 on public access to European Central Bank documents (ECB/2004/3), OJ 18.3.2004, L 80, p. 42; last amended by Decision (EU) 2015/529 of the European Central Bank of 21 January 2015 amending Decision

legitimacy, effectiveness and accountability, thus strengthening the principles of democracy.[56]

At the same time, the ECB draws clear limitations which can already be deduced from the legal protection of the confidentiality by primary law, resulting from the limited scope of application of Art. 15(3) sub-para. 4 TFEU to the ECB as well as the obligation of professional secrecy according to Art. 37 ESCB/ECB Statute.[57]

Therefore, the exceptions in Art. 4 Decision 2004/258/EC, where the ECB refuses access to documents, are also extensive. These exceptions apply, for example, where disclosure would undermine the protection of public interests, for example in relation to the confidentiality of the proceedings of the ECB's decision-making bodies or the Supervisory Board, the financial, monetary or economic policy of the Union or a Member State, the internal finances of the ECB or of the NCBs, protecting the integrity of euro banknotes, the stability of the financial system in the Union or in a Member State, the Union's or a Member State's policy relating to the prudential supervision of credit institutions and other financial institutions, the purpose of supervisory inspections or the soundness and security of financial market infrastructures, payment schemes or payment service providers.[58] In addition to these public interests, the protection of privacy and the integrity of the individual, in particular in accordance with Union legislation regarding the protection of personal data also constitutes a ground for refusal.[59] The same applies for confidential information protected as such under Community law.[60]

More open is Art. Art. 4(2) Decision 2004/258/EC, as it includes a balancing clause. According to this provision, the ECB shall refuse access to a document where disclosure would undermine the protection of the commercial interests of a natural or legal person, including intellectual property, court proceedings and legal advice or the purpose of inspections, investigations and audits, unless there is an overriding public interest in disclosure. Moreover, documents preparing or reflecting the exchange of views with other institutions are also only accessible in the case of an overriding public interest in disclosure.[61]

Moreover, Art. 4(3) Decision 2004/258/EC contains rules on documents relating to deliberations, preliminary consultations and exchanges of views which, in principle, are not accessible even after the decision has been taken, unless there is an overriding public interest in disclosure.

ECB/2004/3 on public access to European Central Bank documents (ECB/2015/1), OJ 28.3.2015, L 84, p. 64.

[56]Recital 1 s. 1 Decision 2004/258/EC.

[57]See also Art. 27(1) SSMR.

[58]Art. 4(1)(a) Decision 2004/258/EC.

[59]Art. 4(1)(b) Decision 2004/258/EC.

[60]Art. 4(1)(c) Decision 2004/258/EC.

[61]Art. 4(3) Decision 2004/258/EC.

In the past, the CJEU has largely considered the ECB's refusal to disclose documents to be in conformity with Union law.[62] It is true that the EGC already held in its decision in the *Thesing/Bloomberg Finance case*, which concerned access to ECB documents relating to the public debt and deficit of the Hellenic Republic, that the exceptions to the right of access to documents referred to in Art. 4 Decision 2004/258/EC derogate from the right of access to documents and must therefore be strictly interpreted and applied.[63] It also stressed, with reference to the case law on Regulation 1049/2001, that where access to a document is refused, the ECB must explain how disclosure of the document would specifically and effectively undermine the interest protected by the supposed exception.[64] Furthermore, the EGC also set out requirements concerning the presumption of a risk of such an undermining, which must be reasonably foreseeable and not purely hypothetical.[65]

Nevertheless, as regards the public interest in protecting the economic policy of the Union or of a Member State under Art. 4(1)(a) 2nd indent Decision 2004/258/EC, the EGC considered, while limiting the scope of its judicial review, that the ECB enjoys "a wide discretion for the purpose of determining whether the disclosure of documents relating to the fields covered by that exception could undermine the public interest".[66]

Also, the protection of confidentiality of information according to Art. 4(1)(a) 1st indent, (c) Decision 2004/258/EC can be a significant constraint. This applies in particular to proceedings of the meetings of the ECB's Governing Council, which are confidential under Article 10.4. ESCB/ECB Statute, unless the Governing Council decides to make the outcome of its deliberations public. The ECJ has recently reinforced this by significantly reducing the requirements for the justification of refusals in the case of Art. 10.4 ESCB/ECB Statute.[67] These confidentiality requirements are also particularly relevant in the area of financial market and banking supervision,[68] where for the ECB as supervisory authority, Art. 53 CRD IV in the shape of the respective national implementing legislation is particularly relevant. In this respect, the ECJ's decision in the *Buccioni case* has made it clear that the ECJ attaches great importance to the protection of confidentiality with a view to the proper functioning of banking supervision[69] and that Art. 53 CRD IV, which

---

[62]See for instance ECJ, Espírito Santo Financial, 19.12.2019, ECLI:EU:C:2019:1117; EGC, Thesing/Bloomberg Finance, 29.11.2012, ECLI:EU:T:2012:635; Versorgungswerk der Zahnärztekammer Schleswig-Holstein, 4.6.2015, ECLI:EU:T:2015:361; Spiegel-Verlag Rudolf Augstein, 27.9.2018, ECLI:EU:T:2018:614; De Masi/Varoufakis, 12.3.2019, ECLI:EU:T:2019:154; see also Lamandini and Ramos Muñoz (2020), pp. 30–31.

[63]EGC, Thesing/Bloomberg Finance, 29.11.2012, ECLI:EU:T:2012:635, para. 41.

[64]EGC, Thesing/Bloomberg Finance, 29.11.2012, ECLI:EU:T:2012:635, para. 42.

[65]Ibid.

[66]EGC, Thesing/Bloomberg Finance, 29.11.2012, ECLI:EU:T:2012:635, para. 43.

[67]ECJ, Espírito Santo Financial, 19.12.2019, ECLI:EU:C:2019:1117, paras. 46, 54–55.

[68]For a comparative overview of the relevant secrecy rules see Smits and Badenhoop (2019), pp. 299–303.

[69]ECJ, Buccioni 13.9.2018, ECLI:EU:C:2018:717, paras. 21–28.

establishes the principle of protection of secrets, lists exceptions to the prohibition of disclosure exhaustively.[70]

However, even where exceptions are open to weighing of interests, the CJEU impose certain requirements as to the existence of an overriding public interest. In the *De Masi/Varoufakis case*, for example, the EGC recently held that the interest of citizens in reviewing the legality of the acts of the Union institutions is a general consideration and is therefore, not such as to demonstrate that the principle of transparency in the present case has a special urgency which could outweigh the reasons for refusing access to the document at issue.[71] In the *Thesing/Bloomberg Finance case*, the applicants alleged infringement of Art. 10 ECHR. Although the EGC drew a parallel with Art. 11 CFR on the basis of Art. 52(3) CFR,[72] it also emphasised the special nature of Art. 42 CFR with regard to access to documents of the institutions, bodies, offices and agencies of the Union.[73] In conclusion, the EGC denied an infringement of Art. 10 ECHR because the applicants did not sufficiently substantiate to what extent the ECB's rejection decision infringed their rights and to what extent the facts of the case were comparable to the designated decisions of the ECHR.[74] Although the decision cannot therefore be understood as a general refusal to grant more extensive rights of access to documents on the basis of specific fundamental rights guarantees, such as freedom of the press, it nevertheless reveals a reluctance to adopt rights of access to documents which go beyond the provisions of secondary legislation.[75]

On the whole, therefore, the right of access to documents is a right of control which is proving to be less effective in terms of democratic control.[76] Even in the case of an amendment to primary law, which removes the excessively general limitation of the scope in Art. 15(3) sub-para. 4 TFEU and thus strengthens democratic legitimation,[77] the sensitivity of the financial markets with regard to information and the degree of confidence in the subject matter are likely to prove to be major barriers to public control in the area of monetary policy and financial supervision.

5.1.3.2 Obligation to State Reasons

A strengthening of central bank transparency could also be achieved by focusing on the obligation to state reasons, as stated in Art. 296 sub-para. 2 TFEU for legal acts. This could be achieved, for example, by publishing the minutes of the meetings of

---

[70]ECJ, Buccioni 13.9.2018, ECLI:EU:C:2018:717, paras. 29–30.

[71]EGC, De Masi/Varoufakis, 12.3.2019, ECLI:EU:T:2019:154, para. 70.

[72]EGC, Thesing/Bloomberg Finance, 29.11.2012, ECLI:EU:T:2012:635, paras. 67–72.

[73]EGC, Thesing/Bloomberg Finance, 29.11.2012, ECLI:EU:T:2012:635, para. 73.

[74]EGC, Thesing/Bloomberg Finance, 29.11.2012, ECLI:EU:T:2012:635, paras. 73–81.

[75]Cf. Heselhaus (2017), Art. 42 CFR para. 4.

[76]For a critical view see also Leino-Sandberg (2019), pp. 195 et seq.

[77]See also the criticism at Wegener (2016), para. 14.

the Governing Council and its bodies,[78] as was done in the follow-up to the *PSPP decision*.[79] This offers the potential for controlling bodies as well as citizens or the media to better understand and evaluate the decisions. Nevertheless, it must be borne in mind that publication does of course have an influence on the deliberation process and the quality of decisions, and that the actors involved, especially members of the Governing Council, are influenced by the extent to which they are held to account at national level.[80] Although such *de facto* pressure is certainly not easily dismissed, a strong independence framework can help to prevent this.

In addition, with a view to monitoring proportionality, consideration should be given to further increasing the publication of information on alternative assessments carried out.[81] For instance, the account of the monetary policy meeting of the ECB's Governing Council in June 2020, published as a follow-up to the *PSPP decision*,[82] showed the dominance of the low interest rate environment over monetary policy room for manoeuvre, mainly due to the global decline in natural interest rates caused by demographic developments and low productivity growth. However, if certain side effects affect all potential monetary policy instruments, this also has an impact on the proportionality, in particular appropriateness, of the programmes, which the FCC has denied in the *PSPP case*.

The form of publication is also open to question. With regard to the obligation to state reasons, the ECJ in its *Weiss decision* not only referred to the PSPP decision itself including its recitals.[83] Moreover, the ECJ emphasised, that "various documents published by the ECB at the time when each of those decisions was adopted supplement the reasoning given in the decisions by setting out, in detail, the economic analyses underpinning the decisions, the various options considered by the Governing Council and the reasons justifying the choices made, in the light, in particular, of the observed and anticipated effects of the PSPP".[84] It has also been crucial that "the successive decisions of the ECB relating to the PSPP have consistently been clarified by the publication of press releases, introductory statements of the President of the ECB at press conferences, accompanied by answers to the questions raised by the press, and by the accounts of the ECB Governing Council's monetary policy meetings, which outline the discussions within that body".[85] Finally, the ECJ held that "[i]n addition to the various documents [...] mention can also be made of the publication, in the ECB's Economic Bulletin, of general

[78]Amtenbrink (1999), p. 365; Peroni (2017), pp. 259–260; Steinbach (2020); see also Amtenbrink (2019), p. 317; IMF (2013), pp. 7, 9.

[79]See supra Sect. 3.1.2.4.

[80]Dawson et al. (2019), pp. 82–83.

[81]Steinbach (2020).

[82]Available at https://www.ecb.europa.eu/press/accounts/2020/html/ecb.mg200625~fd97330d5f.en.html.

[83]ECJ, Weiss, 11.12.2018, ECLI:EU:C:2018:1000, para. 34.

[84]ECJ, Weiss, 11.12.2018, ECLI:EU:C:2018:1000, para. 36.

[85]ECJ, Weiss, 11.12.2018, ECLI:EU:C:2018:1000, para. 37.

analyses of the monetary situation in the euro area and of a number of specific studies dealing with the effects of the APP and the PSPP".[86]

However, it is suggested in the literature that the ECB should publish formal and public records of the decision-making process which go beyond mere press releases, press conferences and monthly bulletins.[87] More formalised reasoning is certainly to be welcomed, as it demonstrates the concrete considerations on which the ECB bases its decisions. A multitude of information, analyses, opinions and explanations may lead to a situation where the relationship between the bases for decisions is not always clear. Greater formalisation, while respecting the ECB's independence, could help to regulate the flow of information and at the same time allow for constant monitoring based on comparable parameters over time.

Whatever the form of the statement of reasons, however, it should be noted that, like the right of access to documents, the obligation provided for in Art. 296 (2) TFEU finds its limits in risks to protected legal interests, in particular the undermining of the ECB's objectives, and the confidentiality of information. The fact that too much information disclosed can lead to the material illegality of measures was made particularly clear in the *Weiss case*. In its order for reference, the FCC not only criticised the lack of "a specific statement of reasons regarding the necessity, scope and duration of the programme",[88] in particular a "reasoning [. . .] showing a balancing of the intended monetary policy effects of the PSPP with the additional foreseeable economic policy effects",[89] but also raised objections to the fact that the details concerning so-called blackout periods according to Art. 4 (1) Decision 2015/774 had not been published, not even *ex post*.[90]

With regard to the absence of any subsequent publication of details relating to the black-out period, the ECJ pointed out, somewhat contentiously that, "since the purpose of such publication would be to show the precise content of the measures adopted by the ESCB rather than the reasons justifying those measures, it cannot be required by virtue of the obligation to state reasons".[91]

More convincing is the argument raised by the FCC itself that "the disclosure of details on the mandatory minimum periods should not undermine the objective of market price formation".[92]

Even though the PSPP started 6 years ago (2021), it has not been terminated, but rather resumed and is far from being fully completed in view of an expected reinvestment phase after termination.[93] A particular challenge in this respect is compliance with Art. 123 (1) TFEU, which prohibits any monetary financing. In

---

[86]ECJ, Weiss, 11.12.2018, ECLI:EU:C:2018:1000, para. 40.

[87]Peroni (2017), pp. 259–260.

[88]FCC, PSPP (order for reference), 18.7.2017, 2 BvR 859/15 et al., para. 123.

[89]Ibid.

[90]FCC, PSPP (order for reference), 18.7.2017, 2 BvR 859/15 et al., paras 93–94.

[91]ECJ, Weiss, 11.12.2018, ECLI:EU:C:2018:1000, para. 43.

[92]FCC, PSPP (order for reference), 18.7.2017, 2 BvR 859/15 et al., paras 95.

[93]Cf. ECB, Press Release of 12 September 2019.

order to consider a purchase of government bonds on the secondary market not as the equivalent of an explicitly prohibited purchase on the primary market, the decision in the *Gauweiler case*, later confirmed in the *Weiss decision*, requires, *inter alia* that the potential purchasers of government bonds on the primary market do not know for certain "that the ESCB was going to purchase those bonds within a certain period and under conditions allowing those market operators to act, de facto, as intermediaries for the ESCB for the direct purchase of those bonds from the public authorities and bodies of the Member State concerned"[94] and that a programme is "such as to lessen the impetus of the Member States concerned to follow a sound budgetary policy".[95]

Certain safeguards are therefore needed to prevent such expectations from arising. Although a comprehensive judicial control, as carried out by the FCC, requires knowledge of the details, the publication of specific information can ultimately lead to certainty for market participants, which results in the unlawfulness of the programmes.[96] The substantive legal framework that governs central bank operations thus also sets limits in terms of the density of reasoning and the transparency requirement as a whole.

5.2 The Principle of Democracy of the Grundgesetz: The "German Way of Democracy" as a Role Model?

Since its foundation, the independent ECB has been accompanied in its actions by the jurisdiction of the FCC. In this respect, the focus is on compatibility with the principle of democracy of the German Constitution (Grundgesetz), which is laid down in Art. 20(1), (2) and whose essential contents are not subject to change even in the context of European integration according to Art. 23(1) s. 3 in conjunction with Art. 79(3) GG.

Therefore, the FCC has set up different standards of review, which particularly emphasise *ultra vires* review and identity review, but do not need to be discussed in detail here.[97] In its *Banking Union decision*, the FCC has clarified at least that, with regard to the "right to democracy" *("Anspruch auf Demokratie"),*[98] which the court derives from Art. 38(1) s. 1 GG in conjunction with Art. 20(1), (2) GG in conjunction with Art. 79(3) GG, "ultra vires review and identity review are [. . .] two sides of the same coin".[99]

---

94 ECJ, Gauweiler, 16.6.2015, ECLI:EU:C:2015:400, para. 104.

95 ECJ, Gauweiler, 16.6.2015, ECLI:EU:C:2015:400, para. 109.

96 See also Dawson et al. (2019), p. 82.

97 An overview in the context of the PSPP order for reference can be found at Gentzsch and Becker (2017), pp. 785 et seq.

98 Cf. FCC, Banking Union, 30.7.2019, 2 BvR 1685/14 et al., para. 92.

99 FCC, Banking Union, 30.7.2019, 2 BvR 1685/14 et al., para. 205.

In terms of substance, however, the question is raised as to whether and to what extent the essential contents of the principle of democracy enshrined in the Grundgesetz conflict with independent European and national authorities.

5.2.1 Democratic Legitimation of Administration and Legality of a "Sphere That Is Not Subject to the Influence of a Ministry"

The case law of the FCC contains clear statements on the democratic legitimation of public authority:

> The principle of the sovereignty of the people (Art. 20(2) first sentence GG) as well as the corresponding right of citizens to be subjected only to such public authority they can legitimate and influence links the right to vote to the exercise of public authority. It requires that any act of public authority exercised in Germany can be traced back to its citizens.[100]

The FCC has specified this requirement in the prerequisite of a sufficient level of democratic legitimation *("hinreichendes Legitimationsniveau")*, which is not determined by the various forms of democratic legitimation of state action themselves, but created by the interaction of those.[101]

However, of central importance is the prerequisite that the constitutionally necessary democratic legitimation requires an uninterrupted chain of legitimation *("ununterbrochene Legitimationskette")* from the people to the organs and officials entrusted with state tasks.[102]

To achieve this, the FCC names various forms that are suitable for establishing democratic legitimation, at least in the national context:

> Under constitutional law, the required relationship of accountability between the people and public authority is established, in particular, by way of parliamentary elections, laws adopted by Parliament setting legal standards for the executive branch, by way of parliamentary influence on government policies and by the fact that the administration is generally bound by government instructions. Public officials have full personal democratic legitimation if they have been elected by the people or by Parliament, or if they have been appointed by or with the approval of another public official who in turn has personal legitimation. Legitimation in functional and substantive terms is achieved by the binding effect of law and by oversight and instructions provided by higher-ranking public authorities.[103]

This shows that beyond institutional legitimation, which derives from the formation of the legislative, executive and judicial powers, each with its own functions and organs,[104] a concrete legitimation in terms of organisation and staff

[100] FCC, Banking Union, 30.7.2019, 2 BvR 1685/14 et al., para. 117 with further references.

[101] Cf. FCC, Banking Union, 30.7.2019, 2 BvR 1685/14 et al., para. 129 with further references.

[102] FCC, Wasserverbände, 5.12.2002, 2 BvL 5/98 et al., para. 156 with further references.

[103] FCC, Banking Union, 30.7.2019, 2 BvR 1685/14 et al., para. 129 with further references.

[104] FCC, Kalkar I, 8.8.1978 = BVerfGE 49, 89 (p. 125); Atomwaffenstationierung, 18.12.1984 = BVerfGE 68, 1 (p. 89); based on Ossenbühl (1968), p. 197.

("organisatorisch-personelle Legitimation")[105] as well as in functional and substantive terms *("sachlich-inhaltliche Legitimation")* terms is required.

As we have seen democratic legitimation in terms of organisation and staff on the one hand and in functional and substantive terms on the other hand do not exist in splendid isolation, but complement and substitute each other within certain limits.[106] Such interrelationship also exists with regard to the binding effect of law *("Gesetzesbindung")* and democratic responsibility, in particular the government's power to issue instructions, which together form the overall level of legitimation in functional and substantive terms. If the power to issue instructions, is reduced, the stronger the binding effect of law is to be required, which is accompanied by a restriction of discretion as found in the judiciary branch. *Vice-versa*, a lesser degree of normative control, e.g. by granting discretion to administrative bodies, corresponds to a greater degree of democratic responsibility, in particular dependence on instructions.

The strong emphasis on the right to issue instructions has repeatedly been criticised in the literature, especially when it comes to the admissibility of a "sphere that is not subject to the influence of a Ministry" *("ministerialfreier Raum")*.[107,108] The debate focuses primarily on the freedom from instructions, so that in this respect there is also mention of "areas free from instructions" *("weisungsfreie Räume")*.[109]

According to the central concept of *Böckenförde*, a former judge of the FCC, decisions that have been excluded from democratic decision-making areas are only acceptable if there are compelling reasons for this, which lie in the nature of the task, or if a special constitutional provision or requirement exists.[110] For those tasks which, due to their specific nature, require such freedom from instructions, the examination system has been highlighted as an example.[111] As constitutional provisions, the independence of the Deutsche Bundesbank (Art. 88 GG) is mentioned,[112] which can be supplemented by the independence of the Federal Court of Audit (Art. 114(2) GG).

Likewise, the FCC did not generally rule out a "sphere that is not subject to the influence of a Ministry", but it did emphasise that there are tasks that must, due to their political significance, remain within governmental responsibility and must not

[105]In the official translation of its decision, the FCC speaks of "democratic accountability as regards organisation and staff matters", see FCC, Banking Union, 30.7.2019, 2 BvR 1685/14 et al., para. 212.

[106]FCC, Wasserverbände, 5.12.2002, 2 BvL 5/98 et al., para. 135; for the following options for substitution see the description of Böckenförde (2004), paras. 22–23.

[107]FCC, Banking Union, 30.7.2019, 2 BvR 1685/14 et al., para. 133.

[108]See for example Schmidt-Aßmann (2006), ch. 5 para. 37; Classen (2011), pp. 301–302; Groß (2012), p. 1091.

[109]In detail Oebbecke (1986).

[110]Böckenförde (2004), para. 22.

[111]Böckenförde (2004), para. 24.

[112]Böckenförde (2004), para. 22.

be conferred upon agencies that are independent of governments and parliaments.[113] Otherwise, it would be impossible for the government to assume its responsibility given that agencies that are not subject to oversight nor accountable to anybody could thus gain too much influence on state administration. It can only be determined in the specific case to which tasks this applies.

Later, the FCC considered the participation of representatives of social groups as justification, because decisions concerning freedom of the press and freedom of the arts should, if possible, be taken at a certain distance from the state and on the basis of a pluralistic formation of opinion.[114] Special features also apply to the constitutionally provided or recognised forms of local resp. functional self-government *("kommunale/funktionale Selbstverwaltung").*[115]

Finally, the FCC used the *Banking Union decision* to make general statements on the possibilities and limits of a "sphere that is not subject to the influence of a Ministry", which will also prove to be decisive in future debates concerning national contexts:

> Art. 20(1) and (2) GG allows for limited modifications of the means of democratic legitimation, which serve to compensate for drops in influence. In particular, this applies to effective judicial review or to parliamentary oversight rights, which give Parliament – within the limits of what is permissible under constitutional law – specific possibilities of influencing public authorities and enable it to amend or repeal the respective legal bases and thus have the final say.
>
> However, diminishing the level of democratic legitimation is not permissible without limits and requires justification. [...]. While drops in influence are permissible for reasons that are recognised as legitimate under constitutional law, they may not undermine the principle of the sovereignty of the people.[116]

5.2.2 *The Europeanisation of National Administrative Structures and the Establishment of Independent Bodies, Offices and Agencies of the European Union*

These requirements developed by the FCC on the basis of the constitutional principle of democracy had to be further advanced in view of the increasing unionisation of the administrative branch. Not only were increasingly independent Union institutions set up and entrusted with administrative tasks, but also Union law provisions on the independence of national administrations were laid down. The latter has been exemplified by the problem of independent data protection supervisory bodies.

---

[113]See also FCC, Bremer Personalvertretung, 27.4.1959 = BVerfGE 9, 268 (p. 282); referring to this FCC, Banking Union, 30.7.2019, 2 BvR 1685/14 et al., para. 133.

[114]FCC, Josefine Mutzenbacher, 27.11.1990 = BVerfGE 83, 130 (p. 150).

[115]Fundamentally FCC, Wasserverbände, 5.12.2002, 2 BvL 5/98 et al., paras. 154 et seq.

[116]FCC, Banking Union, 30.7.2019, 2 BvR 1685/14 et al., paras. 130–131.

In the context of the European Union, the FCC has allowed certain modifications of democratic principles, but has basically adhered to the concept of chains of legitimation and, in particular, has always strongly emphasised the importance of the principle of representative democracy. In its *Maastricht decision*, the FCC conceded that democratic legitimation in the EU cannot be established in the same form as within a state order that is uniformly and conclusively regulated by a state constitution *("Staatsordnung")*.[117] In its *Lisbon decision*, the FCC further detailed the specific nature of the Union's legitimation. Art. 23(1) s. 1 GG shall not require, with regard to the observance of democratic principles by the European Union, any structural congruence *("strukturelle Kongruenz")* or even conformity of the institutional order of the European Union with the order which the democratic principle of the Grundgesetz prescribes for the national level.[118] However, democracy shall require a democratic structure appropriate to the status and function of the Union.[119] It should be noted that the FCC assumes that the exercise of sovereignty by the European Union as an association of sovereign states *("Staatenverbund")* is democratically legitimated primarily by the parliaments of the Member States and (only) supported by the European Parliament elected by the citizens of the Union.[120]

These democratic requirements for the establishment of administrative authorities who are not bound by instructions were further developed by the FCC in the *Banking Union decision* for the European Administration in a Union-specific manner and set certain conditions.

Referring to its case law on a "sphere that is not subject to the influence of a Ministry", it stressed the following:

> In order to guarantee a minimum of democratic legitimation and oversight, the same must apply with regard to the Europeanisation of national administrative structures and the establishment of bodies, offices and agencies of the European Union. In both cases, specific justification is required and both must potentially be compensated by judicial review of acts of public authority, by granting special oversight rights to the European Parliament and to the *Bundestag*, or by accountability requirements which enable Member States and EU institutions to amend the legal bases for independent bodies, offices and agencies.[121]

Nevertheless, the conclusion of the FCC, which has been integrated in part into the 3rd headnote, expresses clear scepticism about the organisational changes in the European administration induced by Union law:

> Thus, there are no fundamental objections to the establishment of independent agencies; however, such practice remains precarious in light of the principle of democracy.

---

[117]FCC, Maastricht, 12.10.1993 = BVerfGE 89, 155 (p. 182).

[118]FCC, Lisbon, 30.6.2009, 2 BvE 2/08 et al., paras. 266–267.

[119]Ibid.

[120]Cf. FCC, Maastricht, 12.10.1993 = BVerfGE 89, 155 (pp. 184–186); Lisbon, 30.6.2009, 2 BvE 2/08 et al., paras. 262 et seq., 298 et seq.

[121]FCC, Banking Union, 30.7.2019, 2 BvR 1685/14 et al., para. 134.

At least where institutions, bodies, offices and agencies of the European Union drift towards a complete disconnect from democratic oversight, they come up against the limits of the EU's principle of democracy. This also applies to the ECB.[122]

5.2.3 Evaluation

Despite these reservations, the FCC is approaching those voices in the literature which already demand modifications for the administration's legitimation concept under Art. 20(1), (2) GG, but at least for legitimation in the context of Union law. A *petitum* repeatedly put forward in the literature is the identification, evaluation and implementation of alternative or at least complementary means to hierarchical control, such as greater legal embedment or instruments of direct control, e.g. parliamentary rights of appointment or direct accountability of administration towards parliaments.[123]

Nevertheless, despite its commitment to an independent Union-democratic concept of legitimation, the FCC seems to assume, on the basis of the forms of legitimation it has developed, that there is a standard state of legitimation which is then reduced by granting independence to authorities. A specific justification is required for this, so that general reasons demanding independence, in particular the increase in complexity, do not suffice.

The FCC assumed such a specific justification in its *Maastricht decision* precisely for the establishment of the ECB, which is committed to the objective of price stability, and also confirmed in its *Banking Union decision* "that the ECB's independence is justified under constitutional law as it reflects that an independent central bank can be a better guarantor for monetary stability, and thus for the general economic foundation of budgetary policy, than institutions that depend on money supply and monetary value and which require the short-term approval by political forces as has been proven within the German legal order and is also supported by scientific research".[124]

This approach does not take sufficient account of the autonomy of the Union's institutional order, which is not characterised by a ministerial administration bound by instructions and cannot be so due to a lack of similarity to the state and the absence of a government. It is all the more problematic because the FCC also applies the forms of democratic legitimation which result from the constitutional principle of democracy to the legal review of Union's institutions.[125]

---

[122]FCC, Banking Union, 30.7.2019, 2 BvR 1685/14 et al., paras. 138–139.

[123]See for example Groß (1999), pp. 187–188; Lübbe-Wolff (2001), p. 283; Hermes (2005), pp. 471, 483; Schmidt-Aßmann (2006), ch. 5, para. 35; Masing (2010), p. 215; Classen (2011), p. 301; Ruffert (2011), p. 411; Trute (2012), para. 68.

[124]FCC, Banking Union, 30.7.2019, 2 BvR 1685/14 et al., para. 134 with reference to FCC, Maastricht, 12.10.1993 = BVerfGE 89, 155 (pp. 208–209) and the subsequent case law.

[125]See FCC, Banking Union, 30.7.2019, 2 BvR 1685/14 et al., paras. 212 et seq.

However, at the same time, it has become apparent that the FCC imposes hardly any material requirements with regard to the existence of specific justification and exercises judicial review very cautiously, as has been demonstrated with regard to independent banking supervision.[126]

Thus, contrary to the repeatedly emphasised view that the independence of the ECB in the area of monetary policy cannot be applied to other policy areas,[127] the FCC refrains from analysing both the correlation between independence and financial stability as well as the functional specificities of banking supervision.[128]

However, it is positive that the FCC recognises what it describes as "limited modifications of the means of democratic legitimation, which serve to compensate for drops in influence"[129] or "further elements of legitimation",[130] which enables and at the same time safeguards an independent administration. The fact that the FCC refers explicitly to the ECJ's *Data Protection Authorities decision* and to French academic literature[131] indicates a clear convergence of European and national standards.

As regards parliamentary scrutiny, however, there may be challenges, as this study has already shown. Nevertheless, it seems necessary that where independence requirements exist under Union law, national administrative action should also be safeguarded by reporting and accountability obligations modelled on Union law. An example of this is the BaFin, which, although no longer fully subject to the legal and technical supervision *("Rechts- und Fachaufsicht")* of the Federal Ministry of Finance (Bundesministerium der Finanzen) (§ 2 Finanzdienstleistungsaufsichtsgesetz [FinDAG]) due to Art. 19(1) SSMR in the area of SSM supervision,[132] is not subject to reporting and accountability obligations comparable to Art. 20 SSMR.

In addition, the FCC's commitment to judicial control as a compensatory mechanism is ambivalent. Although judicial control can strengthen the binding effect of law,[133] this must not lead to a demand for the greatest possible degree and density of judicial control. The analysis has already revealed that courts can reach their limits in this respect, especially in the area of monetary policy and banking supervision.

However, the FCC meets with approval here, as it underlines the importance of representative democracy, which includes parliamentary legitimation and oversight

[126] FCC, Banking Union, 30.7.2019, 2 BvR 1685/14 et al., para. 223; see the criticism at Gentzsch and Brade (2019), p. 629.

[127] FCC, Maastricht, 12.10.1993 = BVerfGE 89, 155 (pp. 207 et seq.); OMT (order for reference), 14.1.2014, 2 BvR 2728/13 et al., para. 59; PSPP (order for reference), 18.7.2017, 2 BvR 859/15 et al., para. 59.

[128] See supra Sect. 3.3.1.2.4.2.

[129] FCC, Banking Union, 30.7.2019, 2 BvR 1685/14 et al., para. 130.

[130] FCC, Banking Union, 30.7.2019, 2 BvR 1685/14 et al., para. 285.

[131] FCC, Banking Union, 30.7.2019, 2 BvR 1685/14 et al., para. 130.

[132] FCC, Banking Union, 30.7.2019, 2 BvR 1685/14 et al., para. 130; previously Dechent (2015), p. 771.

[133] See for instance Lübbe-Wolff (2001), p. 273.

of public authority.[134] This model of government, which is deeply rooted in the political history of ideas in Europe,[135] is an essential component of the Union's conception of democracy. Nevertheless, if it is not to lose its powers of persuasion, this conception should not be reduced to formal relations, but should work together with elements of participation and transparency, thus ensuring democratically accountable action by independent institutions, especially central banks.

5.3 Clarification of the ECB's Mandate

In addition to representation, transparency and participation, the central bank mandate as a source of democratic legitimation will now be examined more closely. Although the term "mandate" is not explicitly mentioned in the Treaties or the ESCB/ECB Statute, it is nevertheless found in jurisdiction and the literature and, contrary to some voices,[136] is also a reasonable concept with regard to central bank action. It not only defines the scope of the tasks to be performed, but also sets out the objectives to be pursued and the means and instruments to be used, providing central banks with democratic authorisation.[137]

The study has revealed important findings on the central bank mandate. A sufficiently clear mandate is required not only for democratic control by the representative bodies and the people, but also for judicial and administrative control. The clearer the scope of the mandate, the objectives to be pursued and the means/ instruments provided, the better it will be possible to monitor compliance with the limits of the mandate and the achievement of the objectives. This depends, for example, on how many different, conflicting objectives are assigned to a decision-making body for achievement and the extent to which targets are set in the event of conflicting objectives. The clearer the objectives are formulated and any decisions to weigh up the interests involved are avoided, the better the objectives can be pursued and an *ex post* control of actions can be achieved. This applies, for example, to parliamentary control with regard to the right to question and hearings, but also to judicial control with regard to the legality of action.

The extent to which the attainment of objectives can be measured also plays an essential role in this context. In the case of concrete benchmarks, such as price stability marked with the inflation target, the monitoring is more transparent than in the case of target definitions open to interpretation.

A sufficiently clearly conceived mandate is thus in a position to generate legitimation through a (measurable) output despite the fact that central bank actions are removed from a direct representative-democratic context of responsibility. The study

[134]FCC, Banking Union, 30.7.2019, 2 BvR 1685/14 et al., para. 135.

[135]See Müller et al. (2006), pp. 3 et seq.

[136]Cf. Siekmann (2020), p. 495.

[137]Cf. De Boer and van 't Klooster (2020), pp. 1690, 1697–1698.

has shown that, especially in the second decade of its existence, the ECB has not only been entrusted with additional tasks, but also applies means in an environment for which these are not provided for. Above all, a mandate has emerged which is situated in the triad of price, financial and fiscal stability, but which is not to be found in the Treaty regime of central bank law. These objectives are not without tension, although functional aspects may justify concentration in one institution.

In the following, the fields of tension, especially the relationship between monetary policy and the other tasks, will be examined in more detail. This should build the basis for identifying development perspectives of the ECB's mandate.

5.3.1 Relationship Between Monetary Policy and Banking Supervision/Financial Stability

A major part of the discussion on the establishment of the SSM was the controversy about the opportunities and risks of ECB micro-prudential supervision.[138] The legislator considered that the ECB's capacity as a supervisory authority was mainly based on its "extensive expertise in macroeconomic and financial stability issues".[139] The establishment of the ESFS and the related conferral of macro-prudential tasks on the ECB in the framework of the ESRB already highlighted the intersections and synergies between stability-oriented monetary policy and macroeconomic early warning with regard to financial stability.[140] At the same time, it was emphasised that the conduct of certain monetary policies may pose a threat to financial stability and that the ECB may therefore be exposed to conflicts of interest.[141]

The existence of such trade-offs in the case of the identity of the central bank and supervisory authority was discussed even more extensively.[142] The use of institution-related data collected and analysed for monetary policy purposes for micro-prudential purposes is considered useful from an economic perspective.[143] It should also be noted that price stability is a necessary, albeit insufficient, condition for financial stability and that price stability cannot be achieved without a stable financial system.[144] For this reason, it is argued in the literature that the maintenance of financial stability is already included in the price stability mandate of Art. 127

[138] Cf. Ferran and Babis (2013), pp. 12–16; Lehmann and Manger-Nestler (2014), p. 18.

[139] Recital 13 s. 1 SSMR.

[140] Lehmann and Manger-Nestler (2011), p. 23; see also Steinbach (2016), pp. 366–367; Goldmann (2018), pp. 286–287.

[141] Lehmann and Manger-Nestler (2011), p. 23.

[142] See for example Goodhart and Schoenmaker (1995), pp. 545–548; Hahn and Häde (2010), § 17 paras. 98–99; Heun (2012), p. 240; for another view see Glatzl (2009), pp. 245–246.

[143] Cf. Thiele (2014), pp. 198–199.

[144] Steinbach (2016), p. 367.

(1) TFEU, which is to be confirmed and also delineated by Art. 127(5) TFEU.[145] If, however, the different objectives require divergent measures, primary law provides a clear hierarchy of objectives with the primacy of price stability, which is clarified in secondary law by the fact that the Governing Council can object to draft decisions of the Supervisory Board, "in particular stating monetary policy concerns".[146]

However, the risk of a conflict between prudential supervision focused on the stability of institutions and a monetary policy bound by the price stability directive cannot be dismissed.[147]

These concerns cannot, in any case, be dispelled by the fact that the dilemma becomes virulent, particularly in the event of a crisis, when resolution measures appear possible, and that the Union's responsibility for resolution and recovery has not been conferred on the ECB. Indeed, this does not *a priori* exclude the possibility that the ECB may pre-empt any resolution measures through monetary policy measures.

The legislator wanted to address these concerns by separating monetary policy and supervisory tasks[148] as wells as setting up a supervisory body.[149] Art. 25(2) sub-para. 1 SSMR provides for a separation of monetary policy and supervisory tasks, which is expressed in particular by an organisational separation of the respective staff as well as by a physical separation in the form of different meetings and agendas of the Governing Council.[150]

From an institutional point of view, the establishment of the Supervisory Board as an internal body of the ECB shall contribute significantly to the prevention of conflicts of interest by preparing draft decisions, the adoption of which will be decided by the Governing Council in a no-objection procedure.[151] In order to avoid conflicts of interest in terms of personnel, the Chair of the Supervisory Board may not be a member of the Governing Council, and the representatives of the ECB may not be directly involved in monetary policy functions.[152]

However, the Vice-Chair is also a member of the Executive Board[153] and in this capacity is entrusted with the implementation of monetary policy in accordance with guidelines and decisions laid down by the Governing Council.[154]

---

[145] Psaroudakis (2018), pp. 130–137; see also Lamandini et al. (2017), pp. 21–22, who, however, highlight restrictions arising from the principle of proportionality.

[146] Art. 26(8) SSMR.

[147] Cf. Thiele (2015), pp. 157–158; Lamandini and Ramos Muñoz (2020), pp. 49–51; see also Kern (2015), p. 171, referring to the empirical correlation between the supervisory mandate and a low number of bank insolvencies on the one hand and higher inflation on the other.

[148] Art. 25 SSMR.

[149] Art. 26 SSMR.

[150] Art. 25(2) sub-para. 2, (4) SSMR.

[151] See supra Sect. 3.3.1.1.

[152] Art. 26(3) sub-para. 1 s. 3, (5) s. 1 SSMR.

[153] Art. 26(3) sub-para. 3 s. 4 SSMR.

[154] Art. 12.1. sub-para. 2 s. 1 ESCB/ECB Statute.

Despite these precautions, there are serious doubts as to whether the intended separation of functions has actually been sufficiently achieved.[155] For example, in a special report the ECA criticised in particular the fact that "some ECB departments provide services to both functions without clear rules and reporting lines that would minimise possible conflicts of objectives".[156]

With regard to the final decision-making competence, it must be emphasised that the Governing Council takes final decisions on both prudential measures and monetary policy. Whether this problem can be eased by the Governing Council carrying out its respective tasks in separate meetings and agendas may be questionable in view of the continued identity of the persons involved.[157]

Provided that the objective of sufficient separation is still pursued, the supervisory body should be established as the final decision-making body in the Treaties in order to establish coherent competences.[158] *De lege lata*, the Governing Council and the Executive Board are the only decision-making bodies of the ECB,[159] so that the establishment of further final decision-making bodies is not open to the EU legislator.[160] The delegation of tasks to the Supervisory Board, as envisaged by the Commission,[161] also raises concerns, according to the ECJ's case law on the internal delegation of decision-making powers.[162]

The establishment of the Supervisory Board as a separate decision-making body in the Treaties could be supported by a formalised procedure before a mediation panel to ensure coordination between monetary policy and banking supervision. However, in order to preserve the accountability of the respective decision-making bodies and link them back to the pursuit of the objectives assigned to them, it seems preferable not to give such a mediation body final decision-making powers. Approaches to such a mechanism already exist in the current SSMR. If the Governing Council of the ECB objects to draft decisions of the Supervisory Body, the NCAs may refer the matter to a mediation panel.[163] This body consists of one member per participating Member State, chosen by each Member State among the members of the Governing Council and the Board of Supervisors.[164] However, the

---

[155] See for example Sacarcelik (2013), pp. 355, 360, Ruthig (2014), pp. 471–472; for another view see Kämmerer and Starski (2013), pp. 321–331.

[156] ECA (2016), p. 10, paras. 7–8; for details see pp. 29–32, paras 40–46.

[157] German Council of Economic Experts (2012/13), p. 175; Lehmann and Manger-Nestler (2014), p. 18.

[158] In general Psaroudakis (2018), pp. 151–153.

[159] *Arg. ex* Art. 129(1) TFEU, Art. 9.3. ESCB/ECB Statute.

[160] FCC, Banking Union, 30.7.2019, 2 BvR 1685/14 et al., paras. 199–202; see also Ferran and Babis (2013), pp. 14–15; Gurlit (2014), p. 15.

[161] Art. 19(3) Proposal for a Council Regulation conferring specific tasks on the European Central Bank concerning policies relating to the prudential supervision of credit institutions of 12 September 2012, COM(2012) 511 final.

[162] ECJ, Tralli, 26.5.2005, ECLI:EU:C:2005:306, paras. 41 et seq.

[163] Art. 25(5) ss. 1, 2 SSMR.

[164] Art. 25(5) s. 3 SSMR.

decisions of the mediation panel are not binding and must be adopted by the Governing Council of the ECB in order to become legally binding.[165] The dialogue between the decision-making bodies could have the potential to better understand the views of the other bodies and improve the quality of their own decisions. This is especially true if one assumes that the pursuit of the price stability mandate, irrespective of prudential competences, enables and possibly requires taking financial stability considerations into account.[166]

However, if the Supervisory Board were to be enshrined in the Treaty as the final decision-making body, it would have to be carefully considered to what extent provisions on (external) independence and democratic control should also be included in primary law. The academic literature has emphasised that financial and price stability are ultimately two sides of the same coin and that independence from both the central bank and the (regulatory and) supervisory function mutually reinforce the respective objectives.[167] However, it is important to note that it is precisely the shaping options available to the legislator that constitute an essential element of democratic legitimation and control of banking supervision, which should not be equated unreflectively with the independence and accountability in the field of monetary policy.

Especially in the event that the Governing Council of the ECB continues to have the right of final decision, but also in the event of a greater separation between the Governing Council and the Supervisory Board, it would be appropriate, in view of the existing conflicts of objectives, to lay down the objective of financial stability as a separate specification in the ECB's set of objectives and to situate it in relation to other objectives.[168] In this context, it would seem preferable to subordinate the ESCB/Eurosystem's pursuit of the financial stability objective to the price stability objective[169] so that the latter is not undermined.[170] A further strengthening of the financial stability mandate can be achieved by underpinning it with instruments similar to those used for monetary policy. Such a comprehensive approach to the use of monetary policy instruments for financial stability policy, regulated by Union law, in particular to tackle serious and emergent systemic crises, would help to reduce the risk of antagonism, particularly in the relationship between the ECB and the ESRB.[171]

---

[165]Cf. Tröger (2013), p. 29.

[166]Psaroudakis (2018), p. 141.

[167]Quintyn and Taylor (2007), pp. 4, 9.

[168]Cf. Lamandini et al. (2015), p. 44, n. 172; Häde (2016), para. 24; Rodi (2018), para. 19; see also Kaufhold (2016), pp. 209–210, who calls for a legal obligation to protect the financial system *de lege ferenda*.

[169]Goldmann (2018), p. 299 ("intermediate, second-order goal of monetary policy"); Psaroudakis (2018), pp. 150–155, who examines a financial stability mandate of equal standing with price stability, but favours a secondary mandate.

[170]Cf. Manger-Nestler and Böttner (2014), p. 629.

[171]See also Psaroudakis (2018), p. 143, favouring a stronger involvement of central banks in macroprudential supervision.

5.3.2 *Relationship Between Monetary Policy and Banking Resolution*

The tense relationship between the primacy of price stability under primary law and macro-prudential and even more micro-prudential banking supervision becomes even more challenging when considering the tasks related to bank resolution. It has already been shown that the ECB triggers resolution by assessing whether an institution is failing or likely to fail.[172] In this respect, however, the ECB's activity is limited to analysis, without giving it any decision-making powers. However, a tension between banking supervision and bank resolution is created by the fact that, according to Art. 4(1)(i) SSMR, the ECB performs supervisory tasks with regard to recovery plans and early intervention when a credit institution or group for which the ECB is the consolidating supervisor does not meet or is not likely to meet the applicable prudential requirements, as well as—only in the cases explicitly stipulated in the relevant Union law for competent authorities—with regard to necessary structural changes at credit institutions to prevent financial stress or failures. While such early intervention measures may be necessary to prevent deterioration of the financial and economic situation of a credit institution at an early stage and thereby preserve financial stability,[173] the simultaneous and primary pursuit of the price stability objective may nevertheless create conflicting objectives.[174] Such tensions are reduced, but not excluded, by the fact that the ECB coordinates its activities with the competent resolution authorities[175] and ultimately does not have any resolution powers at its disposal, as Art. 4(1)(i) SSMR explicitly states.

In addition to possible conflicts of objectives between early intervention measures to be taken by the ECB and the pursuit of the price stability objective, there are further tensions arising from the granting of ELA.[176] Starting from a competence point of view, the ELA granted by the NCBs, especially in the course of the financial crisis, was hardly criticised. However, primary law does not explicitly provide for support for individual, especially overindebted institutions.[177] While the provision of liquidity support at the macro level is mainly attributed to monetary policy,[178] ELA is partly attributed to the task of promoting the smooth operation of payment systems according to Art. 127(2) 4th indent TFEU[179] or to the support competence

[172]See supra Sect. 3.3.5.1.

[173]Cf. Recital 27 s. 1 SSMR.

[174]See Lamandini et al. (2017), pp. 28–31 ("twilight zone").

[175]Recital 27 s. 2 SSMR; see also Art. 13 SRMR.

[176]See supra Sect. 3.1.2.1.

[177]Cf. See Siekmann (2013), para. 124 with further references, who points out that there is no single LoLR function and that, moreover, primary law does not provide a sufficient basis for this.

[178]Cf. Psaroudakis (2018), p. 144.

[179]Siekmann (2013), para. 125.

with regard to financial stability under Art. 127(5) TFEU.[180] In any case, the ECB has only a shared competence where the principle of subsidiarity provided for in Art. 5(3) sub-para. 1 TEU applies.[181] If one assumes with the probably prevailing opinion in literature that the granting of ELA, which does not serve the implementation of monetary policy, does not fall within the competence of the Eurosystem as outlined by the Treaties,[182] the NCBs can nevertheless perform this function on their responsibility and liability according to Art. 14.4. ESCB/ECB Statute.

However, ensuring ELA is also not without problems in relation to the ECB's micro-prudential mandate and, even more so, to the objectives of the SRM. Such loans can have a stabilising effect, but they can also delay insolvency and thus counteract the objectives of the SSM and the SRM.[183,184] This danger is particularly serious because the distinction between illiquid and insolvent institutions often cannot be made beyond doubt, especially in crisis situations.[185] A distinction is also, and precisely for this reason, necessary against the background that ensuring liquidity in the event of insolvency is in principle to be assigned to fiscal policy as a competence of the Member States.[186]

It is therefore welcome that the ECB has now adopted principles on the stricter treatment of ELAs by NCBs, creating a single legal framework with the rules on restructuring and resolution.[187] Nevertheless, trade-offs between the provision of emergency support on the one hand and the mandate of monetary policy and banking supervision on the other cannot be excluded.

Although the ELA measures may be considered as a part of central bank tasks, it seems doubtful whether such a competence should continue to exist within the institutional framework of European monetary, financial and fiscal union.[188] This holds all the more true in view of the envisaged intertwining of the SRM and the ESM resp. European Monetary Fund (EMF) as will be shown below.[189] In the conceived concept, the ESM/EMF provides a common backstop and functions as lender of last resort. If a further LoLR function is considered necessary, it should preferably be located at the Union level, which is not only supported by the close

---

[180] Steinbach (2016), pp. 369–370; Mersch (2018), p. 349; for classification as a monetary policy measure Selmayr (2015), para. 66, n. 239; Beukers (2013), pp. 1591–1592, 1616; both discussed by Psaroudakis (2018), pp. 145 et seq.

[181] Steinbach (2016), p. 380; see also Psaroudakis (2018), p. 146.

[182] ECB (1999), p. 98; Keller (2013), para. 108; Ohler (2015), § 4 para. 37; for another view see Smits (1997), p. 269.

[183] Cf. Art. 14 SRMR.

[184] In detail O'Connell (2013), pp. 261 et seq.

[185] Ohler (2015), § 4 para. 39; Steinbach (2016), pp. 364, 373.

[186] Cf. European Commission, Communication of 30 July, OJ 30.7.2013, C 261, p. 1; Mersch (2018), p. 350; for a critical view Steinbach (2016), pp. 373–374 especially with reference to ECJ, Gauweiler, 16.6.2015, ECLI:EU:C:2015:400, para. 52.

[187] ECB, Agreement on emergency liquidity assistance of 17 May 2017.

[188] Similarly Ohler (2015), § 4 para. 37.

[189] See infra Sect. 5.3.3.

connections to monetary policy and the now highly integrated fields of banking supervision and bank resolution, but also by the high degree of integration of the credit system in the euro area.[190] At least the LoLR function, which is attributed not only to central banks but also, to some extent, to the IMF,[191] should be more clearly enshrined in the legal framework of EMU.

In this respect, however, it must always be borne in mind that granting ELA, especially to significant institutions and especially those operating across borders, can have a considerable impact on monetary policy.[192] Unless the competence remains with the central banks, at least certain rules, such as procedural ones, are needed which take account of the ECB's mandate.

5.3.3 *Relationship Between Monetary Policy and Fiscal Stability*

Not only the relationship between monetary policy and banking supervision or resolution, but also the role of the ECB in the area of fiscal stability must be located in the ECB's mandate. Here it became apparent in the study that the ECB plays a merely analytical but nevertheless essential role in the area of granting financial aid, which at least so far has been carried out on the basis of an international treaty, as well as in macroeconomic surveillance.

The fact that the ECB has no decision-making powers within the framework of the ESM is intended to prevent central bank independence in the area of monetary policy from being corrupted,[193] but it is only insufficiently able to resolve tensions. These shortcomings resulting from the inconsistency between the ECB's primary mandate and its tasks in the field of economic policy and financial stability were reflected in particular in the envisaged reform of the ESM.

On 6 December 2017, the Commission presented a comprehensive package of communications and proposals, succeeding the Five Presidents' Report of June 2015 and the reflection paper on deepening Economic and Monetary Union.[194] One of the four main initiatives was a Council Regulation on the establishment of a European Monetary Fund,[195] which aimed at transposing the ESM into the Union legal order

[190] Psaroudakis (2018), pp. 147–148.

[191] See for details Lastra (2015), paras. 14.162 et seq.

[192] Cf. Siekmann (2013), para. 124 with references to the economic literature; Steinbach (2016), pp. 370–371, therefore advocating for a division of competences between the ECB and the NCBs concerning ELA according to significance (pp. 379–380); Psaroudakis (2018), p. 147.

[193] Zilioli (2016b), p. 179.

[194] For an overview see European Commission, Communication of 6 December 2017, COM(2017) 821 final.

[195] Proposal for a Council Regulation on the establishment of the European Monetary Fund Brussels of 6 December 2017, COM(2017) 827 final (hereinafter: EMFR Draft).

and transforming it into a separate legal entity under Union law,[196] succeeding to and replacing the ESM.[197]

This reform, as envisaged by the Commission, extended the mandate of the ESM/EMF, so that it would also be a common last-resort backstop for the SRF, activated in the case the SRF proved to be insufficient to finance the resolution of the banks concerned.[198] The proposed regulation has received a positive response, in particular from the ECB[199] and the European Parliament.[200]

However, the Eurogroup continued to maintain an intergovernmental structure for the ESM and only reached an amendment to the TESM, which was ratified by the contracting Member States.

The most significant change is that "the ESM will provide the common backstop to the Single Resolution Fund ('SRF') and be strengthened on the basis of the elements set out in the letter of the President of the Euro Group dated 25 June 2018".[201] In particular, the mandate of the ESM will be extended[202] and a backstop facility will be added to the ESM's toolbox.[203] As regards the mandate and independence of the ECB, however, there are hardly any relevant changes.[204] For instance, one should note the clarification in Recital 10 s. 2 TESM new version that "the duties conferred within this Treaty on the European Commission and the ECB do not entail any powers to make decisions of their own and that the tasks executed by those two institutions on the basis of this Treaty solely commit the ESM". In addition, the ECB's merely supportive role vis-à-vis the Commission in the assessments required for the granting of stability support is further accentuated.[205] As regards substance, Art. 13(1) s. 3 (b) s. 2 TESM new version now provides that the assessment of debt sustainability and repayment capacity "shall

---

[196]See Art. 1 Statute of the European Monetary Fund, Annex to EMFR Draft (hereinafter: EMF Statute Draft).

[197]Art. 2(1) EMFR Draft.

[198]EMFR Draft, p. 4; Arts. 3(2)(b), 22 EMF Statute Draft.

[199]ECB, Opinion of 11 April 2018 on a proposal for a regulation on the establishment of the European Monetary Fund (CON/2018/20), OJ 25.6.2018, C 220, p. 2.

[200]European Parliament, Resolution of 14 March 2019 on the proposal for a Council Regulation on the establishment of the European Monetary Fund, P8_TA(2019)0218.

[201]Recital 5a TESM new version.

[202]Art. 3(2) TESM new version.

[203]Arts. 18a, 12(1a) TESM new version.

[204]Remarkable, however, is Art. 7(4) s. 3 TESM new version, which provides that "[t]he Managing Director and the staff of the ESM shall be responsible only to the ESM and shall be completely independent in the performance of their duties". According to Recital 16 TESM new version the independence of the Managing Director and staff of the ESM which is recognised by that Treaty "should be exercised in a manner such that, where relevant and as provided for in this Treaty, consistency is preserved with European Union law, whose application is overseen by the European Commission". This mode of independence excludes the persons concerned, in particular the Managing Director, from the accountability framework of the Union, without, however, establishing complete freedom of instruction and influence.

[205]Cf. Recital 11b s. 4 TESM new version.

be conducted in a transparent and predictable manner while allowing for sufficient margin of judgment". Such a restriction of the margin for decision making through transparency requirements requires further concretisation, but is a first step towards proceduralisation which can provide democratic legitimation to some extent.[206] With regard to the backstop facility instrument, no tasks are entrusted to the ECB except for the assessment whether the conditions for an urgency procedure are met.[207] In this way, as with the separation of SSM and SRM, the ECB is protected from (further) trade-offs. Especially, the ECB which is entrusted with banking supervision is still not responsible for refinancing possible settlement measures as LoLR.[208] An albeit slight improvement in accountability is achieved by making the annual report of the Board of Auditors accessible not only to national parliaments and supreme audit institutions of the ESM Members and the ECA, but also to the European Parliament.[209]

The agreement reached on the reform of the ESM falls well short of the proposed regulation in respect of institutional and organisational changes.[210] Apart from the designation as European Monetary Fund, which was deemed misleading by the ECB in particular with regard to the economic policy orientation of the institution,[211] the thus reformed ESM/EMF was to become an institution under Union law on the basis of Art. 352 TFEU.[212]

A delegation of tasks and powers to a body not provided for under primary law may raise concerns with regard to the ECJ's *Meroni doctrine*, which cannot be fully resolved by the requirement of a final decision of the Council.[213] Nevertheless, it is convincing, as we have seen,[214] to judge Union action solely on the basis of the principle of democracy enshrined in Union law and to consider the delegation of discretionary powers to be permissible in so far as it is sufficiently constrained by democratic mechanisms.

In this respect, the proposed regulation shows welcomed improvements.[215] This concerns in particular the strengthened reporting and accountability obligations of the ESM/EMF towards the European Parliament, the Council and the Commission

[206]See supra Sect. 5.1.3.2.

[207]Art. 18a(6) sub-para. 1 s. 1 TESM new version.

[208]Manger-Nestler and Böttner (2019), pp. 57–58.

[209]Art. 30(5) TESM new version.

[210]For an in-depth analysis see Manger-Nestler and Böttner (2019), pp. 43 et seq.; Pennesi (2018), pp. 530 et seq.

[211]ECB (n. 187), no. 3.

[212]For details concerning the legal basis Manger-Nestler and Böttner (2019), pp. 62–72.

[213]See Art. 3(1) EMFR Draft for decisions which require an approval of the Council; for details see Manger-Nestler and Böttner (2019), pp. 74 et seq.; similarly Pennesi (2018), pp. 532–534 with a comparison to the powers of ESMA.

[214]See supra Sect. 4.4.3.

[215]A strengthening of the political monitoring mechanisms for the ECB's activities in the ESM is also called for by Lettanie (2019), pp. 330–331.

as well as national parliaments,[216] which have clear parallels with the democratic accountability within the SSM. In addition, the integration of the ESM/EMF into the legal order of the Union goes hand in hand with control by the ECA and—without arbitration jurisdiction under Art. 273 TFEU—the CJEU,[217] but also with improvements concerning transparency.[218] Transposing the ESM into the Union's legal order would thus terminate the coexistence of the EU institutions and an intergovernmental "annex" institution and would resolve a split legal situation characterised by inconsistency in terms of democratic accountability, respect for fundamental rights and legal protection.[219] MoUs concluded on behalf of the ESM/EMF would also fall under the system of Union acts and would thus be fully subject to judicial control by the CJEU although the hurdles for individuals remain high.[220]

The proposed regulation also introduced more far-reaching changes to the ECB's participation in the ESM/EMF, which should not be lost sight of in view of future reforms of the central bank mandate. In particular, it was intended that the President of the ECB as well as a member of the Commission would participate in the meetings of the BoG as non-voting members.[221]

However, both the proposed regulation and the draft amendment to the TESM now available do not take into account an important aspect highlighted by the ECB in its opinion:

> The ECB recommends that, in the light of further development and enhancement of the Union's permanent crisis management framework in a post-crisis environment, any contributory role of the ECB should be further clarified to better reflect the ECB's tasks and independence under the Treaties and the clear allocation of technical expertise and responsibilities in the future framework of the ESM. Going forward, the ECB may deal, in an appropriate manner and where necessary, in accordance with its competences, with financial sector policies and macro-critical issues, such as headline fiscal targets and sustainability and financing needs.[222]

This requirement is fully accepted here and shall be extended the ECB's other tasks, mainly those conferred by secondary legislation. It is precisely the terminological and semantic openness of financial stability that requires a clear separation of institutional competence from monetary policy, with which it is closely related.[223]

This could also help to resolve to some extent the competence ambivalence of bond purchase programmes in the context of macro-financial assistance programmes. Not without reason did the Advocate General, in his opinion on the

---

[216]See Arts. 5, 6 EMFR Draft; cf. Manger-Nestler and Böttner (2019), pp. 58–60.

[217]For details see Manger-Nestler and Böttner (2019), pp. 77–78; Pennesi (2018), pp. 541–542.

[218]For ESM's transparency see Simone (2017), pp. 205–208, 210.

[219]Cf. Manger-Nestler and Böttner (2019), p. 49.

[220]Pennesi (2018), p. 540.

[221]Art. 5(3) EMF Statute Draft. With regard to the Board of Directors, however, the ECB should retain observer status, according to Art. 6(2) EMF Statute Draft.

[222]ECB (n. 187), no. 1.3.

[223]Manger-Nestler and Böttner (2019), p. 62.

Gauweiler case, criticise the ECB's "'dual role', as (i) holder of a claim the basis for which is a government bond issued by a State and (ii) supervisor and negotiator of a financial assistance programme applied to the same State, with macroeconomic conditionality included".[224] Ultimately, the ECB's support to macro-financial assistance programmes could lead to a presumption that the terms and conditions of such programmes are not exclusively determined by third parties, with the result that legally separate bond purchase programmes may no longer be covered by the monetary mandate.[225]

The Advocate General should therefore be agreed with in so far as he considers "that the OMT programme is to be regarded as a monetary policy measure, provided that the ECB refrains — once the time has come to put that programme into effect — from any direct involvement in the financial assistance programmes of the ESM or the EFSF".[226]

5.3.4 *Consequences for Current Challenges*

5.3.4.1 Deepening of the EMU After the COVID-19 Crisis

The primary objective of the ESCB/Eurosystem is to maintain price stability. The reason why the ECB is increasingly also carrying out tasks in the area of economic policy and economic supervision is not only due to the analytical resources at its disposal, but is caused by the fact that fundamental conditions for a properly functioning monetary policy are created by macro- and micro-prudential banking supervision, which is primarily aimed at financial stability, as well as participation in the granting of financial assistance and macroeconomic surveillance, which is primarily intended to ensure the stability of the Member States' budgets. The same applies to formal monetary policy action, which may reduce the Member States' economic leeway.

It is therefore even more important that the ECB's actions are based on a strong legal framework that identifies these objectives, sets them in relation to each other and underpins them with a clear range of tasks and set of instruments.

This also applies to the secondary goals assigned to the ESCB according to Art. 127(1) s. 2, (5) TFEU, which at the same time reflect the conceptual asymmetry between economic and monetary union. Admittedly, the competences associated with this prove to be supportive because they require decisions to be taken autonomously by other actors, especially the Member States, so that clear limits are thus placed on the central banks' room for manoeuvre. At the same time, these

---

[224]Advocate General Cruz Villalón, Gauweiler, 14.1.2015, ECLI:EU:C:2015:7, para. 142.

[225]Cf. Advocate General Cruz Villalón, Gauweiler, 14.1.2015, ECLI:EU:C:2015:7, para. 145; however, on the contrary, ECJ, Gauweiler, 16.6.2015, ECLI:EU:C:2015:400, para. 60.

[226]Advocate General Cruz Villalón, Gauweiler, 14.1.2015, ECLI:EU:C:2015:7, para. 151.

competences are characterised by the fact that their broad wording allows for a conceivably wide range of objectives and measures. This becomes particularly clear with regard to the secondary objective standardised in Art. 127(1) s. 2 TFEU, which explicitly refers to the objectives of the Union laid down in Art. 3 TEU and thus inscribes numerous objectives on the ECB, *inter alia* to work for the sustainable development based on balanced economic growth and price stability, a highly competitive social market economy, aiming at full employment and social progress, and a high level of protection and improvement of the quality of the environment (Art. 3(3) sub-para. 1 s. 1 TEU) and to promote economic, social and territorial cohesion, and solidarity among Member States (Art. 3(3) sub-para. 3 TEU). However, even to the extent that central bank action can be based on sufficient competence, it is nevertheless clearly limited by the vertical distribution of competences. This finds expression in the prohibition of monetary financing according to Art. 123 (1) TFEU, whose aim is "to encourage the Member States to follow a sound budgetary policy, not allowing monetary financing of public deficits or privileged access by public authorities to the financial markets to lead to excessively high levels of debt or excessive Member State deficits".[227]

This context becomes particularly clear in view of the measures taken by the ECB in the wake of the COVID-19 pandemic, including in particular the Pandemic Emergency Purchase Programme (PEPP),[228] which, according to its current design, provides for the purchase of bonds with a total volume of EUR 1,850 billion under the conditions of the EAPP/PSPP until at least the end of March 2022.[229] According to the ECB, this is a "response to a specific, extraordinary and acute economic crisis, which could jeopardise the objective of price stability and the proper functioning of the monetary policy transmission mechanism".[230] Concerning the objective of the PEPP, which is explicitly not identical to that of the EAPP/PSPP,[231] the ECB therefore underlines the declining economic development in the euro area as a result of the pandemic and its negative impact on the monetary policy transmission mechanism and the inflation outlook.[232] Against this background, the PEPP is considered a proportionate measure to address the initial risks to price stability, to the monetary policy transmission mechanism and to economic developments in the euro area arising from the outbreak and the rapidly increasing spread of COVID-19.[233]

However, the purchase modalities for public sector bonds, which differ from the PSPP concept, raise doubts about conformity with primary law.[234] This applies in

[227]ECJ, Gauweiler, 16.6.2015, ECLI:EU:C:2015:400, para. 100.

[228]For further measures see Mersch (2020), pp. 9–16.

[229]ECB, Press Release of 4 June 2020c; Press Release of 10 December 2020f.

[230]Recital 3 s. 3 Decision (EU) 2020/440.

[231]Recital 3 s. 4 Decision (EU) 2020/440.

[232]Recital 4 ss. 1–5 Decision (EU) 2020/440.

[233]Recital 4 s. 6 Decision (EU) 2020/440.

[234]For details see Gentzsch (2020), pp. 583–584; Mooij (2020), pp. 713 et seq.; for another view see Mersch (2020), pp. 11–12.

particular to the extent that purchases under the PEPP "shall be conducted in a flexible manner allowing for fluctuations in the distribution of purchase flows over time, across asset classes and among jurisdictions".[235] Moreover, the ECB announced that "[t]o the extent that some self-imposed limits might hamper action that the ECB is required to take in order to fulfil its mandate, the Governing Council will consider revising them to the extent necessary to make its action proportionate to the risks that we face".[236]

Admittedly, the PEPP may be covered by Art. 127(1) s. 2 TFEU, in so far as it also counteracts the risks to economic development beyond the maintenance of price stability, especially if one considers the support of economic policy in the light of the objectives of the Union, in particular economic, social and territorial cohesion and solidarity among Member States (Art. 3(3) sub-para. 3 TEU). Nevertheless, the flexible handling, according to which, for example, in deviation from the capital key, Italian government bonds were acquired to a disproportionately high extent, while French government bonds were acquired to a disproportionately low extent,[237] and the renunciation of legally binding guarantees to ensure market price formation that seems questionable even on the basis of the rather less strict ECJ jurisprudence, raise doubts with regard to the compatibility with Art. 123(1) TFEU, which can probably only be eliminated by a re-interpretation of the provision's purpose, taking into account the exceptional nature of the crisis.[238]

However, the COVID-19 pandemic has revealed that the retention of fiscal policy competence by Member States is a major hurdle in the management of crises triggered by external factors.[239] It is therefore all the more important that the conceptual asymmetry between economic and monetary union is understood as a challenging task for the future and that the economic union is strengthened and further developed into a genuine banking, fiscal, capital market and financial union.[240] Admittedly, this requires a stronger political interlocking within the Union, which tends towards the limits of European integration,[241] but is ultimately indispensable for a functionally adequate, independent performance of the ECB's tasks in the service of the public good.[242]

This would at the same time tackle the problem discovered by the FCC, according to which a judicial control approach that largely considers a distinction between economic and monetary policy to be impossible could jeopardise central bank independence, "as it possibly exposes the ECB to political pressure that it make

[235]Art. 5(2) Decision (EU) 2020/440.

[236]ECB, Press Release of 18 March 2020b.

[237]www.ecb.europa.eu/mopo/implement/pepp/html/index.en.html (26 February 2021).

[238]See Gentzsch (2020), pp. 584–585 with further references.

[239]See also Lastra and Kern (2020), p. 19.

[240]Manger-Nestler (2020), para. 232.

[241]Cf. FCC, Lisbon, 30.6.2009, 2 BvE 2/08 et al., para. 228.

[242]See also Louis (2016), p. 78; Goodhart and Lastra (2017), p. 55 (central banks as "only game in town").

use of the leeway afforded it by the CJEU".[243] The FCC ruled that, "[t]he broader the scope of the ECB's mandate, and the further it reaches into areas reserved to economic and fiscal policy, the greater the risk that interested parties try to influence the ECB's decision-making".[244,245] Although the correlation between broad scope for action and actual influence proves to be a mere assertion, basic economic and fiscal policy decisions should be assigned to the representative bodies, to whose realisation the ECB can contribute.

5.3.4.2 Perspectives for a Sustainable ECB

This relates in particular to the challenges for the ECB arising from climate change. Since 2018, the ECB has been a member of the Network of Central Banks and Supervisors for Greening the Financial System (NGFS), which takes climate change issues into account in various workstreams focusing in particular on macro- and micro-prudential supervision, as well as green financing.[246]

In the area of banking supervision, for example, investments in carbon-intensive economic sectors must be adequately considered with regard to losses due to climate change (physical risks) on the one hand, and the transition to a low-carbon economy (transition risks) on the other.[247] In this respect, an important step has been taken with the ECB's "Guide on climate-related and environmental risks".[248]

In the area of monetary policy, the purchase of green bonds is increasingly being discussed, although the Asset Purchase Programme (APP) in particular is designed to be market-neutral and does not discriminate either positively or negatively against environmental, social and governance criteria.[249] For this, normative basis, which is admittedly rather a generally formulated requirement,[250] is found in Art. 127(1) s. 3 TFEU, according to which "[t]he ESCB shall act in accordance with the principle of an open market economy with free competition, favouring an efficient allocation of resources, and in compliance with the principles set out in Article 119". Nevertheless, the principle of market neutrality does not *a priori* prohibit certain measures, such as the mispricing of climate-related financial risks, as it is not conceived as a strict prohibition such as Art. 123(1) TFEU.[251]

---

[243]FCC, PSPP, 5.5.2020, 2 BvR 859/15 et al., para. 161.

[244]Ibid.

[245]Similar concerns raised by Lamandini et al. (2017), p. 17 with regard to OMT.

[246]An overview is available at https://www.ngfs.net/en/about-us/governance/origin-and-purpose (26 February 2021).

[247]Cf. Enria (2020); Smoleńska and van 't Klooster (2020); Bovenschen and Lieshout (2020), p. 125.

[248]ECB, Guide on climate-related and environmental risks of 27 November 2020e.

[249]ECB, Economic Bulletin, Issue 7/2018.

[250]De Boer and van 't Klooster (2020), p. 1709.

[251]Cf. Várhelyi (2020), pp. 161–162.

However, combating climate change becomes an objective that must find grounding in the mandate, if the ECB intends, for example, not only to "better safeguard the banking sector's resilience",[252] but by adequate pricing of climate risks to "drive a smoother and faster transition to a more sustainable economy".[253] It would also be an actively pursued goal if the ECB were to use monetary policy tools and instruments including the collection of collateral and the establishment of relationships with Eurosystem counterparties whose activities are considered sustainable, or to maintain monetary policy asset purchase portfolios with an overall footprint compatible with the EU's numerical emission reduction targets.[254]

Although Art. 11 TFEU provides that environmental protection requirements must be integrated into the definition and implementation of the Union's policies and activities, in particular with a view to promoting sustainable development, climate protection cannot be easily integrated into the ECB's mandate.[255] That pursuing a carbon-neutral economy can be relevant for maintaining the primary objective was recently highlighted by *Isabel Schnabel*, a member of the ECB's Executive Board, who pointed out that "climate risks – including physical and transition risks – may affect medium-term inflation dynamics as well as central banks' ability to protect price stability against large and persistent climate shocks in the vicinity of the lower bound".[256]

If such a reference to the primacy of price stability cannot be proved, only the competence to support the general economic policies in the Union according to Art. 127(1) s. 2 TFEU may allow the ECB to actively favour low-carbon sectors and bond issuers in its actions.[257] However, the competence to support does not allow the ECB to pursue autonomous environmental policy objectives, but limits it to contribute to the relevant economic policies in the Union.[258] In this respect, the targets set out in the European Green Deal, in particular that of no net emissions of greenhouse gases by 2050,[259] may form an important guide for a complementary monetary policy, but still need to be implemented in concrete standards.

In any case, it would be important for the ECB's action to be determined by clear and measurable criteria, whereby the EU taxonomy for sustainable activities as enshrined in Regulation (EU) 2020/852[260] sets the right path.

---

[252]Cf. Enria (2020).

[253]Ibid.

[254]Cf. Arruga Oleaga (2020), pp. 115–116.

[255]For a critical view see also Smoleńska and van 't Klooster (2020); Nees (2021), pp. 127 et seq.; for another view Cerrato et al. (2020), understanding Art. 11 TFEU as a strict obligation for the ECB; similarly Arruga Oleaga (2020), p. 114.

[256]Schnabel (2020); see also Bovenschen and Lieshout (2020), pp 122–123.

[257]De Boer and van 't Klooster (2020), p. 1709; see also Lastra and Kern (2020), p. 5.

[258]Bovenschen and Lieshout (2020), p. 124.

[259]Details are available at https://ec.europa.eu/info/strategy/priorities-2019-2024/european-green-deal_en (26 February 2021).

[260]Regulation (EU) 2020/852 of the European Parliament and of the Council of 18 June 2020 on the establishment of a framework to facilitate sustainable investment, and amending Regulation

5.3.4.3 Impact on the Issuance of a Digital Euro

Fanned by the flames of the debate regarding crypto-currencies, like Bitcoin or Diem (former: Libra), the scope of the central bank mandate, and thus central bank independence, must also be considered in view of the planned introduction of a digital euro.[261] This issue of so-called central bank digital currency (CBDC) is the answer to the advance of blockchain-based private payment instruments using distributed ledger technology (DLT), which are already conceptually difficult to grasp and are referred to as crypto-currencies, crypto-assets, digital currencies or virtual currencies.[262]

After extensive analysis, the ECB published a comprehensive report on the possible issuance of a digital euro in early October 2020, which should provide the basis for a subsequent experimental phase and a broad public and inter-institutional debate.[263] The currently proposed concept envisages an electronic form of central bank money that will be made available to all citizens and companies and can thus act as a cash equivalent (not a substitute).[264] Before the introduction of a digital euro, however, the "if" needs to be clarified, taking into account various conditions such as usage behaviour, acceptance of CBDC and possible threats to monetary policy, financial stability and the smooth functioning of payment systems.[265] On the other hand, the "how" of the introduction in its technical and legal form must be examined more closely.[266] With regard to the digital euro, a centralised solution supported by a central bank account is being considered on the one hand, while on the other hand a decentralised solution involving more closely the supervised financial intermediaries, possibly via DLT, is being considered.[267] In either case, the back-end infrastructure and thus the issuance of the digital euro should be controlled by the central banks.[268]

At all events, the choice of the proper legal basis will depend on whether the digital euro is actually issued to final customers or whether access is only granted to those entities that already have access to central bank money. In the former case in particular, the ECB prefers to apply Art. 128(1) in conjunction with Art. 16 ESCB/ECB Statute, but also envisages a legislative act under Art. 133 TFEU to regulate the

(EU) 2019/2088, OJ 22.6.2020, L 198, p. 13; for details see Bovenschen and Lieshout (2020), pp. 119–122.

[261] See for details Manger-Nestler (2021a), pp. 4 et seq.; on the monetary classification of crypto-assets, see Manger-Nestler (2021b), paras. 58 et seq.

[262] A special form of appearance are so-called stablecoins, such as the project Diem (former: Libra) project, which was announced mainly on the initiative of Facebook.

[263] ECB (2020d), p. 2.

[264] ECB (2020d), p. 6.

[265] ECB (2020d), pp. 9–15; see also Omlor and Birne (2020), pp. 1–2.

[266] Omlor and Birne (2020), pp. 2–4.

[267] ECB (2020d), pp. 36 et seq.; previously Bindseil (2020), p. 4.

[268] ECB (2020d), pp. 4, 8, 36.

conditions for the Eurosystem to issue a digital euro with legal tender status.[269] However, the Advocate General in the *Dietrich case* provides support here, mentioning as *obiter dictum* that the Union may also "assign, alongside euro banknotes (and coins), the status of legal tender to other forms of currency that are not necessarily physical".[270]

With regard to the independence of the ECB, however, decisive limits can be detected. In terms of democratic legitimation and control, the fundamental rights relevance of any measures must be taken into account. This is particularly true if the digital euro creates an asset position whose value stability market participants can trust. Furthermore, it should not be overlooked that CBDC and the disintermediation it entails may have a negative impact on banks' financing costs and thus on interest rates and credit volumes. The creation of CBDC thus has the potential to challenge the very foundations of the national and supranational monetary order, thus undermining the traditional division of tasks in the two-tier system between central and commercial banks. Considerable economic effects are conceivable, which could also provoke further proceedings before the FCC with a view to safeguarding Member State competences. A democratic embedment of the process is therefore necessary, but must also carefully consider the competences of the ECB.

Depending on its design, the introduction and distribution of CBDC may also belong to the basic tasks of the ECB. If, as currently envisaged, a digital euro could be exchanged at par value for other forms of the euro and thus be stable in value,[271] it would directly participate in the stability primacy of Art. 127(1) s. 1 TFEU. In this way, CBDC may strengthen the transmission of monetary policy, for instance when the Eurosystem sets a remuneration rate, thereby directly influencing consumption and investment decisions.[272] On the other hand, "digital runs" away from scriptural currency and towards the digital euro can lead to liquidity and thus settlement risks, especially in times of crisis.[273] Especially for the ECB, which operates in the triad of monetary policy, macro-supervision and micro-supervision,[274] the implementation of CBDC proves to be challenging. All models of CBDC more or less shake up the historically evolved division of tasks between central and commercial banks and thus the cornerstones of the supra- and national monetary and financial system. Even as an alternative payment technology, CBDC would have to demonstrably create added value, both in terms of functioning and efficiency, in order to outweigh the

[269]ECB (2020d), pp. 24–25, cf. 6–7; for provisions regarding virtual money/crypto-currency based on Art. 133 TFEU, although without explicit reference to CBDC, see Wutscher (2019), para. 2.

[270]Advocate General Pitruzzella, Dietrich, 29.9.2020, ECLI:EU:C:2020:756, para. 96; on conformity with Art. 128 TFEU see Omlor and Birne (2020), p. 4.

[271]ECB (2020d), p. 50.

[272]ECB (2020d), pp. 12–13, but with reservation; previously Bindseil (2020), pp. 6–7.

[273]ECB (2020d), pp. 16 et seq.; Bindseil (2020), pp. 22 et seq. pleading for a „Two-tier remuneration of CBDC".

[274]Manger-Nestler and Böttner (2014), pp. 628 et seq.

threats to financial stability (Art. 127(5), (6) TFEU) that would simultaneously accompany its innovative power.

References

Amtenbrink F (1999) The democratic accountability of central banks – a comparative study of the European central banks. Oxford University Press, Oxford

Amtenbrink F (2019) Independence and accountability in the new age of European central banking – revisiting Gormely and de Haan's 'The democratic deficit of the European Central Bank'. In: Amtenbrink F, Davies G, Kochenov D, Lindeboom J (eds) The internal market and the future of European integration – essays in honour of Laurence W. Gormley. Cambridge University Press, Cambridge, pp 305–321

Amtenbrink F, Markakis M (2019) Towards a meaningful prudential supervision dialogue in the euro area? – a study of the interaction between the European Parliament and the European Central Bank in the Single Supervisory Mechanism. Eur Law Rev 44:3–23

Arruga Oleaga I (2020) Introduction to the panel on the EU taxonomy and action plan on sustainable finance – what uses for the ESCB? In: ECB, Legal Conference 2020, Frankfurt a. M., pp 112–117. https://www.ecb.europa.eu/pub/pdf/other/ecb.escblegalconferenceproceedings2020~4c11842967.en.pdf?b70332cb34a349c717ca2d50cf1dc521. (26 February 2021)

Beukers T (2013) The new ECB and its relationship with the Member States of the euro area – between central bank independence and central bank intervention. Common Mark Law Rev 50:1579–1620

Bindseil U (2020) Tiered CBDC and the financial system, Working Paper Series. https://www.ecb.europa.eu/pub/pdf/scpwps/ecb.wp2351~c8c18bbd60.en.pdf (26 February 2021)

Böckenförde E-W (2004) § 24 Demokratie als Verfassungsprinzip. In: Isensee J, Kirchhof P (eds) Handbuch des Staatsrechts der Bundesrepublik Deutschland, Band II Verfassungsstaat, 3rd edn. C.F. Müller, Heidelberg

Bovenschen W, Lieshout R (2020) EU taxonomy, action plan & supervisory developments on sustainable finance – what uses may these have for the E(S)CB? In: ECB, Legal Conference 2020, Frankfurt a.M., pp 118–129. https://www.ecb.europa.eu/pub/pdf/other/ecb.escblegalconferenceproceedings2020~4c11842967.en.pdf?b70332cb34a349c717ca2d50cf1dc521. (26 February 2021)

Calliess C (2016) Kommentierung zu Art. 296 AEUV. In: Calliess C, Ruffert M (eds) EUV/AEUV, 5th edn. Beck, Munich

Caranta R, Andenas M, Fairgrieve D (eds) (2004) Independent administrative authorities. British Institute of International and Comparative Law, London

Cerrato E, Agostini F, Jaberg N (2020) Why the PSPP judgment of the German Federal Constitutional Court gives the ECB another incentive to integrate climate change considerations into monetary policy, European Law Blog of 27 May 2020. https://europeanlawblog.eu/2020/05/27/why-the-pspp-judgment-of-the-german-federal-constitutional-court-gives-the-ecb-another-incentive-to-integrate-climate-change-considerations-into-monetary-policy/. (26 February 2021)

Classen CD (2011) Unabhängigkeit und Eigenständigkeit der Verwaltung – zu einer Anforderung des Europarechts an das nationale Recht. In: Müller-Graff P-C, Schmahl S, Skouris V (eds) Europäisches Recht zwischen Bewährung und Wandel – Festschrift für Dieter H. Scheuing. Nomos, Baden-Baden, pp 293–308

Curtin D (2017) 'Accountable independence' of the European Central Bank – seeing the logics of transparency. Eur Law J 23:28–44

Dawson M, Maricut-Akbik A, Bobić A (2019) Reconciling independence and accountability at the European Central Bank – the false promise of proceduralism. Eur Law J 25:75–93

De Boer N, van 't Klooster J (2020) The ECB, the courts and the issue of democratic legitimacy after Weiss. Common Mark Law Rev 57:1689–1724

Dechent FA (2015) Bundesanstalt für Finanzdienstleistungsaufsicht und Bundesanstalt für Finanzmarktstabilisierung – Unabhängige Behörden in der Bankenaufsicht. Neue Zeitschrift für Verwaltungsrecht, pp 767–772

Eijffinger S, de Haan J (1996) The political economy of central-bank independence, Special Papers in International Economics No. 19. https://www.researchgate.net/publication/5072793_The_Political_Economy_of_Central-Bank_Independence. (26 February 2021)

Enria A (2020) ECB banking supervision's approach to climate risks – Keynote speech at the European Central Bank Climate and Environmental Risks Webinar of 17 June. https://www.bankingsupervision.europa.eu/press/speeches/date/2020/html/ssm.sp200617~74d8539eda.en.html. (26 February 2021)

European Central Bank (1999) Annual report. https://www.ecb.europa.eu/pub/pdf/annrep/ar1999en.pdf. (26 February 2021)

European Central Bank (2017) Agreement on Emergency Liquidity Assistance of 17 May. https://www.ecb.europa.eu/pub/pdf/other/Agreement_on_emergency_liquidity_assistance_20170517.en.pdf?23bb6a68e85e0715839088d0a23011db. (26 February 2021)

European Central Bank (2018) ECB Economic Bulletin, issue 7 – update on economic and monetary developments. https://www.ecb.europa.eu/pub/economic-bulletin/html/eb201807.en.html#IDofOverviewes_Eb. (26 February 2021)

European Central Bank (2019) Press Release of 12 September. https://www.ecb.europa.eu/press/pr/date/2019/html/ecb.mp190912~08de50b4d2.en.html. (26 February 2021)

European Central Bank (2020a) Press Release of 24 February. https://www.ecb.europa.eu/press/pr/date/2020/htm/ecb.pr200224~752f11038e.en.html. (26 February 2021)

European Central Bank (2020b) Press Release of 18 March. https://www.ecb.europa.eu/press/pr/date/2020/html/ecb.pr200318_1~3949d6f266.en.html. (26 February 2021)

European Central Bank (2020c) Press Release of 4 June. https://www.ecb.europa.eu/press/pr/date/2020/html/ecb.mp200604~a307d3429c.de.html. (26 February 2021)

European Central Bank (2020d) Report on a digital euro, October. https://www.ecb.europa.eu/pub/pdf/other/Report_on_a_digital_euro~4d7268b458.en.pdf. (26 February 2021)

European Central Bank (2020e) Guide on climate-related and environmental risks of 27 November – supervisory expectations relating to risk management and disclosure. https://www.bankingsupervision.europa.eu/ecb/pub/pdf/ssm.202011finalguideonclimate-relatedandenvironmentalrisks~58213f6564.en.pdf. (26 February 2021)

European Central Bank (2020f) Presse Release of 10 December, https://www.ecb.europa.eu/press/pr/date/2020/html/ecb.mp201210~8c2778b843.en.html. (26 February 2021)

European Court of Auditors (2016) Single Supervisory Mechanism – good start but further improvements needed, Special Report No. 29. https://www.eca.europa.eu/Lists/ECADocuments/SR16_29/SR_SSM_EN.pdf. (26 February 2021)

Ferran E, Babis V (2013) The European Single Supervisory Mechanism, University of Cambridge Faculty of Law, Legal Studies Research Paper Series, Paper No. 10/2013. https://papers.ssrn.com/sol3/papers.cfm?abstract_id=2224538. (26 February 2021)

Fromage D, Ibrido R (2018) The 'banking dialogue' as a model to improve parliamentary involvement in the monetary dialogue? J Eur Integr 40:295–308

Gentzsch M (2020) Die EZB ultra vires? – Die PSPP-Entscheidung und ihre Konsequenzen für das Recht der Währungsunion. Zeitschrift für Bank- und Kapitalmarktrecht, pp 576–585

Gentzsch M, Becker M (2017) PSPP – curtain up for a new act in the drama "German Federal Constitutional Court versus European Court of Justice". German Yearb Int Law 60:785–797

Gentzsch M, Brade A (2019) Die Bankenunion vor dem Bundesverfassungsgericht – Neue Impulse für grundlegende Fragestellungen des Verfassungs- und Unionsrechts. Europarecht, pp 602–636

German Council of Economic Experts (2012/13) Annual report. https://www.sachverstaendigenrat-wirtschaft.de/fileadmin/dateiablage/gutachten/ga201213/ga12_ges.pdf. (26 February 2021)

Glatzl S (2009) Geldpolitik und Bankenaufsicht im Konflikt – Die Pflicht der Mitgliedstaaten zur Unterstützung der EZB im Bereich der Preisstabilität unter besonderer Berücksichtigung der Bankenaufsicht. Nomos, Baden-Baden

Goldmann M (2018) United in diversity? – the relationship between monetary policy and prudential supervision in the Banking Union. Eur Const Law Rev 14:283–310

Goodhart C, Lastra RM (2017) Populism and central bank independence. Open Econ Rev 29:49–68

Goodhart C, Schoenmaker D (1995) Should the functions of monetary policy and banking supervision be separated? Oxford Econ Pap 47:539–560

Gormley LW, de Haan J (1996) The democratic deficit of the European Central Bank. Eur Law Rev 21:95–112

Groß T (1999) Das Kollegialprinzip in der Verwaltungsorganisation. Mohr Siebeck, Tübingen

Groß T (2012) Unabhängige EU-Agenturen – eine Gefahr für die Demokratie? Juristenzeitung, pp 1087–1093

Gurlit E (2014) The ECB's relationship to the EBA. Europäische Zeitschrift für Wirtschaftsrecht Beilage, pp 14–18

Häde U (2016) Kommentierung zu Art. 127 AEUV. In: Calliess C, Ruffert M (eds) EUV/AEUV, 5th edn. Beck, Munich

Hahn HJ, Häde U (2010) Währungsrecht, 2nd edn. Beck, Munich

Hermes G (2005) Legitimationsprobleme unabhängiger Behörden. In: Bauer H, Huber PM, Sommermann K-P (eds) Demokratie in Europa. Mohr Siebeck, Tübingen, pp 457–488

Heselhaus S (2017) Kommentierung zu Art. 15 AEUV sowie Art. 42 GRCh. In: Pechstein M, Nowak C, Häde U (eds) Frankfurter Kommentar zu EUV, GRC und AEUV. Mohr Siebeck, Tübingen

Heun W (2012) Finanzaufsicht im Wandel. Juristenzeitung, pp 235–242

Huber PM (2005) Demokratie in Europa – Zusammenfassung und Ausblick. In: Bauer H, Huber PM, Sommermann K-P (eds) Demokratie in Europa. Mohr Siebeck, Tübingen, pp 491–512

IMF (2013) European Union – issues in transparency and accountability, March. https://www.imf.org/external/pubs/ft/scr/2013/cr1365.pdf. (26 February 2021)

Kämmerer JA, Starski P (2013) Die Europäische Zentralbank in der Bankenunion oder: Vor Risiken und Nebenwirkungen wird gewarnt. Zeitschrift für Gesetzgebung, pp 318–338

Kaufhold A-K (2016) Systemaufsicht – Anforderungen an die Ausgestaltung einer Aufsicht zur Abwehr systemischer Risiken entwickelt am Beispiel der Finanzaufsicht. Mohr Siebeck, Tübingen

Keller C (2013) Kommentierung zu Art. 18 ESZB/EZB-S. In: Siekmann H (ed) EWU – Kommentar zur Europäischen Währungsunion. Mohr Siebeck, Tübingen

Kern A (2015) European Banking Union – a legal and institutional analysis of the Single Supervisory Mechanism and the Single Resolution Mechanism. Eur Law Rev 40:154–187

Lamandini M, Ramos Muñoz D (2020) SSM and SRB accountability at European level – what room for improvements? Banking Union Scrutiny. https://www.europarl.europa.eu/RegData/etudes/STUD/2020/645711/IPOL_STU(2020)645711_EN.pdf. (26 February 2021)

Lamandini M, Ramos Muñoz D, Solana Álvarez J (2015) Depicting the limits to the SSM's supervisory powers – the role of constitutional mandates and of fundamental rights' protection. Quaderni di Ricerca Giuridica No. 79. https://ssrn.com/abstract=2733620. (26 February 2021)

Lamandini M, Ramos Muñoz D, Solana Álvarez J (2017) The European Central Bank (ECB) (powers) as a catalyst for change in EU law – the ECB's mandates (part 1), SSM, SRM and fundamental rights (part 2). Columbia J Eur Law 23:1–54. and 199–263

Lastra RM (2015) International financial and monetary law, 2nd edn. Oxford University Press, Oxford

Lastra RM, Kern A (2020) The ECB mandate – perspectives on sustainability and solidarity, Monetary Dialogue Papers, June 2020. https://www.europarl.europa.eu/RegData/etudes/IDAN/2020/648813/IPOL_IDA(2020)648813_EN.pdf. (26 February 2021)

Lehmann M, Manger-Nestler C (2011) Das neue Europäische Finanzaufsichtssystem. Zeitschrift für Bankrecht und Bankwirtschaft, pp 2–24

Lehmann M, Manger-Nestler C (2014) Einheitlicher Europäischer Aufsichtsmechanismus – Bankenaufsicht durch die EZB. Zeitschrift für Bankrecht und Bankwirtschaft, pp 2–21

Leino-Sandberg P (2019) Public access to ECB documents – are accountability, independence and effectiveness an impossible trinity? In: ECB, Legal Conference 2019 – building bridges: central banking law in an interconnected world, Frankfurt a.M., pp 195–219. https://www.ecb.europa.eu/pub/pdf/other/ecb.ecblegalconferenceproceedings201912~9325c45957.en.pdf?258d648ffcf1be39f9d927e5c13f393f. (26 February 2021)

Lenaerts K (2013) The principle of democracy in the case law of the European Court of Justice. Int Comp Law Q 62:271–315

Lettanie U (2019) The ECB's performance under the ESM Treaty on a sliding scale of delegation. Eur Law J 25:317–332

Louis J-V (2016) The EMU after the Gauweiler judgment and the Juncker Report. Maastricht J Eur Comp Law 23:55–78

Lübbe-Wolff G (2001) Europäisches und nationales Verfassungsrecht. Veröffentlichungen der Vereinigung der Deutschen Staatsrechtslehrer 60:246–289

Lupia A (2006) Delegation and its perils. In: Strøm K, Müller WC, Bergman T (eds) Delegation and accountability in parliamentary democracies, 2nd edn. Oxford University Press, Oxford, pp 33–54

Majone G (1998) The regulatory state and its legitimacy problems, Institute for Advanced Studies Vienna, Political Science Series No. 56. https://nbn-resolving.org/urn:nbn:de:0168-ssoar-246700. (26 February 2021)

Manger-Nestler C (2020) § 25 Das Recht der Europäischen Währungsunion. In: Müller-Graff P-C (ed) Enzyklopädie Europarecht Vol. 4. Europäisches Wirtschaftsordnungsrecht, 2nd edn. Nomos, Baden-Baden

Manger-Nestler C (2021a) Digitales Zentralbankgeld aus währungsrechtlicher Sicht. Recht der Zahlungsdienste, pp 4–11

Manger-Nestler C (2021b) Kapitel 9 Währungsrecht. In: Omlor S, Link M (eds) Kryptowährungen und Token. Fachmedien Recht und Wirtschaft, Deutscher Fachverlag, Frankfurt am Main

Manger-Nestler C, Böttner R (2014) Ménage à trois? – Zur gewandelten Rolle der EZB im Spannungsfeld zwischen Geldpolitik, Finanzaufsicht und Fiskalpolitik. Europarecht, pp 621–637

Manger-Nestler C, Böttner R (2019) Der Europäische Währungsfonds nach den Plänen der Kommission. Zeitschrift für ausländisches öffentliches Recht und Völkerrecht, pp 43–84

Maricut-Akbik A (2020) Contesting the European Central Bank in banking supervision – accountability in practice at the European Parliament. J Common Mark Stud 58:1199–1214

Masing J (2010) Unabhängige Behörden und ihr Aufgabenprofil. In: Masing J, Marcou G (eds) Unabhängige Regulierungsbehörden – Organisationsrechtliche Herausforderungen in Frankreich und Deutschland. Mohr Siebeck, Tübingen, pp 181–219

Mersch Y (2017) Central bank independence revisited, Keynote at the "Symposium on Building the Financial System of the 21st Century: An Agenda for Europe and the United States", Frankfurt a.M., 30 March 2017. https://www.ecb.europa.eu/press/key/date/2017/html/sp170330.en.html. (26 February 2021)

Mersch Y (2018) The limits of central bank financing in resolution – speech at the IMFS Distinguished Lecture Series, Goethe Universität Frankfurt a.M., 30 January 2018. Europäische Zeitschrift für Wirtschaftsrecht, pp 349–352

Mersch Y (2020) Legal aspects of the ECB's response to the coronavirus (COVID-19) pandemic – an exclusive but narrow competence. In: ECB, Legal Conference 2020, Frankfurt a.M., pp 9–17. https://www.ecb.europa.eu/pub/pdf/other/ecb.escblegalconferenceproceedings2020~4c11842967.en.pdf?b70332cb34a349c717ca2d50cf1dc521. (26 February 2021)

Mooij AAM (2020) The legality of the ECB responses to COVID-19. Eur Law Rev 45:713–731

Müller WC, Bergman T, Strøm K (2006) Parliamentary democracy – promise and problems. In: Strøm K, Müller WC, Bergman T (eds) Delegation and accountability in parliamentary democracies, 2nd edn. Oxford University Press, Oxford, pp 3–32

Nees D (2021) Klimaschutz durch die EZB? Reichweite und Grenzen des Mandats der EZB in Bezug auf den Erwerb sogenannter "grüner" Anleihen, Europarecht, pp 119–136
O'Connell M (2013) The legal framework for the provision of Emergency Liquidity Assistance within the ESCB. Zeitschrift für Europäische Studien, pp 261–328
Oebbecke J (1986) Weisungs- und unterrichtungsfreie Räume in der Verwaltung. Deutscher Gemeindeverlag, Köln
Ohler C (2015) Bankenaufsicht und Geldpolitik in der Währungsunion. Beck, Munich
Omlor S, Birne A (2020) Digitales Zentralbankgeld im Euroraum. Recht Digital, pp 1–10
Ossenbühl F (1968) Verwaltungsvorschriften und Grundgesetz. Gehlen, Bad Homburg/Berlin/ Zürich
Pennesi F (2018) The accountability of the European Stability Mechanism and the European Monetary Fund – who should answer for conditionality measures? Eur Pap 3:511–545
Peroni G (2017) The European Central Bank (ECB) and European democracy – a technocratic institution to rule all European states. In: Daniele L, Simone P, Cisotta R (eds) Democracy in the EMU in the aftermath of the crisis. Springer, Heidelberg, pp 249–264
Peters A (2001) Elemente einer Theorie der Verfassung Europas. Duncker & Humblot, Berlin
Petersen N (2010) Demokratie und Grundgesetz – Veränderungen des Demokratieprinzips in Art. 20 Abs. 2 GG angesichts der Herausforderungen moderner Staatlichkeit. Jahrbuch des öffentlichen Rechts 58:137–171
Peuker E (2011) Bürokratie und Demokratie in Europa – Legitimität im Europäischen Verwaltungsverbund. Mohr Siebeck, Tübingen
Psaroudakis G (2018) The scope for financial stability considerations in the fulfilment of the mandate of the ECB/Eurosystem. J Financ Regul 4:119–156
Quintyn M, Taylor MW (2007) Robust regulators and their political masters – independence and accountability in theory. In: Masciandaro D, Quintyn M (eds) Designing financial supervision institutions – independence, accountability and governance. Elgar, Cheltenham/Northampton, pp 3–40
Rodi M (2018) Kommentierung zu Art. 127 AEUV. In: Vedder C, Heintschel von Heinegg W (eds) Europäisches Unionsrecht EUV/AEUV/GRCh/EAGV, Handkommentar, 2nd edn. Nomos, Baden-Baden
Ruffert M (2011) Die neue Unabhängigkeit – Zur demokratischen Legitimation von Agenturen im europäischen Verwaltungsrecht. In: Müller-Graff P-C, Schmahl S, Skouris V (eds) Europäisches Recht zwischen Bewährung und Wandel – Festschrift für Dieter H. Scheuing. Nomos, Baden-Baden, pp 399–414
Ruthig J (2014) Die EZB in der europäischen Bankenunion. Zeitschrift für das gesamte Handelsrecht und Wirtschaftsrecht 178:443–484
Sacarcelik O (2013) Europäische Bankenunion – Rechtliche Rahmenbedingungen und Herausforderungen der einheitlichen europäischen Bankenaufsicht. Zeitschrift für Bank- und Kapitalmarktrecht, pp 353–360
Schmidt MG (2019) Demokratietheorien – Eine Einführung, 6th edn. Springer, Heidelberg
Schmidt-Aßmann E (2006) Das allgemeine Verwaltungsrecht als Ordnungsidee – Grundlagen und Aufgaben der verwaltungsrechtlichen Systembildung, 2nd edn. Springer, Heidelberg
Schnabel I (2020) Never waste a crisis – COVID-19, climate change and monetary policy, Speech at the INSPIRE virtual roundtable 'Sustainable Crisis Responses in Europe' on 17 July 2020. https://www.ecb.europa.eu/press/key/date/2020/html/ecb.sp200717~1556b0f988.en.html. (26 February 2021)
Selmayr M (2015) Kommentierung zu Art. 282 AEUV. In: von der Groeben H, Schwarze J, Hatje A (eds) Europäisches Unionsrecht, 7th edn. Nomos, Baden-Baden
Siekmann H (2013) Einführung. In: Siekmann H (ed) EWU – Kommentar zur Europäischen Währungsunion. Mohr Siebeck, Tübingen
Siekmann H (2020) Gerichtliche Kontrolle der Käufe von Staatsanleihen durch das Eurosystem – Anmerkungen zum PSPP-Urteil des BVerfG vom 5.5.2020. Europäische Zeitschrift für Wirtschaftsrecht, pp 491–500

Simone P (2017) Respecting the democratic principle in ESM activities related to the context of the economic and financial crisis. In: Daniele L, Simone P, Cisotta R (eds) Democracy in the EMU in the aftermath of the crisis. Springer, Heidelberg, pp 195–214

Smits R (1997) The European Central Bank – institutional aspects. Kluwer Law International, The Hague

Smits R, Badenhoop N (2019) Towards a single standard of professional secrecy for financial sector supervisory authorities – a reform proposal. Eur Law Rev 44:295–318

Smoleńska A, van't Klooster J (2020) Greening banks in the face of uncertainty – on the ECB's new supervisory approach to environmental and climate-related risks, VerfBlog, 2020/11/16. https://verfassungsblog.de/greening-banks-in-the-face-of-uncertainty/. (26 February 2021)

Steinbach A (2016) The lender of last resort in the Eurozone. Common Mark Law Rev 53:361–383

Steinbach A (2020) Ultra schwierig, VerfBlog, 2020/5/06. https://verfassungsblog.de/ultra-schwierig/. (26 February 2021)

Strøm K (2006) Parliamentary democracy and delegation. In: Strøm K, Müller WC, Bergman T (eds) Delegation and accountability in parliamentary democracies, 2nd edn. Oxford University Press, Oxford, pp 55–106

Thiele A (2014) Finanzaufsicht – Der Staat und die Finanzmärkte. Mohr Siebeck, Tübingen

Thiele A (2015) Krise der Europäischen Integration? – Die Bankenunion als Beleg für die Handlungsfähigkeit der EU. Gewerbearchiv, pp 111–116, 157–160

Tröger TH (2013) The Single Supervisory Mechanism – panacea or quack banking regulation?, SAFE Working Paper No. 27. https://papers.ssrn.com/sol3/papers.cfm?abstract_id=2311353. (26 February 2021)

Trute H-H (2012) § 6 Die demokratische Legitimation der Verwaltung. In: Hoffmann-Riem W, Schmidt-Aßmann E, Voßkuhle A (eds) Grundlagen des Verwaltungsrechts, vol 1, 2nd edn. Beck, Munich

Várhelyi G (2020) EU taxonomy and the monetary policy prism. In: ECB, Legal Conference 2020, Frankfurt a.M., pp 144–165. https://www.ecb.europa.eu/pub/pdf/other/ecb.escblegalconferenceproceedings2020~4c11842967.en.pdf?b70332cb34a349c717ca2d50cf1dc521. (26 February 2021)

von Bogdandy A (2000) Gubernative Rechtsetzung – Eine Neubestimmung der Rechtsetzung und des Regierungssystems unter dem Grundgesetz in der Perspektive gemeineuropäischer Dogmatik. Mohr Siebeck, Tübingen

Wegener B (2016) Kommentierung zu Art. 15 AEUV. In: Calliess C, Ruffert M (eds) EUV/AEUV, 5th edn. Beck, Munich

Wutscher C (2019) Kommentierung zu Art. 133 AEUV. In: Schwarze J, Becker U, Hatje A, Schoo J (eds) EU-Kommentar, 4rd edn. Nomos, Baden-Baden

Zilioli C (2016a) The independence of the European Central Bank and its new banking supervisory competences. In: Ritleng D (ed) Independence and legitimacy in the institutional system of the European Union. Oxford University Press, Oxford, pp 125–179

Zilioli C (2016b) The ECB's power and institutional role in the financial crisis – a confirmation from the Court of Justice of the European Union. Maastricht J Eur Comp Law 23:171–184

Zilioli C, Selmayr M (2001) The law of the European Central Bank. Hart Publishing, Oxford/Portland

Zuleeg M (1993) Demokratie in der Europäischen Gemeinschaft. Juristenzeitung, pp 1069–1074

Chapter 6
Conclusion

Central bank action in the EMU is provided with far-reaching guarantees of independence, which are primarily found in the Treaties and are expressed in institutional, personal, financial and functional independence. Of particular importance is the dimension of functional independence, which is expressed by an extensive freedom of instructions and influence, but which is strictly bound back to the objectives, tasks and duties provided for in the Treaties and finds its actual justification in the primacy of price stability.

The singularity of this *modus operandi* became apparent in the comparison between the independence of the ECB and other institutions, bodies and agencies of the Union. Admittedly, there are normative parallels in which, for example, the other institutions are also anchored by primary-law provisions that are difficult to amend, are characterised by long terms of office and high threshold options for dismissal, and are to be protected from influence perceived as improper by prohibitions on giving instructions.

Nevertheless, the ECB's independence can be regarded as exceptional in its unique combination of regulations on the construction of institutional autonomy, the granting of financial autonomy, the implementation of a far-reaching scope for monetary policy-making, the factually uninfluenced performance of tasks and the absence of direct parliamentary control through the dismissal of members or the overruling of decisions.

The concrete function proves to be the pivotal issue of the democratic legitimation and control of central bank action, which follows from the democratic requirements under Union law and in the Member States and is primarily intended to ensure a reconnection with the citizens of the Union and the organs representing them by establishing responsibility.

Especially the functional change of the ECB towards the use of unconventional monetary policy instruments as well as the performance of further tasks for safeguarding financial and fiscal stability on the basis of secondary law or extra-contractual agreements has made visible the necessity of a task-related differentiation, which contrasts with a legal conception and examination of central bank action

C. Manger-Nestler, M. Gentzsch, *Democratic Legitimation of Central Bank Independence in the European Union*, https://doi.org/10.1007/978-3-030-75115-9_6

solely by reference to *topoi* such as independence, efficiency, flexibility, specialisation, institutional balance, accountability and judicial self-restraint.[1]

The scope of democratic legitimation and control to be demanded depends on various factors. For example, the specific performance potential of central banks, as has become apparent above all with regard to open-structured, target-oriented and forecast-based monetary policy, can influence the steering and control function of the contrasting bodies, especially parliaments and courts, because the density of steering and control is lower and is reduced to the definition and review of procedural requirements. In contrast, regulatory matters in which controllable conditional programmes are applied, such as in micro-prudential banking supervision, enable a greater degree of regulation and parliamentary, judicial and administrative control.

In addition, the impact on fundamental, especially constitutional, principles or protected interests may require a stronger democratic commitment. This applies not only to measures that—such as banking supervision as a component of economic supervision – encroach on fundamental rights but also to those that—such as large-volume bond-buying programmes that are not limited in time—are on the edge of monetary policy competence and threaten to interfere with the Member States' competences.

Which counterbalances are to be put in place against this on the basis of the Union's principle of democracy (Arts. 2, 10–12 TEU) also depends on the function of central bank action and may vary in the course of time and the challenges posed. For as Congressman *John Lewis* put it: "Democracy is not a state. It is an act, and each generation must do its part."[2]

In principle, various mechanisms that can be summarised under the concept of democratic accountability enable political, judicial and administrative control by taking into account the concept of institutional differentiation, cooperation and control laid down in the European Treaties (Art. 13(1), (2) TEU) and ultimately ensuring that objectives (output) provided for in the Treaties and by law are pursued and achieved. This is an important difference to the requirements for the democratic legitimation of administrative bodies according to the principle of democracy enshrined in the Grundgesetz, according to which—at least in the interpretation by the FCC—democratic legitimation is decisively established by the governmental power to issue instructions. The fact that the FCC has nevertheless opened itself up to other forms of democratic control referred to as compensation mechanisms, in particular parliamentary accountability and judicial control, shows the profound influence of central bank independence and control on the entire administration in Germany determined by Union law.

The study has also revealed that the Union democratic principle provides further forms of democratic control, which are expressed above all in the democratic

[1]Cf. Müller-Graff (2018), p. 239 with regard to judicial control.

[2]John Lewis, Together, You Can Redeem the Soul of Our Nation, New York Times of 30 July 2020, https://www.nytimes.com/2020/07/30/opinion/john-lewis-civil-rights-america.html (26 February 2021).

principles of Arts. 10–12 TEU. In addition to the principle of representative democracy, which undoubtedly forms the core of democratic requirements, participation and transparency enable further forms of civic participation and public control that can usefully complement the democratic principle. With regard to central bank action, however, the limits of these forms were also pointed out, which result in particular from the fact that the decision-making process is characterised by economic as well as legal complexity and requires confidentiality to a high degree.

A decisive factor in measuring the guarantee of independence on the one hand and governance and control on the other is the existence of a mandate that is characterised by clear and measurable objectives, the hierarchy of which is determined from the outset, and which also reserves the weighing of fundamental concerns affecting the common good for the representative bodies. This also serves the principle of representative democracy by ensuring that the mandate of independent authorities endowed with expertise ultimately only extends as far as it is necessary to realise certain objectives. Even if this does not necessarily have to go hand in hand with a narrow mandate, one-goal mandates and exempting central bank action from fundamental balancing decisions can ensure democratic embedment all the better. These aspects must be given particular consideration in the future orientation of the ECB and the NCBs in the globally challenging fields of European integration, sustainability and digitalisation.

Reference

Müller-Graff P-C (2018) Die Bankenaufsicht der EZB vor Gericht. Zeitschrift für das gesamte Handelsrecht und Wirtschaftsrecht 182:239–251

Printed by Printforce, the Netherlands